FROM
MONK TO
MONEY
MANAGER

PRAISE FOR *FROM MONK TO MONEY MANAGER*

"A monk, a Marine, and a money manager walk into a bar . . . actually, they wrote a book and they are all the same person! Doug Lynam is one of the most interesting people I know. His diverse life experiences have led to an easy-to-read book on personal finance that is unlike anything else you will read. Combining philosophy, common sense, and a writing style that allows you to get lost in stories rather than dry, recycled platitudes, *From Monk to Money Manager* takes you on a personal finance journey toward financial enlightenment. I wish I had this personal finance book when I was younger."

Scott Dauenhauer, CFP, MSFP, AIF
Meridian Wealth Management

"Doug Lynam perfectly combines spiritual and practical advice to get your financial house in order. He explains that money is not the root of all evil and guides you through fixing your investments, making some money, and helping to save the world. Think of this as your own Investment Policy Statement with a heart. Ignore the wise words of an ex-monk turned financial adviser at your own peril."

Anthony Isola, CFP
Investment Advisor Representative,
Ritholtz Wealth Management

"Doug Lynam's *From Monk to Money Manager* contains the kind of sane talk and practical advice about money that so many of us didn't get when we were starting out as earners. But it's much more than just another money management book. It also addresses a question that has plagued me all my life: How is a moral person supposed to think and feel about money when we were taught in school or church that poverty is blessed and wealth is a spiritual encumbrance?

Doug's very unique perspective as a former Benedictine monk removes the guilt and helps us understand just how important it is to be a little bit wealthy because only when our own needs are addressed can we begin to help others. If, like me, you've ever felt trapped between participating in the heartless economic rat race of modern society and the desire to live a spiritually and morally balanced life, you'll find this book will give you a way to understand: yes, you can be a good person and still be a little bit wealthy. This is not a book about becoming rich. It's about learning how to help make the world a better place by understanding the role money can play in the life of a spiritually aware person."

Bill Kowalski
Bestselling author

"When it comes to money, most people are in a dark monastery of their own—cloistered from reality regarding money management or saving for college or retirement. In *From Monk to Money Manager*, Doug Lynam not only tells you what you need to do with your money, he also takes the devil out of the details and makes the subject a spiritual pursuit. Read this book and you won't need to pray for more money ever again!"

John Wasik
Journalist, editor, speaker, and author, *Lightning Strikes*

"While it's generally unwise to discuss religion or money with strangers, Doug Lynam, who is an expert in both, joins the world of God and mammon for your benefit. Read, absorb, and enjoy *From Monk to Money Manager*, and you'll enrich both your spirit and your pocketbook."

William Bernstein
Author, *The Investor's Manifesto*

"It should be no surprise that a former monk and educator would have the perfect recipe for a healthy relationship with money."

Dan Otter, PhD
Founder of 403(b)wise and author, *Teach and Retire Rich*

"I should have never sent him to speech therapy. Now he won't stop telling people what to do."

Lois
Doug's proud mom

FROM
MONK TO
MONEY
MANAGER

A FORMER MONK'S FINANCIAL GUIDE TO BECOMING A LITTLE BIT WEALTHY— AND WHY THAT'S OKAY

DOUG LYNAM

W PUBLISHING GROUP

AN IMPRINT OF THOMAS NELSON

Published in Nashville, Tennessee, by W Publishing Group, an imprint of Thomas Nelson.

Thomas Nelson titles may be purchased in bulk for educational, business, fund-raising, or sales promotional use. For information, please e-mail SpecialMarkets@ThomasNelson.com.

Unless otherwise noted, Scripture quotations are taken from the Holy Bible, New International Version®, NIV®. © 1973, 1978, 1984, 2011 by Biblica, Inc.® Used by permission of Zondervan. All rights reserved worldwide.

Scripture quotations marked NRSV are from New Revised Standard Version Bible. © 1989 National Council of the Churches of Christ in the United States of America. Used by permission. All rights reserved.

Scripture quotations marked KJV are from the King James Version. Public domain.

Scripture quotations marked BSB are from the Holy Bible, Berean Study Bible, BSB. © 2016, 2018 by Bible Hub. Used by permission. All rights reserved worldwide.

The names and some descriptive details of real people and events have been changed to protect the identities of the guilty and the innocent.

Any Internet addresses, phone numbers, or company or product information printed in this book are offered as a resource and are not intended in any way to be or to imply an endorsement by Thomas Nelson, nor does Thomas Nelson vouch for the existence, content, or services of these sites, phone numbers, companies, or products beyond the life of this book.

ISBN 978-0-7852-2388-7 (eBook)

Library of Congress Cataloging-in-Publication Data

Names: Lynam, Doug, 1973- author.
Title: From monk to money manager: a former monk's financial guide to becoming a little bit wealthy—and why that's okay / Doug Lynam.
Description: Nashville, Tennessee: W Publishing Group, [2019] | Includes bibliographical references. |
Identifiers: LCCN 2018045505 (print) | LCCN 2018047874 (ebook) | ISBN 9780785223887 (E-book) | ISBN 9780785223870 (softcover)
Subjects: LCSH: Finance, Personal. | Wealth.
Classification: LCC HG179 (ebook) | LCC HG179 .L9565 2019 (print) | DDC 332.024—dc23
LC record available at https://lccn.loc.gov/2018045505

Printed in the United States of America

19 20 21 22 23 24 LSC 6 5 4 3 2 1

*To everyone at LongView Asset Management—
for taking a risk on me.*

*And to Ron Lieber—for showing me my
own story for the first time.*

CONTENTS

PART 4: IT'S TIME TO BECOME A LITTLE BIT WEALTHY

PART 5: HELP OTHERS BECOME A LITTLE BIT WEALTHY TOO

AUTHOR'S NOTE

If you find making financial calculations just a little too much like getting a root canal, please visit my website, douglynam.com, to use any of these calculators for free:

Retirement Planner
Retirement Planner for Two Working Spouses
Snowball Debt Elimination
401(k)
403(b) Savings
Benefit of Spending Less
College Savings
Emergency Savings
Home Rent vs. Buy
Social Security Benefit
Time Value of Money

WHAT IS IT ABOUT MONEY?

I've always hated talking about money. In fact, I don't like to think about my own money at all. Helping others with money is fine, but I procrastinate on paying my bills and balancing my checkbook each month. I get it done (and do it well), but sometimes I need to reward myself by pouring a stiff drink afterward—one of the few times when I drink. It settles my nerves and gives me the courage to face my own personal finances.

You're probably wondering, *Why does a professional money manager have so much trouble finding the energy to pay his bills even when he's in good financial shape?* Honestly, I think I have a form of financial PTSD. Money has caused me so much stress, anxiety, and hardship that giving my own finances attention triggers all the horrible memories and experiences I've had. And I've had a lot of them. But I've learned that if you ever want to have the peace of mind that comes from being financially secure, you need to face this stuff head on. Triggers be damned.

So here goes.

I used to be a monk. Now I'm a financial adviser. For a while, I was both a monk *and* a financial adviser. For some reason, those facts make me a sort of unicorn to most people. But the fact of that paradox is why this book is so important. For too long, religion and money have been held separate, as if the very existence of one sullies the other. But the cold hard truth of modern life is that we need money. We can't live our lives and serve others without it. Everyone needs a little bit of wealth—even monks, as you'll soon learn.

I grew up in a family that had a lot of money. It was a nightmare. I know, cry me a river, but the truth is, it was awful. My parents had messed-up attitudes about money—they were self-centered and materialistic, and they gave wealth a bad name. I entered the monastery to get away from that world. But even in the monastery I had financial problems. While there, I learned a lot about religion, selfless service . . . and money. It began with the monastery's financial troubles. Once I got the hang of that, I started helping monastic guests with their finances. I saw how much people suffer when they don't have money and knew I had the tools and knowledge to help folks get on the right track.

The irony is that I learned the most important financial lessons of my life *because* of my time in the monastery, not despite it. The lessons I learned as a monk made me realize that the most powerful way for me to have an impact in the world was to leave the monastery and advise people about their finances full time. If I can help you achieve basic financial security, then I am serving the world by alleviating a small part of its suffering. If you can then take what you've learned and help someone else, together we'll have an exponential impact for the good. We each have our calling, and I've finally found mine. I know—the humor of this reversal isn't lost on me either.

We can't ignore money. Believe me, I tried. So now I'm ready to address the subject of finances in a way I hope is helpful, thoughtfully and mindfully.

My goal for this book is to give people who struggle with money the courage to face their fears and anxieties, tackle their crushing debt, find financial security, and start building personal wealth. The route doesn't need to be perfect or pretty—and maybe you'll need to pour yourself a stiff drink at the end too—but the journey needs to be taken. It is necessary to help reduce your suffering and the suffering of the world.

By the way, in case you're wondering, this book isn't a get-rich-quick scheme, and anyone promising you a quick and easy path to wealth is a liar. Run far away from those people because here's the truth: building a strong and healthy financial future for yourself and those you love is difficult. In fact, it mostly sucks. But the good news is that it has nothing to do with your level of education. It's mostly a question of how hard you want to work to build good habits. With discipline, determination, and a little luck, you can end your financial suffering by becoming a little bit wealthy.

I love hearing from folks, so please feel free to reach out to me with questions or comments via e-mail: doug@douglynam.com.

PART 1

WHY WE ALL NEED TO BE A LITTLE BIT WEALTHY

CHAPTER 1

MY HATE AFFAIR WITH MONEY

Ironically, most of my money troubles occurred because I tried to escape worrying about money. I didn't want to deal with any of it. I grew up in a rich family where money was abundant but weaponized. Like a common virus engineered to be a weapon of mass destruction, money was the tool we used to hurt, control, manipulate, and dominate one another. It was horrible.

Growing up, I learned through the behavior of those around me that money and materialism were evil. So when I started studying philosophy and religion in high school and read the words of Paul the apostle, "For the love of money is the root of all evil," I believed Paul was right.

Throw a Jesus quote into the mix and you have a proto-monk in the making. That would be Matthew 19:21: "If you want to be perfect, go, sell your possessions and give to the poor, and you will have treasure in heaven. Then come, follow me." This seemed like the answer I was looking for.

I was a long way from becoming a monk because, at the time, I was an agnostic and a teenager. So I became an anti-materialist wannabe hippie instead. I covered my car with rain forest murals, peace signs, and rainbows. I grew out my hair, wore ratty clothing, and tried to drop out of society. It seemed like a clever idea at the time, plus it annoyed my parents. The only problem was that many of my new liberal brethren were just as selfish, self-centered, and materialistic as my conservative parents. They just wanted different stuff. They didn't want to be told what to do, and their anti-establishment attitude was often ego in disguise. They wanted the freedom to be as self-centered as possible and seek as much personal pleasure as possible without any responsibility. Despite the "one world" rhetoric, which I greatly admired, they didn't seem to give a darn about anyone but themselves. That wasn't much of an improvement.

So then I tried to find selfless service in the military—the perfect egalitarian meritocracy. Excellence is rewarded, but your pay is fixed. In college, I ended up at Officer Candidate School with the US Marine Corps and loved it. I graduated near the top of my class, and I almost stayed to make a career out of the military (I did not go active duty), but I realized that my real job as a Marine was to kill people. I'm not a pacifist, but the Marines taught us to enjoy killing, and that freaked me out a bit. I found the idea of killing people for a living disturbing, but mostly because the adventure part of it thrilled me. Unlike some, I didn't quit the Marines because I hated soldiering. I quit because I got good at the soldiering part and enjoyed it too much. There is a reason many men and women like hunting and playing shooter video games: it is a heck of a lot of fun.

If I was going to quit the Marines and do something better, what could be a higher calling? Where else could I find a life of service and avoid the "greedy capitalistic corporate world"? Just then, I began to have a religious reawakening and started to explore the possibility of becoming a monk.

It seemed a perfect solution. In the monastery, I would have all the structure and discipline I liked about the Marines along with comradery, or esprit de corps, but with an even nobler purpose. God comes before country. Best of all, I would take a vow of poverty and be free from the grip of money and materialism forever.

Or so I thought.

A Surprise Twist

I entered the monastery when I was twenty-two years old and fresh out of college. My original intent was to try it out for a little while, like taking a gap year, as a break before my life started. It was also a rebellious adventure or the "road less traveled." I was looking for the meaning of life, and I decided that if I was ever going to find it, a monastery was the most likely place to do so.

I wasn't disappointed. Being a monk was everything I'd hoped for, and much more. I discovered a remarkable community filled with lovingkindness and wonder at the grandeur of the universe. Each day was rich with meaning, even if poor in spirit.

In my early years at the monastery, it was a struggle to pay the bills and keep the household running smoothly. I was the junior monk by almost thirty years, so I was the lowest person in the pecking order. I had very little power or control over daily events. I was just a happy grunt, trying not to screw up.

Since the other brothers were older, wiser, and smarter, I assumed they knew something about finance and bookkeeping. Sadly, that was not the case. Within a few years it was clear that something was desperately wrong with the community finances. We were all working full time, but somehow there wasn't enough money to pay the bills.

Eventually we hit the breaking point. Calls were coming in from creditors, and I was using my personal credit cards to cover living expenses. I didn't understand what was going wrong. I finally insisted on taking responsibility for the household finances so I could see what the problem was. I had no idea if I would have better luck than the other monks at figuring out a solution, but I had to give it my best shot.

What I stumbled into was a Pandora's box of troubles. I learned that the community had been running in the red for years. There were medical bills, car repairs, student loans, insurance payments, and all the living expenses required for any home. There were also retreats to Rome and help given to those in need. Most importantly, there were several years of underemployment and below-subsistence wages for some of the brothers, along with a failed business venture when finding meaningful work seemed impossible. There wasn't enough money coming in the door. So credit cards became a necessary survival mechanism. Even when our income level improved after we all landed good teaching jobs, it was too late. We were under an avalanche of debt.

Moreover, we were not supported by the church and never accepted any donations. Part of our charism (the style of our religious order) was a commitment to being self-sufficient and to never rely on outside support. Why should someone else donate money so we could live the lifestyle of our choosing?

How did our financial problems get so bad? For two reasons. First was the hope that prayer alone could solve our money problems. If prayer alone was ever going to solve a big money mess, we were first in line. The second reason was we all played an insidious game of hot potato with the community finances. We viewed money as evil and didn't own up to our individual or collective responsibilities. Somehow, everything was going to work out for the best, *or* it was someone else's responsibility to fix. We could always find someone else to shift the responsibility onto, another brother or, worse, God.

The quest for blame is always successful. And "giving everything to God" doesn't mean pushing our responsibilities into his lap. God shows us how to live, but God can't do the living for us. We each have responsibilities to ourselves, our families, and our neighbors. In fact, we have a universal responsibility to all humanity and nature.

Hope and blame are not strategies. Prayer that leads you to the right action is great. Prayer that leaves you sitting on your backside isn't. And prayer used as a form of denial or blame isn't real prayer. I believe in the power of prayer, but praying for the bills to get paid without taking right action is a guaranteed path to failure. You won't have enough money for retirement if you don't put any money into your account or buy lottery tickets as your financial plan.

One of hardest truths for the community to face was the reality that God was not going to magically pay the bills. It didn't matter that we were doing good in the world. It didn't matter that we lived a life of love, service, and self-sacrifice. Visa wanted their money back, with a lot of interest, and they wanted it by the end of the month.

After many months of trying to untangle the financial mess I'd just uncovered, there was only one course of action available—bankruptcy. The community was insolvent, and since much of the debt was on personal credit cards, personal bankruptcy for each monk in the community was the only solution. It was a horror and a logistical nightmare. The process took over two years to file and discharge all the bankruptcies. My part-time job, in addition to teaching full time, was to organize, file, and track all the paperwork.

However, there was an upside. Since we were broke and lived in relative poverty, we had nothing to repossess and nothing to lose. Bankruptcy immediately improved our credit scores and left us with a completely clean slate, able to start over and build anew. In the end, it was a huge blessing. Fortunately, we filed for bankruptcy long before the laws changed in 2005, which made filing harder and more complex . . . as if it was easy before.

After surviving that ordeal, I made it a point to learn everything I could about personal finance. If I was going to be responsible for the community money, I was going to do it right. Determined never to repeat past mistakes, I went to our local bookstore and purchased every credible book on personal finance I could find. The depth of my ignorance on the subject shocked me. I had no idea how the world of money worked. Finance was one of the most crucial aspects of life, and I knew nothing about it. Most schools don't teach it, most parents don't teach it, and most adults are financially illiterate to some extent. Even people who have money often lose it due to poor planning. Financial illiteracy causes untold amounts of suffering.

Over the years my knowledge of money management deepened, then took another unexpected twist. Monasteries have regular guests, and we were no exception. Friends and visitors frequented our dinner table, often pouring their hearts out, seeking solace and support during troubled times. Since I was the most junior monk, I wasn't encouraged to give spiritual counsel to guests. That was for the prior. I mostly just watched and listened during conversations with visitors. And as I listened to those conversations unfold gradually, I realized that almost every visitor who came with a spiritual problem also had a financial problem lurking in the background. More importantly, I could help. So I did.

I started working pro bono with guests to solve their money problems. If guests could afford a real financial planner or lawyer, I sent them to an appropriate professional. I took the clients who were too poor to get attention from anybody in the industry. I knew that I wasn't good enough, yet, to charge anyone, but I was steadily developing my skill set.

The most unusual problems fell into my lap. I probated estates, helped file more bankruptcies, worked out long-term debt repayment, helped with child support, student loans, and identity theft, to name a few.

Financial problems are often entangled with spiritual problems. The financial problem is sometimes a root cause and sometimes a by-product—and sometimes they're so tangled together it's hard to know where one ends and the other begins. For example, when one client was dealing with the death of a loved one, their grief and loss were the primary concern. But there was also an estate to probate and no one to help. Trying to navigate probate while mourning the loss of your dearest loved one isn't practical.

One terminally ill client was dealing with their end-of-life grief process, but they also needed to write a will, assign someone to have power of attorney for health care and finances, and create a Do Not Resuscitate order. Focusing only on the spiritual grief would have been a travesty. Some suffering in life is unavoidable, especially from unforeseen financial catastrophes, but the suffering that poor estate planning produces is avoidable. If I could help avert the lesser tragedy that dying without a will (intestate) produces, I felt a moral obligation to do so.

Frequently guests would ask me to pray for them to get relief from their money crises. I always did, but I also insisted we make a budget. As I have said, we must make real change happen for ourselves. God has given us free will and agency—and the responsibility to use them. God is not going to work a miracle to solve a problem that you have the power to fix.

A New Source of Suffering

The greatest irony of my life is that I joined a monastery, in part, to escape the world of money, and I ended up spending more time worrying about money than almost anyone in the outside world. Another irony, directly related to the first, is that I learned I'm good at helping people with their financial problems.

From these experiences, I learned several rules about money and life. Here are two:

Rule #1: If you ignore money it will always bite you in the backside.
Rule #2: Bad things happen to good people. (Remember that nice guy called Jesus? They nailed him to a tree for saying that we should all be kind to one another.)

Around 2005, my life took another unexpected turn. I was working as a math and science teacher at a private seventh- through twelfth-grade school, and serving as chair of the mathematics department, when the school's statistics/economics instructor left unexpectedly. In a moment of crisis, I took the course on as an overload. I wasn't the most qualified person for the job, but I was good with kids and was familiar enough with the material. Most importantly, I was also the only person available.

Surprisingly, it became my favorite course to teach. I loved it. I was in my element and, unbeknownst to me, on my way to realizing my true calling. The first thing I did was throw out the horribly dry textbooks and teach through projects and real-world examples.

After several years of teaching economics and personal finance, as well as helping countless monastery guests, my colleagues at work began asking me for financial advice. I gladly helped them, free of charge. As a monk I never billed clients. It was just my form of service. And that is when I took one big step closer to where I am today.

Do you ever have "bookmark" moments in your life? Events so profound there will always be a before and an after for that event? Here's one of those moments for me.

I have a good friend and colleague with whom I worked for decades. Around 2008, she asked me for help planning her retirement. At sixty-four, she knew it was past time to start. I asked her to e-mail a convenient time to meet and we'd set something up. But the e-mail never came. We'd pass each other in the hall every few days, and each time she saw me, I would remind her to set up the appointment. She'd promise to e-mail me soon but keep procrastinating. This went on for over a year. She was avoiding a difficult conversation.

After I pressed her on the issue during a faculty event, we were finally able to set up an appointment. A week later, on that fateful winter afternoon, we met after school in her office and tried to plan her retirement.

I'd already had a busy day teaching classes, supervising the cafeteria, and tutoring students on how to use the trigonometric ratios during my free periods. When I walked into her cramped office, the dusty smell of books and Band-Aids lingered in the air. In a small school, everyone wears multiple hats. As the resident den mother, she kept a ready supply of first-aid gear to help bandage bruised knees, tape sprained ankles, and soothe upset stomachs, all piled up alongside stacks of papers and reports.

She greeted me warmly, gave me a big hug, and thanked me for taking the time to meet. In the dark months before spring break, every teacher is exhausted, and we could both see the fatigue in each other's eyes. Still, it was nice to connect with an old friend, and we settled down into squeaky office chairs in front of her computer.

The first surprise: it took about thirty minutes just to log in to her account since she'd never opened it before. We had to get customer service on the phone to set up online access, which is always maddening. After numerous failed login attempts, we were finally in.

Then came the big shock: after thirty years as a private school teacher, her retirement savings was only $16,000. That plus credit card debt put her in a tragic hole. She had never faced this money demon, had never opened her retirement account, and had given the matter zero time and attention. I always suspected it was going to be an unpleasant conversation, but I had no idea it would be dire.

She then politely asked me what I could do to help, as if it were like fixing a broken sink. Just tinker with it a little, slap on some duct tape, and the problem will be solved.

By all accounts, she is one of the strongest women I've ever known. To this day, she is still a national mountain-bike champion for her age bracket. But when I explained the gravity of her situation, as delicately as I could, she broke down in tears and cried. And cried. It was a heartrending moment.

My friend then asked me when she could expect to retire. I lied and said I didn't know. But I did know. The answer wasn't good, and I lacked the courage to speak the truth. I tried not to make a horrible moment worse by letting her see my sadness. I fought back the tears but, as I thought of the life she dedicated to selfless service, I couldn't help it—I started to cry too. I wanted to give her hope and encouragement, not a pity party. Yet I was breaking inside along with her. Worse, I understood the seriousness of her situation more acutely than she did. She was just worried about retiring next year. I saw a mountain of unpayable medical bills in her future and pictured her struggling to get out of bed to go to work in her old age.

The rest of her life was likely to be a financial train wreck, and she was just beginning to realize it. Social Security is great, but it doesn't go far in the expensive town where we live. The best I could do was help her build a workable budget, clear up her debt, increase her savings rate, select better retirement investments, and encourage her to buy a modest home so that her cost of living would go down as she aged. It still wasn't going to be the retirement she deserved.

A New Calling

Luke 6:20:

> Looking at his disciples, he said:

> "Blessed are you who are poor,
>   for yours is the kingdom of God."

I never fully understood the meaning of these words until I was financially desperate. I think the desperately poor are going to heaven because there is no reason for them to go to hell—they've already been there. That might be a theological overreach for some, but maybe they at least get a few decades off purgatory?

After seeing the trouble my friend and colleague had saving for retirement, I began to dig into the retirement plan at my school. I wanted to know what went wrong. How could someone spend a lifetime as a teacher and have no retirement savings? Someone must run the plan and be responsible for it, right? Didn't anyone ever reach out and let her know she was so far offtrack?

What I found when I examined my school's retirement plan shocked me again. It wasn't being run for the benefit of the employees. It was being run for the benefit of the company administering the plan. Then, after more research, I discovered this wasn't a unique situation. Almost every teacher retirement plan in the country is in shambles. For decades, schools and teachers have innocently pumped money into plans they trusted but that are actually broken. Retirement plans have been neglected by school boards in both public and private institutions, providing financial predators an easy feast. As a result, there are currently multiple class-action lawsuits against Ivy League schools for failing to monitor and supervise their retirement plans adequately. The problem is so endemic that even Ivy League schools struggle. Having seen for myself, I can assure you it isn't a pretty situation further down the academic ladder.

(If you want to find out if your school retirement plan company is working for you or against you, just ask one question: Are they a fiduciary? A fiduciary is legally required to act in your best interests. I talk more about them in chapter 14. Run away from the rest. And don't be fooled by any answer that isn't an unequivocal yes. The rest are sharks.)

There was only one solution to this problem I could think of, though it wasn't going to be easy: build my own company and take these plans away from the financial monsters preying on teachers.

So that is what I did, and that is what I continue to do. I formed my own company, Lynam Financial Services, then happily merged with a larger firm, LongView Asset Management. That's when I left the monastery. I'd found a wider community to serve. In my mind, I didn't leave monasticism; I'm just bringing what I discovered in the monastery out into the world.

When I became a monk, I mistakenly believed I had to choose between a life of spiritual abundance *or* material abundance. I was wrong. We need to be a little bit wealthy—meaning, fiscally wise and financially strong—so we can help others and make the world a better place. When money becomes a part of our spiritual practice, used in love and service, it brings us closer to God.

My mission is simple: I don't want anyone to be poor. Poverty sucks—and though I know what the verse says, I can't think of anything blessed about being poor. (Perhaps it is like the blessing we give to those heading off to war. They deserve our compassion because of the suffering they will face, and so they are blessed with our most solemn prayers.) Instead of just praying for the poor, can we find pragmatic solutions that don't require huge government intervention? Every forced poverty reduction plan has failed. Just ask the Russians. But what does it take not to be poor? What do you need to avoid that pain? Moreover, what do you need to ensure you aren't at risk of being poor ever again? The answer is simple: you need to be a little bit wealthy.

For the record, my faith journey is complex. And it isn't over yet! I'm still growing and learning in my spiritual adventure. But I see the divine everywhere and in everyone, regardless of their faith tradition or lack thereof. When I share my faith, it is to help connect you with yours, not convert you to mine.

While this book is grounded in my unique experience of Christian monasticism, the discussion of religion and money impacts you regardless of your religious beliefs. Our Western values are heavily influenced, both consciously and unconsciously, by more than three thousand years of Judeo-Christian history. Sometimes this unintentionally causes pain in the world. So I joyfully welcome people of all faiths, or no faith, to this conversation.

I believe God wants you to be a little wealthy. Not selfish or heartless, like a robber baron, but comfortable, able to pay your bills, care for your loved ones, pay for college, afford health care, give to others, and retire with dignity. Those things require wealth. This idea may strike some as a radical notion. In the next chapters I lay out not only why it's not but how you can do it and still be true to your highest values.

With courage, compassion, and common sense, you can improve your financial situation and even become wealthy while putting your life in service to others. You can also connect deeply and meaningfully with friends, family, and your community while growing in material abundance.

It's okay to be a little bit wealthy. In fact, it's necessary.

CHAPTER 2

MONEY ISN'T BAD— POVERTY IS

In the monastery I discovered that there are many levels of poverty. As monks, we were poor. However, the original poverty of the monastery was just living in simplicity. We always had enough to cover our basic needs, and we didn't need much. I was happy at the poor level. It was when we downgraded from simplicity to desperation that I learned the true meaning of poverty.

Our financial woes pushed us into the ranks of what I call the Desperate. The Desperate are those of us who have to worry about money all the time. We hustle every single day to make ends meet. If you let your guard down, even for a moment, you'll go from desperation to disaster. You can't do anything in a modern economy without money, so money stress dictates every single action of every single moment in your life.

I understand why the Desperate have higher rates of alcoholism, domestic violence, drug abuse, infidelity, obesity, heart disease, accidents, depression, and reckless behavior. They are going insane from

17

the stress of being poor.[1] Any escape, even for a few hours, is a blessed release. If you get that release from a pill, a bottle, a blunt, or a box of Twinkies, so be it. Don't judge unless you've been there.

We have only so much energy and mental fortitude for one day. If all your energy and willpower is concentrated on avoiding complete financial collapse, you don't have the time, energy, or mental strength to make good decisions in other areas of your life. Everything falls apart.

The Desperate don't always look like they are struggling. In fact, some of the Desperate people I know look fine from the outside. They work good jobs, drive respectable cars, and dress well, but they are underwater or are struggling in every financial area of their life. The Desperate are just one mistake—one random and unforeseeable event—away from disaster. That is why they are so stressed out.[2] In some urban parts of America, like San Francisco or New York, even having a six-figure income isn't enough to make ends meet.[3]

After the Desperate are the Dispossessed—those whose lives *are* a disaster. They live out of their cars or on the streets. The Dispossessed are completely unmoored from the social structures that help hold lives and families together. They struggle to find employment, housing, and their daily bread. Once in that financial hellhole, it is extremely difficult to climb out. The stress and the shame are unrelenting.

The monastic community was desperate but never homeless. When our living room roof collapsed during a winter storm, that was stressful. The monastery had homeowner's insurance to cover the interior damage, but a new roof was still $20,000. We couldn't ignore the massive hole in our roof during winter, but where was I supposed to get $20,000 for the roof and $5,000 for the insurance deductible?

Even more devastating and unexpected, the community's highest income earner suddenly needed a quadruple bypass heart surgery and couldn't work anymore. That's when the terrible, stress-filled reality of being desperate starts to sink in.

Lack of money is the key driver for most of the suffering in the world. If we can face that problem squarely, honestly, and with good minds and hearts, we can solve, or at least mitigate, some of the worst problems in the world.

Here's an example. One of the leading causes of divorce is money stress.[4] Every major social problem, such as drug abuse, alcoholism, child abuse, abortion, domestic violence, crime, sex trafficking, poor health, and lack of education, can be reduced, mitigated, or eliminated just by increasing a person's net worth.[5] According to Tom Boyce, Chief of UCSF's Division of Developmental Medicine, "Socioeconomic status is the most powerful predictor of disease, disorder, injury, and mortality we have."[6]

To be fair, this is a chicken-or-the-egg problem. People who have the talent to avoid poverty tend to have more intellectual capital, but money also helps people gain intellectual capital. And even modest increases in a family's net worth can have a profound impact in reducing all social ills and guarantee a better future for the children in those homes.[7] Reducing poverty is good for the world.

Money is a powerful tool. It can be used for ill or good, and we need to use all our economic tricks to make it serve the good rather than cause needless suffering or dismiss it under the presumption that it is evil.

But why do so many people think money is evil? To understand our present attitudes about money, let's take a quick look at our collective historical money baggage.

A Very Brief History of Money and Religion

Few things have caused as much conflict as money, except perhaps religion. Put them together and you have a potentially toxic mix, which makes historical attempts to separate them understandable.

Religion, in its finest moments, stands for love, kindness, and compassion. The world of money is often cruel, unkind, and brutally harsh. No wonder religion often stands in opposition to the world of finance. Our religious views on money are sometimes based on old-world economics and, paradoxically, can create the very suffering they attempt to prevent.

For example, many religious texts, including the Old Testament, New Testament, and the Koran, condemn usury (the practice of lending money with interest).[8] For most of Christian history, usury was a mortal sin equivalent even to murder.[9] Why? Because in the old days, borrowing money was more like borrowing from the mob: very personal and extremely dangerous. If you defaulted on a debt in the time of Jesus, the collection process was brutal and possibly included slavery for you and your family. How could religious leaders justify usury in an era before credit reports, an effective court system, and a "risk-free" rate of return?

Times have changed. For example, corporations didn't exist in the time of Jesus.[10] While I don't like Visa very much, borrowing and lending money is foundational to a robust modern economy. The bond market is almost twice the size of the stock market. (Bonds are a type of debt.) And bonds help fund many of our civic projects and corporate enterprises that make our world run smoothly.

To understand Jesus' warnings about money, it also helps to understand who rich people were back then. It was an era that looked more like Spartacus than Pleasantville. Like today, if you had money, you had power. But, unlike today, power was generally used to oppress and kill poor people. It was also an era of true class warfare. We think class warfare is about tax cuts, but for Jesus' time, it was about killing and enslaving each other. Back then, a rich person was, by necessity, a greedy, selfish, power-hungry jerk. If you weren't a scoundrel, you didn't stay rich for long. In that situation, whose side should God be on? The poor are still oppressed today, but as I'll show, my wealth in a modern economy does not require me to oppress anyone, so we need more nuance in our thinking.

In fact, during Jesus' time, the middle class wasn't invented yet. The middle class wouldn't exist for another 1,700 years.[11] Modern economic theory was equally nonexistent, as were modern democracy, a universal rule of law, modern corporations, or separation of powers. It's hard to have a fair economic system under those circumstances. The conflicts of interest were too great. For example, Pontius Pilate was the prosecuting attorney, judge, and jury in Jesus' trial. It is hard to see how that was ever going to go well.

Since Jesus walked the earth, the playground has changed a lot. We've got more toys to work with, like modern science and economics. So we need some new rules and ways of thinking about how to use these toys fairly and effectively. Tee-ball rules don't work on the football field. It's a very different game now.

The real question of economics is this: How do we balance our innate selfishness with our cooperative need to work together and get along? How do we intelligently integrate those conflicting desires?

Wealth Is No Longer Zero-Sum

One of the most exciting lessons I discovered in economics is that building wealth in a modern economy is not a zero-sum game. Sports is a classic zero-sum example, which is why I don't like sports very much. For someone to win, someone else must lose. $+1 - 1 = 0$. I hate seeing people lose. A competitive workforce often makes us feel like economics is zero-sum—if I get a job, someone else didn't get that job. I win and get hired only if someone else loses.

In the biblical era building wealth was mostly zero-sum. The rise of one wealthy family often meant the fall of another. It was like *Game of Thrones*. Building wealth now is different. It is more like going to the gym. Just because I work out in yoga, on a bike, or in the weight room, doesn't prevent you from doing the same. My physical fitness does not come at the expense of someone else. Likewise, building

personal wealth in a well-regulated economy does not require someone else to be poor.[12]

The poor are poor despite my wealth, not because of it. No one
had to lose for me to save, invest, and make money. And yes, there are
lots of scoundrels who prey on people for profit—there always will be,
which is why we need a robust legal system. But just because corrupt
people are sometimes wealthy doesn't mean wealth makes you corrupt. Wealth alone does not corrupt the soul. A lack of ethics does.

Moreover, the amount of money and wealth in the world is no
longer finite. There was only so much gold or grain during Jesus'
time on the earth, and they needed strong rules to make people share
those limited resources. Now, there is no limit to how much wealth
we can generate. According to public policy expert Charles Wheelan,
"Economics tells us that there is no theoretical limit to how well we
can live or how widely our wealth can be spread."[13]

For example, how much was Google worth at its beginning?
Nothing. What is it worth now? Approaching $1 trillion. Where
did most of that money come from? It was created. Google added
value to the economy, increasing the amount of wealth in the world.
There is no end to the amount of money, or value, we can add to the
global economy. If there is a limit, why does the value of the stock
market keep going up instead of stopping at some specific number?
The stock market will never "top out" at some point where all the
available money is used up. This is a new phenomenon that religious
texts couldn't have addressed at the time.

Money Matters in the Age of Capitalism

Communism and Fascism tried and failed to build utopian societies
in the modern era. All attempts at building a utopia end in tragedy
because a utopian society must remove the free will of people to make

their own decisions, especially "bad" decisions. The only way to stop people from using their free will is with a gun and the threat of violence. Which, in my opinion, is why every attempt at building a "perfect" society produces genocidal horrors.

But could the most powerful engine for generating wealth, a well-regulated free-market economy, also be used to solve our individual and social money problems? Could capitalism help fix the problem of poverty rather than ignore it and accept it as an inevitable by-product?

I think yes! By helping everyone become a little bit wealthy. The *potential* amount of money is infinite, and the world population will always be finite. I like that math.

If the goal is to build wealth, how can someone reconcile that with Matthew 19:24, "Again I tell you, it is easier for a camel to go through the eye of a needle than for someone who is rich to enter the kingdom of God"?

At the risk of being branded a heretic and inviting another round of the Spanish Inquisition to visit my home, please note that I'm simply asking and musing on a question. I wonder how to understand this passage considering modern economic theory. Especially when modern economics requires all of us to be a little bit wealthy in order to have the fullest life possible.

It helps me to reframe this passage to say: *Again I tell you, it is easier for a camel to go through the eye of a needle than for a greedy, selfish, power-hungry scoundrel to enter the kingdom of God.* That makes more sense to me. I've met too many wonderful rich people who are loving, kind, charitable, and work hard to live lives of service to think that wealth equals being a jerk. That doesn't mean there aren't plenty of greedy, selfish, power-hungry jerks out there, but that is equally true among the poor as it is among the rich. (Have you ever visited a slum? That's not a safe place at night for anyone.) Selfishness is endemic in all of us, regardless of our tax bracket.

So let's help everyone make money and share that wealth as best

we can in the context of capitalism without reverting to the radical
wealth redistribution of socialism or communism.

To Fit a Camel Through the Eye
of a Needle—Use a Blender

Let's revisit one of most famous of biblical quotes on wealth, Matthew
19:21: "If you want to be perfect, go, sell your possessions and give
to the poor, and you will have treasure in heaven. Then come, follow
me." How should we read this considering our goal of building wealth
for the world? Especially with the kicker verse that follows about putting a camel through the eye of a needle? What are these passages
trying to tell us about money and property?

Honestly, I don't know. There are as many interpretations of these
passages as there are people to debate them. And the more context
you put the quotes into, the worse the dilemma becomes. Especially
when Jesus praises Peter and the apostles for giving up everything to
follow him a few verses later in the text. These passages are the basis
for much of monasticism and vows of poverty in the religious life.
Absolute poverty, complete helplessness and hopelessness, depending
only on the will of God, may be the last step in the spiritual journey.
When your ego is eliminated, and you've internally and externally
renounced *everything*, then maybe you reach Enlightenment, Nirvana,
union with God, sainthood, or the Beatific Vision. I've never been
there, so I don't know; however, I have been desperately poor, and that
didn't get me any closer to God.

When I entered the monastery, I took these statements literally. I
was a young man from a rich family, who was also a chronic perfec-
tionist. Jesus' statement was the ultimate throw-down challenge. So I
gave up everything to follow Jesus. I don't regret the decision; it was
a beautiful adventure filled with love and meaning. But I no longer

believe poverty is good in and of itself, nor required by Jesus' teachings to reach the highest levels of perfection.

These passages are a riddle, like: "When you can do nothing, what can you do?" They are a mental tripwire. If you don't stumble on the logic, you aren't thinking hard enough. But if you trip and face plant across molten asphalt covered with glass and then rinse your body with rubbing alcohol for extra fun, you might be overdoing it a bit.

Perhaps it is a test of faith. If necessary, could I let myself be thrown to the lions for the love of God? That doesn't mean I need to jump the fence at my local zoo and play Frisbee with a ribeye in the lion cage this weekend. That would be silly.

If I believe that God called upon me to do so, could I give up every material possession in this world for love? Let's look at what it says right after these passages in Matthew 19:29: "And everyone who has left houses or brothers or sisters or father or mother or wife or children or fields for my sake will receive a hundred times as much and will inherit eternal life." Does this mean I must give up all my relatives to be a person with faith? No, of course not. But we need to be able to if necessary. There are situations where someone may need to leave their family to survive spiritually, but that doesn't make it a requirement. If you love anything, including money, to the point where it prevents you from following your highest ideals, then you have a problem. But you don't need to become a homeless beggar to be close to the divine, any more than you need to abandon your children to love and serve the world.

Perhaps we've confused the life of the ascetic with the way to salvation, however *you* define the word *salvation*. Maybe it's true that prophets and mystics must step outside of all dominance hierarchies and reject money, sex, power, fame, achievement, family, recognition, and status. But most of us aren't called to such highly specialized occupations. For us, leading commendable spiritual lives requires us not to step outside of the world, but to figure out how to live well in it.

I don't think a spiritual life requires us to reject a useful tool like economics, just as it doesn't require us to reject science. Both are powerful tools for making the world a better place. Instead, we need to give up the egoism, self-aggrandizement, and oppression of others that money and science often produce. Just because science is great doesn't mean that dropping nuclear bombs on people is good. Likewise, just because economics is great doesn't mean that enslaving people and raping God's creation for profit is good.

The (Other) Money Myths

As we confront the myth that money is evil, we should also examine a few lesser logical fallacies that can distort our relationship to wealth.

1. **The goal is to be rich.** Throughout this book I'm going to make a distinction between being rich and being wealthy. They sound the same, and to some they are, but not to me. Rich people can become poor people very quickly. Just ask Willie Nelson, Mike Tyson, MC Hammer, Larry King, and the pantheon of other celebrities and "rich" people who lost everything and went bankrupt. Why did they lose everything? Because no one has enough money to buy everything. If you spend more than you make, no matter how much money you have, you'll eventually go broke.

Wealthy people use their money to buy investments, not stuff. Those investments then generate more money. If you have good investments, they will generate enough money for you to live off, without needing a paycheck or a movie deal. You are wealthy if your investments and assets generate enough returns for you to be self-sufficient. Then you have freedom and security, and, barring acts of God that you can't control, you should remain wealthy for the rest of your life. Riches are fleeting, wealth can be forever.

Remember how I grew up in a rich family? Guess what happened over the years I was in the monastery? All my father's money disappeared he spent it all. My CEO dad was rich, not wealthy.

2. Less is more. The anti-wealth crowd will sometimes slip this into conversations: "Don't be a materialist. Limit your wants, focus on your needs, and then you can be happy with very little." Like all good lies, this is partially true. This logic assumes that if you only focus on needs and avoid consumerism, you'll have ample amounts of money without stress. That is silly. You can easily end up in a situation where you don't have enough money to cover your needs or your wants, which is insanely stressful. How do you go without something that you need? You suffer. This is especially true when you are responsible for the needs of a family.

For example, during the early years in the monastery, I suddenly cracked a molar on my lower left jaw. We didn't have the $750 necessary for me to get a dental crown. So what did I do without money or insurance? I just stopped chewing on the left side of my mouth for a year until I could get it fixed. In the meantime, I would see stars if I quickly swallowed something cold. What else was I going to do? Pull it out with some pliers? Please believe me, I was limiting my wants, but I really needed a darn root canal. Or what about the brother who really needed a $250,000 surgery? Good insurance is a beautiful thing—and expensive!

The harsh reality is that a modern economy requires a little bit of wealth to live with dignity.

3. Resources must be rationed. For me, the most annoying fallacy is, "Live simply so that others may simply live." It makes for a good bumper sticker but is a terrible way to build an economy.

I remember being shown videos of starving children in Somalia when I was in fifth grade. We watched a documentary of emaciated children with tiny rib bones tight against withered chests contrasted with distended bellies. Their mothers sat by, too weak to keep the flies or rats off their dying children. I was so grief stricken and guilty about having so much material abundance in the face of such suffering, I vowed not to eat lunch, ever. I was going to consume less so starving Somali children could live. Unfortunately, poverty and starvation are not from a lack of global resources—they are from an unequal and unjust distribution of resources. Starvation is often a weapon of war, conflict, and genocide. It is deliberate and often perpetuated by state governments.[14] And those conflicts aren't always caused by us. Racism and tribal hatred were not invented in America, even if they flourish here.

The reason some countries or communities have abundance and other people starve is that prosperous nations with a strong middle class have well-run economies and effective governments. It is the job of our governments to regulate society and set the rules of the game. If the game is generally fair and free, then there is never mass starvation. Bad things still happen, just not that bad.[15]

For those who think we should feel guilty because we have an abundance of food and resources in the developed world, please know that we have abundance *despite* the suffering around the globe, not because of it. This is a subtle but crucial point in macroeconomic theory that many miss. While there are too many historical injustices perpetrated on developing nations to list, if we all stop buying stuff completely, the world is not going to be a better place. It would be so much worse.[16] Civilization would collapse because your spending is someone else's income, and someone else's spending is your income.

4. **Poor people are lazy or stupid.** The poor may be ignorant about finance, but they work hard. The whole point of being wealthy is that your money makes money for you, so you don't have to do as much. The middle class and the poor aren't so lucky. They have to hustle every day to avoid finanical calamity. Oddly, in a modern economy, many doctors, lawyers, teachers, and professors claw their way up a career ladder, struggling for everything they have, but they, too, are

one accident, one personal catastrophe away from ruin.[17] I see it happen regularly in my financial practice.

That isn't a great way to live. I'd like to fix that.

A New Attitude Toward Money

Unless we want to condemn all wealthy people to hell, which is just silly, then we need a healthier attitude toward money.

Here is my suggestion: If we know that building wealth can alleviate suffering, then it should be our goal to help everyone become a little bit wealthy and alleviate that suffering, including for you. I promise that life has plenty of pain in store for you, and everyone else, without needing to add an extra layer of suffering by being poor.

Just don't become a greedy, selfish, power-hungry scoundrel. In fact, the tradeoff is this: If you know wealth alleviates suffering, including your own, then try to help your friends, family, neighbors, and wider community become a little bit wealthy too. This makes Jesus' statement in Mark 12:31, "Love your neighbor as yourself," even more powerful. Your job isn't to think of yourself and destroy your neighbor, society, or planet. Just the opposite. You need to help everyone you can become a little bit wealthy while you are caring for all of God's creation. It's a big task that requires all of us to work together, regardless of our faith tradition or political persuasion.

We need to accept that money is not evil and that there is no virtue in being poor. It may take great virtue to endure being poor, but there is nothing inherently virtuous about poverty. Jesus lived the life of a pauper in solidarity with the poor. I call that a crucifixion. We don't nail ourselves to crosses to follow in Christ's footsteps, so there is no reason we should strive to be poor either. Instead, we need to help the poor not be poor. But again, what is the best way to do that? I believe it is by making everyone a little bit wealthy.

When I became a monk, I thought only greedy, selfish, self-centered people worried about money. It took me a long time to realize that, no matter where you go in life, money issues will follow. There is no escaping it, even in a monastery, so you might as well face it with as much grace and dignity as you can muster. Ignoring money is so much worse.

In a modern economy money is like oxygen. Without it you can't survive. So, like on an airplane, it is a good idea to put your oxygen mask on first before you assist others. You don't need to feel ashamed about breathing, but you do need to feel ashamed if you let others suffocate next to you when you have the power to help. And remember, just because you have an oxygen mask on in a crashing plane doesn't mean the story has a happy ending.

I think this is what God wants: for us to love and serve each other while caring for ourselves. It is a healthy balance between self-compassion and selfless service. Remember, "Love your neighbor as yourself." God also gave us the necessary tools, good hearts and good minds, to do it right.

So let's go forth and serve.

CHAPTER 3

LOVING MONEY WITH THE RIGHT KIND OF LOVE

Some Christians will cherry-pick quotes from the Bible or parse a single passage to justify being wealthy. One of the more popular justifications is to reinterpret key passages, such as 1 Timothy 6:9–10:

> But those who want to be rich fall into temptation and are trapped by many senseless and harmful desires that plunge people into ruin and destruction. For the love of money is a root of all kinds of evil, and in their eagerness to be rich some have wandered away from the faith and pierced themselves with many pains. (NRSV)

I've heard preachers say that it is the *love* of money that is the problem, not money itself. For me, this is like saying sex isn't a problem, enjoying sex is the problem: have all the sex you want, just don't like it very much. That's a little silly too. I love having sacks of money! But that doesn't mean there aren't serious spiritual dangers around money and sex. Rampant selfishness at the expense of others is unspiritual, unkind, and in opposition to the core teaching of the world's religions. We need to find a way forward that allows us to be a little bit wealthy and care for the poor and our planet, without feeling guilty about money, and enjoying it *wholeheartedly* for the good it produces in the world and our personal lives.

Be mindful about your money by giving your money some love—the right kind of love. Not avarice or greed but spiritual love. Love that is attentive, patient, and kind.

In ancient Greek, the original language of the New Testament, there are four different words for *love*, each with a unique flavor and nuance. But in English we have only one word for love. All four Greek terms get jumbled together, creating much confusion about the love of money. This is a topic worthy of an entire book, but it seems reasonable to distinguish between selfish, narcissistic love of money for self-aggrandizement and a higher love of money that is mindful, filled with gratitude for our blessings, and increases our capacity for service.

The phrase "love of money" in 1 Timothy 6:10 comes from the word *philargyria*, which literally means "love of silver." *Phil* is one of the Greek roots for love, and *argyria* is "silver," the metal that ancient Greek coins were made from. (*Argyria* rhymes with *Algeria*.) *Philargyria* has a profoundly negative connotation and refers to avarice.

What I suggest is that we need *agape-argyria*: divine love of money.[1] Agape is the highest form of love and also means "charity." It is a selfless love fervently devoted to the service of others. Agape allows us to love that which is intuitively unlovable: the sinner, the criminal, the fool, the leper—and perhaps even money.

Why shouldn't money and God work together? It is true that "no one can serve two masters. Either you will hate the one and love the other, or you will be devoted to the one and despise the other. You cannot serve both God and money" (Matt. 6:24). But here's a cool trick: you can make money serve God. Just not the other way around.

The journey from *philargyria* to *agape-argyria* is a life's work. To transform ourselves and our communities from avaricious greed to a healthy love and respect for the beauty and power of wealth is not easy. And the work is never done because eliminating our self-centered egoism, increasing our capacity for love and service, is the spiritual journey.

Agape-argyria is a daily practice, not a line item on your taxes. It is a spiritual practice that aligns our actions with our highest ideals. And because money is the tool that allows us to move and act in the world, it must be infused with our highest spiritual values to help bring love to fruition. By honoring the power of wealth, we give ourselves opportunities to enhance our spiritual practice.

For example, one brother would stop and say a prayer of gratitude every time he passed through the doorway to his room. This small, simple act was part of his daily spiritual practice, helping him stay mindful. (In the monastic tradition, gratitude is the heart of prayer.) To instill gratitude into my financial life I offer a quick prayer of thanks every time I give or receive money. It's especially hard to do when paying the bills and mean it, but it helps me be grateful that I can pay my bills. It also makes me pause and think when I'm shopping, *Does this purchase align with my goal of being a little bit wealthy and helping others?* If not, I step away from that money decision.

Try it for a week and see how big an impact it has on every aspect of your life. Gratitude is easy to express as a prayer or mindfulness exercise, giving thanks for all things. You'll be surprised by how well it works to pause momentarily on each financial transaction. People think monks are spiritual because they pray several times a day. But if you say a prayer of gratitude or take a moment of mindfulness every time you use money, you'll be meditating more than most monks I know.

Jacob's Ladder: *Agape-argyria* in Action

Building a healthy, loving relationship to money requires a clear framework to judge our beliefs and behavior. I like to use an analogy I call Jacob's Ladder, referring to the Old Testament story of Jacob seeing a ladder, in a dream, that reaches up to heaven. I'm going to ignore the actual meaning of that story, which isn't exactly clear, and just steal the metaphor. (Biblical scholars, please don't stone me.)

The symbol of a ladder reaching to heaven is a good way for me to think about values in action because you can't reach the highest rungs until you've climbed up through the lower rungs. The lower rungs on the ladder represent our baser, more self-centered needs and desires. Each rung up the ladder is a higher form of love, service, self-sacrifice, and charity. There are many rungs on Jacob's Ladder, and the higher you reach, the harder the next step is to take. Like a real ladder, it gets frightening the higher you climb, and every step takes courage and strength. Which is why so many people are stuck at the bottom.

The higher you go, the more effectively you can love and serve others, and the more exciting the journey becomes. It is a virtuous ascension and a form of grace. That grace draws us up, encourages us, bringing greater joy and contentment, even when the journey is difficult. We are destined for greater and greater capacities of love and service. And the more wealth and abundance we are able to share with our neighbors and communities, the wider our potential impact on the world.

Jacob's Ladder is our journey from selfishness to selflessness. It allows us to understand how we can care for ourselves, while also growing in our love and service to others. Most people think that selfless service requires complete self-renunciation, but that isn't how it has to work. The higher rungs up the ladder of selfless service are supported by the lower rungs and require healthy self-care, or appropriate selfishness. But getting stuck at the bottom is a form of hell.

Your progress on the ladder is completely unconnected to your wealth. If you have wealth, you can do a lot more good in the world, which is amazing. Money is power. However, it is impossible to climb the ladder and be wealthy if you aren't using your power in service of others. Instead, greed becomes an impossibly heavy weight that pulls you down and prevents you from reaching the top. That is *philargyria*. The higher you climb, the more *agape-argyria* you need to have.

This analogy helps me better understand the statement, "Love your neighbor as yourself." You can love yourself and care about your needs and the needs of your family, while reaching out to others. You don't have to renounce all wealth and live a life of poverty, but you do need to fight, and fight hard, to help the needy in your community. *Agape-argyria* requires charity—lovingkindness toward those we don't even like.

We are all in this game of life together.

If you are a person of faith, it's important to keep in mind that being wealthy doesn't mean that God loves you more (or less) than anyone else. I'm always a bit peeved at rich people who were born into rich families and then feel superior to others. Achieving wealth by your own efforts is worth celebrating, but remember that outcomes are different for everyone and are affected by a wide range of circumstances. In the monastic tradition, God doesn't "bless" anyone with money. God isn't viewed as a parent giving out rewards for good behavior. (Anyone remember the book of Job?)

Believing in a God who blesses you with money is spiritual narcissism. It implies that God didn't bless the poor with money because God doesn't like or trust them as much as he does the wealthy. Remember that Jesus and the apostles were all poor, and they got crucified (literally and metaphorically) by the world. Clearly, worldly success is not related to spirituality in Christianity. Caligula had a lot of money, and early Christians got tossed to the lions—they didn't win the Roman Empire lottery. The idea that prosperity is God's blessing on your family is just rich people trying to find a theological justification to relieve their perceived guilt. My point is that they have nothing to feel guilty about if they passionately love and serve others!

For those with faith, crediting all the work to God because God loves you more than the rest of us is egotistical horse manure. (It's also the sin of pride.) If we accept that logic, then God is cursing poor people with poverty since he is blessing others with wealth. In my opinion, God doesn't curse people with poverty any more than God curses people with cancer. We need science to cure cancer and economics to cure poverty.

God is calling us *all* to be a little wealthy and master the art of money management because it will reduce our suffering and allow our acts of service to have a larger impact, bringing more love and joy into the world. But that doesn't make a wealthy person spiritually superior. A wealthy person can be anywhere on Jacob's Ladder, even at the bottom. But a wealthy person at the top of the ladder can have a wider circle of influence and live a life of service that impacts more people.

How to Progress Up the Ladder

As our journey relates to money, there are numerous rungs on the ladder. It is also important to note that upward progress on Jacob's Ladder is not guaranteed. You can fall to the bottom at any time. You can also step down to a lower rung, and then move back up. It is rarely a linear progression. You can have each hand and foot on a different rung, representing different aspects of your life. You may be more generous with your family than with your coworkers. You may have a burst of charity to a homeless shelter, then on the same day treat a homeless person with disdain.

Making progress up the ladder takes great effort, and we each have a unique journey to travel. But two key traits are essential to everyone's journey: courage and kindness. You need both in heavy doses. It's a scary climb, and sometimes we get exhausted on the journey and then make mistakes, which is why faith communities, prayer, and contemplation are so important for renewal. The spiritual journey is hard. It isn't for the weak of heart.

Most importantly, we need to be clear about the goal. The greatest damage to our world, country, communities, and families is that we've lost sight of a common goal. Many times, we don't realize that we have a common goal and tear one another apart instead.

The point is to see our common humanity. Spiritual heroes feel a kinship with every brother and sister on the planet. They recognize their own pain inside everyone they meet. When the spiritual hero sees our shared suffering, they weep, and then they act. In the context of this book, I'm talking about acting in a way to alleviate suffering by increasing wealth.

Why is it so hard to climb the ladder of selfless service? Why do we struggle so much to be loving, kind, and compassionate when most of us agree that it is our highest ideal? There are a few damaged souls who think compassion is wrong, but they've probably never experienced true lovingkindness. Ignore them. For the rest of us, what's the deal? Why is lovingkindness so hard, sometimes even toward those closest to us?

The challenge is with our egoism. Loving and caring *for* others requires us to care *about* the needs of others. That requires self-sacrifice, and self-sacrifice is painful.

But here is the key distinction we need to make: self-sacrifice to help others is very different from self-denial. Sacrificing for others is key, but denying yourself basic comforts just to feel spiritual isn't very helpful and can even be damaging. For example, making money and then helping a person in need can take you higher up the ladder. Renouncing money as a form of self-denial and doing nothing else won't get you very far.

Worse, I've seen some people develop dangerous spiritual egos because of the pride they take in their extreme ascetic practices. They falsely believe that because they can endure some bizarre act of self-denial or self-harm that they are more spiritually advanced than the rest of us. This is the exact opposite of the spiritual journey. The whole point of the spiritual adventure is to see and feel your common connection to everyone and everything else, not to judge everyone else as inferior.

The spiritual life is about mastering the art of selfless service, and money is a very effective tool for serving others.

A Healthy Love of Money Requires Moral Virtue

Let me illustrate the rungs of the ladder in a different light. Have you heard of the book *Rich Dad Poor Dad*? It is one of the most popular finance self-help books of all time and was one of the first things I read when educating myself about the world of money. I've always struggled with it. For years I've tried to figure out why and how to thoughtfully frame my distaste. It is a difficult text to argue with because some lessons in personal finance and business are excellent, and I've tried to capture the best ideas in my own writing. But the book is morally bankrupt. Let me try to explain *Rich Dad Poor Dad* for those of you who haven't read it and provide a quick recap if you have.

The true story follows a young man from relative rags to great riches. His biological father was poor, working paycheck to paycheck as a school superintendent and a union leader. He was a hardworking, middle-class American who didn't have a lot of financial savvy. As the author grows up, he finds an older mentor, a "Rich Dad," who takes him under his wing and teaches him the ropes of the business world, helping him climb the ladder of material success. The book then shares with the reader the financial lessons learned from the Rich Dad and the financial mistakes made by the Poor Dad. Fine so far.

The problem with the book is the utter contempt the author has for his biological father. Whether he intended to or not, the author threw his real father under the proverbial bus and made a complete mockery of him. His poor father is portrayed as an ignorant freeloader and fool for not discovering the secrets of entrepreneurial success. When I read *Rich Dad Poor Dad*, I was still a high school teacher and monk, struggling paycheck to paycheck. I felt ashamed of myself when I finished it. I thought I was a chump. A fool. A lazy leech who ignorantly and stupidly toiled away serving others instead of being smart, looking out for only number one, and making lots of money at all costs. How silly is that? Why should a monk feel ashamed of living a life of service?

While I must applaud the tools for financial success that the author learned from his Rich Dad, the moral implications are horrific. The book elevates the Rich Dad to sainthood and encourages us to follow his example. However, I sympathize with the Poor Dad. He may not have made much money, and that isn't ideal, but he worked hard in education and for social justice. On Jacob's Ladder, the Poor Dad is higher up.

The best solution would be to bring the two dads together. Learn the money management skills of the Rich Dad and the social justice virtues of the Poor Dad, and then you have a powerful force in the world. Both dads lack a key skill. If I'm forced to choose, which I really don't want to do, then I'd rather be like the Poor Dad. The Rich Dad sounds like a selfish, narcissistic jerk.

Rich Dad Poor Dad is a powerful symbol of what has gone wrong with money and ethics. It idolizes and elevates a moral coward above a moral hero, simply because the coward has more money and creates jobs. That is confusing for most of us. It makes heroes out of villains. That may explain much of the moral chaos we see in the world and in politics today.

Money Love: One of Today's Best Tools to End Suffering

Was Saint Francis of Assisi correct when he embraced the leper but rejected his father's wealth? For his era—yes. In a modern economy, I'm not so sure. Not when money can cure the leper. Drugs, not hugs, will cure leprosy. Isn't that a miracle and blessing worth celebrating?

For those who don't see a spiritual conflict between religion and money, here's a concept to ponder: Judas's sin of avarice caused him to help murder God in human form for thirty pieces of silver. *Philargyria* is *the* sin that drives the plot of the New Testament story. Thirty pieces of silver created the Last Supper, the Garden of Gethsemane, and the Crucifixion.[2] No wonder we have such a strange relationship to money and why many Christians quietly push this topic under the proverbial rug or twist the Bible's message. This is scary stuff!

We can't let excessive ambition allow us to harm and destroy others, but that doesn't mean ambition is bad. If we made that claim, nothing would get accomplished, even the ambition to feed the poor. Likewise, excessive self-interest or greed is very dangerous, especially when it harms others. As I discussed in chapter 2, that doesn't mean that wealth is evil. Wealth is just a tool that expresses our values. Right values are what matter. And having right values and wealth is much better than having right values and no wealth. How many people have you desperately wanted to help but couldn't because you didn't have the resources?

We now know that the Bible is not a scientific textbook, but we can't use it as an economics textbook either. The spiritual practices of lovingkindness and mindfully cherishing God in all ways still apply, but the world is different now. We need an operating system update and reboot or else the spiritual world can't talk to the financial world, leaving everyone much worse off. We need a new model for spiritual bravery that doesn't involve renunciation or hatred of money.

Money is simply how we store work. We work to earn money. Money stores that work, and we then exchange money for the goods and services we need from others rather than barter. If you deny the dignity of money, you deny the dignity of work. If we can bring God into our work, then we can bring God into our money.

We should cherish money. Respect money. Be mindful of money. Be grateful for the blessings it brings and use it in the service of others. Love it like a child you want to see grow, mature, and be a gift you can share with the world.

Have you ever tried truly loving your money? When we love someone or something, each interaction is a joy. But when a relationship is toxic, every nuance, every pull for our attention is annoying as heck. Even the way someone chews their food or picks their teeth can drive you insane when you dislike them. If thinking about money fills you with anxiety and dread, you may have a toxic relationship with your finances. We do everything we can to avoid toxic relationships, which leads to financial neglect, which makes the relationship even worse.

Do you hate money? Will that relationship ever turn out well?

We are automatically attentive to the things we love. When you love and respect your money, you'll intuitively want to understand the ways of money more and more, helping to grow your wealth—which you can use to build a better world.

Jesus was correct when he said that the poor will always be with us, but he didn't say how many of us need to be poor! Isn't less poverty better than more poverty?

Economic theory is clear: there is no reason anyone must be poor. The economic systems that a well-regulated free market can produce, when combined with good government, are among the most powerful anti-poverty tools in the history of human civilization. In fact, the greatest success story of the modern era is that increases in free trade and improved economic structures have pulled large swaths of the world's population out of dire poverty. In just the past twenty years alone, capitalism pulled one billion people around the world out of extreme poverty! That is a stunning achievement. Free markets and good governance are vastly more powerful than any international aid or assistance programs.[3]

Saint Teresa of Calcutta's self-sacrifice caring for Jesus in the distressing guise of the poorest of the poor is one of the noblest spiritual accomplishments of the twentieth century. No question about it. But building a better economic infrastructure in Calcutta would be far more effective at eliminating the poverty there.

The blood of Christ may take away the sins of the world, but a little bit of wealth takes away much of the pain. If the choice is up to me, I'll take both, thank you very much. I don't need any more pain; I've had all I want.

Economics, like science, is one of the most effective tools available to alleviate suffering. We've updated our religious and moral framework to include scientific discovery and the scientific method in our worldview. Given the demands of a modern economy, is it possible to update our religious and ethical worldviews to have a healthier attitude toward money? One that doesn't layer all money talk with guilt and shame but views it as a tool to reduce suffering both individually and collectively?

Money crystalizes and amplifies our most selfish desires, which is why money is so dangerous to our spiritual development and so frequently admonished in religious texts. But spiritual bravery requires us to face the power and importance of money with charity and lovingkindness toward ourselves and the world. We need a better way forward.

PART 2

YOU AND YOUR MONEY

CHAPTER 4

IDENTIFY YOUR MONEY PERSONALITY

As with other areas of self-improvement, before we can change, we have to understand where we are. Money, of course, is complicated, and people's relationship with money is often influenced by how they grew up. My childhood is a prime example.

Up was down for my parents when it came to money. The more money we had, the tenser things became. After my parents divorced, they each fell over themselves to make it seem like the other parent had all the money and that they were the poor one. Each parent wanted to hurt the other. Money was their weapon of choice, and they used their children as bullets in a financial battle of the sexes. I wore ratty shoes with holes in the sides all through middle school because it was too much trouble to buy new ones. Any money spent on me, even for an ice cream cone, felt like a huge burden that was going to bankrupt the family.

Worse, when a parent did finally pay for something, I was expected to treat the event like it was the greatest moment of generosity imaginable. As if they were a martyr who had just fallen on their sword or a soldier who jumped onto a grenade.

Meanwhile, they were driving nicer and nicer cars, booking expensive vacations, and chartering planes for trips. Even though my father was a CEO, had a private office suite that was bigger than my current home, and appeared on the cover of a business magazine, each parent told me they were broke. I should ask the other to pay for any needs I had. It was really confusing. As a kid, I believed them when they said they were broke because the truth was too hard to bear: they had money, they just didn't want to spend any of it on me.

Even weirder was that my father didn't have any trouble lavishing his next girlfriend or wife with whatever she wanted. And there were lots of them. So where did that put me on his list of priorities?

Their money battles went beyond smaller things, like shoes. My senior year of college, I was twenty-four hours away from being expelled for not paying my tuition because my parents were playing a game of financial chicken. The divorce settlement dictated terms of financial support only until I reached twenty-one years of age. By my senior year, I was twenty-one, so there were no rules about who had to pay for my final year of college. Each parent wanted the other to pay up. The bill finally got paid by my father, with just moments to spare.

Eventually I just stopped asking for stuff. As soon as I was tall enough, I mowed lawns for neighbors to earn spending money. Then, when I was fifteen, I got my first real job working in a Baskin-Robbins. In the summers when school was out, I picked up an extra shift at Wendy's. For a little while, I also waited tables at a local breakfast joint. It was less work to have a job than try to get money out of my parents. It also gave me some autonomy and freedom, even as I wore ratty clothes and drove a junk car that was barely roadworthy.

In college I worked two part-time jobs that I never told my family about. My parents would have made me use the money toward my tuition, with no consideration that I needed money for things like books, toothpaste, and basic living necessities. I never understood how some college students can afford to party so much. Where do they get the money for all that beer and pizza?

But my feelings about money didn't start and stop with my parents. I even struggled with my relationship to the money I earned. Subconsciously, I understood that my parents did have money. I just wasn't good enough to deserve it. So why should I deserve someone else's money, even for honest work, if I didn't deserve my parents' money?

To be fair, my parents grew up with distorted notions of money from their own parents. It is a vicious cycle, and I'd like to break it. Parents who have money issues are likely to pass them on to their children. This should be motivation enough to tackle your money issues head-on. Why would you want that suffering for your children?

Both of my parents grew up in struggling immigrant families, but my dad's family was particularly poor. The son of an Irish flour salesman near Buffalo, New York, my dad was often sent out with his siblings after school to look for discarded soda bottles that they could exchange for a few pennies or a nickel, which would help pay for dinner that night. He grew up with a lot of shame around money. This motivated him to make a pile of it and build a successful career to impress his father. Sadly, his father was too much of a narcissist to notice.

My mom wasn't in much better shape as a child. Habitually ignored or criticized by her parents, she was left to fend for herself and never had any financial support from her family. Her father would pay for a son to attend college but wouldn't waste his money on a daughter even though she was extremely talented. He was also a secretive man. His immigration to America is still a family mystery. We learned, only after his death when going through his records, that he grew up in Sicily. But because of anti-Italian prejudice in America, he lied about his ancestry. Because of his swarthy complexion, he passed himself off as Spanish. He kept up this ruse his entire life, and not even his wife or kids knew! Growing up, I thought I was part Spanish. My mom grew up in a household with even more secrecy and shame about money than I did.

I don't blame them anymore. I love them very much because they are good people. But unhealthy attitudes toward money are toxic, and most of us have them in some form.

Slay Your Money Monsters

Before you can tackle your financial demons, you must be able to recognize them. And to recognize them you need to look at your history. You can't get into financial shape if you don't acknowledge your own unique set of baggage. To help you spot those vulnerabilities, I want to share some of the negative archetypes toward money that we all exhibit at times. I'm still guilty of some of these, and I know better. You don't need to get a cat-o'-nine-tails and whip your back bloody because you make these mistakes. Rather, learn how to work around your issues and reach your financial goals anyway. We all have challenges to overcome. You are not alone, but your money wounds will never heal until you face them.

Facing your money issues can be tough. You may even need professional mental health assistance to heal your money wounds. If so, accept that reality. Mental wounds can be far more crippling than physical ones, and we all have them to some degree. With money, it helps to start by not judging yourself too harshly or else you are adding to the shame and secrecy that causes money problems. If you are a good person, it can be harder to forgive yourself than forgive others. Asking for, and receiving, forgiveness for our mistakes also allows us to forgive ourselves and move forward with grace.

One place to start the healing is by bringing the divine love of money, *agape-argyria*, into your life. Be attentive to your inner emotional landscape and gently explore the values and attitudes that create a toxic relationship with money. Try making mindfulness, compassion, and humility the virtues you value around money, with the goal of becoming a little bit wealthy, to relieve your suffering and the suffering of the world.

Here are a few of the wealth-destroying and suffering-producing emotional archetypes I've encountered over the years. We all tend to slip into one, or a confusing combination, of these financial attitudes. Once you can recognize them in yourself, you are one step closer to building healthy money habits.

The Blinger

The Blinger uses money and luxuries as status symbols to pump up their ego. It makes them feel good when other people notice their conspicuous consumption. Having things that others don't have makes some folks feel superior, inflating their egos. While there is nothing wrong with material comforts, the spiritual journey should help us embrace our common humanity—not separate us from others. The Blinger enjoys domination and status. It is both a spiritual and financial trap.

If you spend all your money on stuff, you'll always be broke. Simple as that. And if you always compare your status symbols or wealth to those of others, someone will always beat you, and you'll be on a constant roller coaster of emotional highs and lows. It will destroy your wealth and your happiness.

One way to tame the Blinger impulse is to imagine yourself alone in the woods. If no one could ever see you with the thing you want to purchase, would you still buy it? How enjoyable would a Ferrari, a diamond ring, or a fur coat be if no one saw you with them? The Blinger impulse is a social beast. It needs company to survive. Remove your concern for what other people think of you and focus on things that spark joy in your heart and bring meaning into your life, and the Blinger cravings will become far less intense.

No one really cares about your stuff. You may think they do, but they don't. The rest of the world is too absorbed in their own mess to think about you much at all. Why destroy your wealth, freedom, and happiness to impress other people who don't give a darn?

My dad is broke and living with the help of relatives because the Blinger impulse captivated him, creating the image of wealth through the accumulation of stuff. He was never truly wealthy, just rich. To become a little bit wealthy, you'll need to save and invest money wisely, not spend it trying to impress others. Remember the virtue of humility? It can help you spiritually and financially.

Rich people can become poor people overnight. Wealthy people stay wealthy. They know how powerful money is and use it to create more value in their lives, ad infinitum. They use their capital (money) to generate more capital, which is why our economic system is called capitalism. Capitalists buy investments; consumers buy stuff.

The Hole in the Pocket

The Hole in the Pocket often looks and acts like the Blinger but has different origins.

The Hole in the Pocket uses money to feel good about themselves in the moment. If something is new and shiny, they want it. This is mindless consumerism at its worst. It is especially a problem for people with poor impulse control. The Hole in the Pocket impulse makes people feel good for a little while, but the high is short lived and financially damaging. Buying stuff becomes a sugar fix for the ego. It feels good for a moment, but then there is a crash. The way out of the crash is more sugar. It's a vicious cycle.

The Hole in the Pocket often suffers from low self-esteem and a sense of inadequacy and has a burning need to feel good for a little while. The Hole in the Pocket builds an illusion of fulfillment with each purchase. There are no simple fixes for this problem, but the best healing tool I know of is lovingkindness.

Instead of filling the void of emptiness inside with material purchases, try serving and thinking of others instead. The finite world of stuff can never fill the infinite void of loneliness and alienation.

If you spend all your money on things, you can't invest your money and generate wealth. You will always struggle, no matter how hard you work or how much money you make, if you can't control your spending.

That is why the trappings of wealth, such as big cars, big houses, and fancy vacations, don't mean a thing. They are wealth destroyers. They will bleed you dry. Avoid them like the plague (or at least until they are only a tiny portion of your total net worth). I will drive my used Toyota into the ground and keep my modest, but nice, condo for as long as possible. Why care about the trappings of wealth? I'd rather have my money carefully invested.

Stuff won't make you happy. I promise. When we buy stuff, it provides short-term pleasure, but we quickly adapt to a new normal and revert to our original mental state. This is a well-documented phenomenon called the "pleasure treadmill." It causes us to strive for the next sugar rush of consumption. Wealth, on the other hand, can permanently change your mental state by providing financial freedom, reduced stress, and greater security.

Although the media often focuses on the billionaires living extravagant lifestyles, the truth is that the average wealthy person doesn't have lots of bling. The fallacy of wealth equals stuff was destroyed by a famous book called *The Millionaire Next Door* by Thomas J. Stanley and William D. Danko. The book is timeless, and the conclusions are profound. Most wealthy people don't give a darn about stuff. They care about investments that grow their wealth. That's why they're wealthy, and you aren't. That said, some luxuries are great but only if they add personal, intrinsic value. Things with intrinsic value have a deep personal, pragmatic use for you, such as a college education or a safe, reliable car.

Objects with extrinsic value are just shiny things that consumer culture tells you to buy, like an expensive, impractical car or an enormous house. For example, I recently bought an amazingly expensive laptop. Why? Because I use it every day, and a poorly performing computer drives me crazy. I get a lot of personal value from it. It is worth the expense. But I don't walk into a coffee shop, pull my laptop out, and wait for people to notice how much money I spent on my computer. I don't care what other people think. I need my computer and phone to be excellent because my livelihood depends on them. I don't care about my car at all because, from where I live, I can walk to work and stores. So why do I need a fancy car? I drive about 3,500 miles a year. But that's me. You and I are not the same. You may need a good truck for work or a van for your kids, or maybe cars are your hobby. Just make sure your purchases have great personal value. Not because you are "keeping up with the Joneses." The Joneses are broke and in debt.

Better yet, if you want some material comforts and have the disposable income, use your play money to purchase luxury services rather than luxury goods. For example, once I earned a decent living, the greatest gift I've given myself is a house-cleaning service. I love it. It saves me time, stress, and energy, and it also keeps me from throwing out my lower back. It is worth every penny. I used to iron my own shirts to be frugal, but once I could afford it, I sent them out to the cleaners. The time and energy I save can be better used elsewhere.

Reinvest that extra energy into your career or something else that brings real happiness, like your family, friends, or volunteer activities. As an added bonus, paying for luxury services is a way of giving back to your local economy. It creates service-industry jobs that help pull people out of poverty and that can replace manufacturing jobs, which are increasingly lost to overseas competition.

I call this the Outsourcing Effect. You have a finite amount of time and energy in a day. The more junk you can take off your plate and the simpler you can make your lifestyle, the more time and energy you have for building your wealth, caring for yourself, and caring for others. Those are the important things. They help make life lovely.

When you have some extra disposable income, instead of buying things, outsource one task you hate (e.g., housecleaning). Then, as your income and wealth continue to grow, and you want to splurge some more, skip the consumer goods and outsource another task, such as yard work. Reinvest your newfound time into something more meaningful and lucrative, and then the following year you might be able to afford a good bookkeeper/accountant to handle your monthly bills. That's a big stress reliever. Reinvest that saved effort again and perhaps you'll start becoming outrageously wealthy and can hire a laundry service, nanny, cook, and driver. Then hire a personal assistant to manage all the people you've hired. Your world gets better, your time is increasingly spent on the things that are meaningful to you, and you're giving back to your local economy.

When making purchasing decisions, stop and think: Does the value I get from this good or service outweigh the power I'm losing by giving up my money? Maybe say a brief mindfulness prayer for guidance and inspiration. Remember: money is power. If a purchase truly adds value to your life, and you have the extra money to spare, that's fine, but don't assume that every purchase will add value. Most don't in the long term.

I meet a lot of rich people who buy big houses (or even several houses), and then the upkeep, maintenance, and big mortgage cause them huge amounts of stress and restrict their freedom. What is the point of having money if you let it complicate your life?

The Deer in the Headlights

The Deer in the Headlights archetype suffers from decision paralysis based on fear. The root cause can have several possible origins, but, generally speaking, financial stuff is terrifying for them—so they do nothing. There are also legitimate psychological conditions, such as arithmophobia, dyscalculia, and dyslexia, that make managing money extremely difficult for some. For others, the paralysis may stem from years of accumulated financial problems that seem too immense to untangle or from a family history that includes an abusive relationship to money. For these folks, a bookkeeper, financial adviser, or trusted family member can play a helpful role in making money management easier.

For those with significant money anxiety, my heart goes out to you. I love my money, but I still hate paying my bills and balancing my checkbook. It takes tremendous mental effort and is emotionally draining. I also procrastinate a lot. *Agape-argyria*, the divine love of money I discussed in chapter 3, helps me have compassion for myself and feel empowered to build a little wealth as a means of serving others. If you can find a way to make money management a form of service to others and the world, it can be a selfless act. It makes the burden a little easier. Not easy—just easier.

Think of how much more generous you can be toward your family and loved ones once you master your finances. How will your spouse, children, or friends benefit from your courage to become a little bit wealthy?

The Blob

The Blob is a financial couch potato—they have the resources and the means to get in financial shape, but they don't act. As I've said, physical fitness and financial fitness are extremely similar. If you don't put in the work, you won't get results. Simple as that. All physical fitness routines require two consistent elements: diet and exercise. All financial fitness routines require three consistent elements: earning, saving, and investing wisely. There is no escaping these truths. We've forgotten that sloth is one of the most problematic of vices. Yes, greed is bad, but sloth isn't a better alternative.

Motivational speeches are not my greatest strength, but for

those of you struggling with financial inertia, try to break down big problems into small baby steps. You don't have to master all of finance at once, just tackle one small task a day, every day. Putting good habits in place is far more important than a short flurry of activity. Is there one simple task, like organizing your work space, that you can do right now?

The Poor Me

The Poor Me has a favorite pastime: self-pity. They blame themselves, fate, bad luck, or difficult circumstances for all their troubles. It is a form of egoism because it allows people to justify being focused on themselves all the time. These folks are a bit like Eeyore in the Winnie the Pooh children's stories. It is hard to get them to act because they are convinced that it won't help much. It is odd that low self-esteem is a form of egoism, but it is. The story inside the Poor Me head is still all about them.

But here's the reality: the world doesn't revolve around you, and most people aren't out to get you. In fact, they aren't thinking about you that much at all. Sure, keep giving yourself excuses for why you can't succeed—you'll always be correct. But that doesn't mean your financial house will ever get in order. You need to get this money monster off your back and stop playing the victim. It is a form of disempowerment that invariably infects all aspects of life.

God is love and wants you happy. But God can't go to the gym for you, and God won't fix your finances for you. God will not work a miracle to solve a problem you created and that you have the power to solve. Constantly looking for miracles is a form of egoism. It is an attempt by your pride to prove that God likes you more than the rest of us. Instead, let some divine love into your life. Be kinder, more compassionate, and mindful in your financial life. You may be surprised at what talents you've been given. Don't hide them under a bushel. Besides, you don't have a choice—this money stuff isn't going away. Ever.

A refrain I often heard when I was a teacher was that students would rather be bad than stupid. By not trying, not doing the work, some people allow themselves the mental excuse of being "bad with money." They never give it their maximum effort. They are afraid that really trying will prove they are just dumb. If you've made it this far in the book, I doubt you're dumb. The best way to help students is to show them that you love and care for them, no matter what. Even if they try and fail, they will still be loved. It helps remove their fear of failure.

I don't know you, but I love you as a spiritual brother or sister. God loves you too. So how about trying to master the art of money with all the strength you've been given and see what happens? You'll never know if you never try.

Start by making a money promise to yourself you know you can keep. As soon as you've done it, make another one. Challenge yourself bit by bit, and you'll find that you are better at dealing with money than you thought. You might even get really good at it.

The Dude or Damsel in Distress

The Dude or Damsel in Distress is similar to the Poor Me but with a twist. They have a form of learned helplessness but are not necessarily depressed. In fact, they can even be very cheerful. The Dude or Damsel in Distress doesn't know how to manage money and hopes (or expects) someone else will solve their financial problems. It is a type of intellectual laziness or sloth. These folks abdicate their responsibility for their life and financial future.

Worse, they set themselves up to be financially abused by a partner, spouse, or charlatan, which reinforces their need to be rescued. They are waiting for their Angel of Mercy or White Knight to save the day. They will even project their learned helplessness onto God, expecting God to magically solve their problems. It is a type of financial immaturity.

The hard truth: no one will ever care as much about your finances as you do. If you are too lazy to take care of this stuff yourself, no one is going to do it for you—or do it better than you can.

To conquer this money demon, you'll need to develop more self-confidence in your ability to manage your money and your life. The best way to build confidence is through success. Start small and look for easy wins, like balancing your checkbook, clearly listing and organizing your debts, or accurately tracking your expenses. Then build from there.

The Angel of Mercy or White Knight

The Angel of Mercy or White Knight is the mirror image of the Dude or Damsel in Distress and is benevolent, even appearing kind. However, they need to have someone depend on them. They get an ego boost from running into a burning building and saving the day. That doesn't mean their actions are heroic—they can be stupid and self-defeating, and they may create bitterness and animosity in relationships. It is easy for an Angel of Mercy or White Knight to match up with a Dude or Damsel in Distress. They work well together to create a codependent relationship filled with mutual resentment.

In time, the Angel of Mercy or White Knight becomes annoyed at always having to care for the Dude or Damsel in Distress with no reciprocity. And the Dude or Damsel in Distress becomes resentful and angry at being financially dependent and infantilized. When these relationships blow apart, the shrapnel rips everyone involved to pieces. Fairy-tale characters never have a happily-ever-after ending in real life.

Giving and receiving charity are the cornerstones of all spirituality, but gifts given from the heart have no strings attached. The Angel of Mercy and White Knight like the dependence on themselves and enjoy the feelings of superiority their gifts create. They enable

codependence to flourish instead of ending the conditions of dependence, which is the goal of authentic charity. They appear extremely
benevolent and kind, so they can be hard to spot.

The best solution is to practice nonattachment to all acts of charity
and kindness. They are beautiful all by themselves. They don't even
need acknowledgment. Give generously, then let go.

The Philosopher

I run into this money archetype in academia or in pretentious
pseudointellectuals who haven't given up their high school fascination with Karl Marx. The rest of us can't afford that luxury. The
Philosopher twists reality, seeing only one side—money as the root of
all evil. Chapter 2 explains what I think about that. The Philosopher
has no real savings and no financial plan because they believe thinking deeply about money is wrong. When these folks retire, they often
face disaster, which reinforces their false beliefs.

I knew a monk who, for many years, took pride in the fact that
he never touched money or credit cards. That made everyone around
him deal with money more often to take care of him. However, his
"purity" was intact, regardless of what impact it had on others. It is
like another friend who refuses to own a car because he doesn't want
to give any money to Big Oil. But he asks his friends to drive him
around when he needs to run errands—using their car, their time,
and their gas. That's the spiritual high road? I don't think so.

Philosophers are often idealists who either refuse to accept the
realities of the world as they are or who have allowed cynicism to enter
their hearts. Either way, their behavior is hypocritical to what they
claim to believe. If you recognize this archetype in yourself, try going
back to the basics. Why are you an idealist? Couldn't money help
you achieve those lofty goals? How does rejecting the world make it
a better place?

The Hoarder

The Hoarder is so afraid of not having enough money that they don't spend money on anything that isn't necessary. The Hoarder amplifies and indulges their greed and stinginess. As a result, they fail to live life fully. Think Ebenezer Scrooge.

One of the misconceptions about money is that it's somehow wrong for it to bring enjoyment. But don't you think that, within reason, we should be able to reap comfort and pleasure from our work? Remember Genesis 1:31: "And God saw every thing that he had made, and, behold, it was very good" (KJV). Good things can be enjoyed, relished, and mindfully appreciated, and the things of this world are very good indeed.

We had a recurring guest at the monastery who was so cheap that he wouldn't spend money on anything that wasn't critical. This person didn't help pay for anything even though we were cooking, feeding, entertaining, and housing him. On every trip to the grocery store, he gave us a shopping list and then never offered to pay for anything. I know he wasn't broke. In fact, he had a solid pension and had inherited some money. So, after many visits like this, we didn't invite him back. His chronic cheapness pushed friends and family away. Ironically, this person was also a minister.

To tame this money monster, we need to learn generosity of spirit and *agape-argyria*, divine love of money that is devoted to the service of others. This requires empathy, selflessness, and compassion. Including self-compassion. There is no simple answer to how to become more generous toward one's self and others, but lovingkindness goes a long way.

Hoarders need to face their fears and develop more self-confidence. They often have financial PTSD, either from childhood poverty or money trauma later in life. Hoarding is a survival mechanism gone awry. One way to overcome the hoarding tendency is to have a fee-only fiduciary financial planner complete a detailed analysis of your financial situation. Let them show you your financial strength and then suggest specific dollar amounts you can use each month for generous acts of charity and kindness. It may ease some of your anxieties, allowing you to give more freely.

The Weaponizer

The Weaponizer is like the Greek god of war, Ares, but with money as a sword. This archetype uses money as a tool for control, power, and punishment. The children of Ares are, appropriately, Fear and Terror. If using, giving, or receiving money is accompanied by fear or terror, then a Weaponizer is at work.

Money can become an extension of your ego to bend people to your will. One of the great problems for the Weaponizer is that even if you get what you think you want, especially in personal relationships, your actions teach the people around you that your love is transactional. It comes with a price. "I'll give you what you want financially if you give me what I want emotionally." Money and love become perversely intertwined. This is the opposite of the spiritual journey, where the highest love is serving others, not making others serve you.

Weaponizers forget that the people around them have egos too. Their victims start to see the Weaponizer as a tool to get what they want and turn the tables. Victims of a Weaponizer will learn to manipulate back, giving what is desired (even love) in exchange for money and gifts. They love conditionally in return, but the Weaponizer is only useful if they still have money. (Think of King Lear and his backstabbing daughters Regan and Goneril.) And if the Weaponizer is sick and dying, a feeding frenzy will ensue. Or they lose their wealth and become useless to those around them.

Why do so many people fall victim to the Weaponizer archetype? Because at their deepest level everyone wants love, acceptance, and acknowledgment. The Weaponizer thinks that money can buy these things. Money is a great tool, but even the Beatles expressed this point in the song "Can't Buy Me Love." They should know. They had more money than most.

The best way to exorcize this money monster is to give up the need to control others, as the Prayer of Saint Francis aptly states:

> O divine Master, grant that I may not so much seek
> to be consoled as to console,
> to be understood as to understand,
> to be loved as to love.

There is always an internal rebellion when someone tries to control and manipulate you emotionally. You don't like it at all. Why would someone else? The result is a giant backfire, producing the opposite result of what the Weaponizer wants: hatred and resentment.

If you recognize the Weaponizer tendency inside yourself, you probably have unmet emotional needs. Try to recognize when you use money to punish or incentivize the people you love, then look for alternative strategies. Money incentives are for employees—not family. How can you express your emotional needs without involving money at all?

The Blamer

The Blamer has too much pride to admit their faults. They don't want to take responsibility for their financial troubles because admitting fault is too big a blow to their egos. Instead, they yell, scream, shout, and rant at everyone else around, blaming others for their troubles. The Blamer makes everyone else around them miserable. Basically, they feel entitled to things they haven't earned.

The Poor Me distorts reality to construe every misfortune as bad luck or bad judgment, creating unrealistic pessimism. The Blamer thinks they are amazing, believes the world owes them everything, and points the finger at everyone else for their problems.

Blamers are childish. They want money, but they don't want to take the responsibility for failure. We all fail; it is part of the journey to success. The hard truth: if we think all our money problems are someone else's fault, we are probably wrong.

Defeating the Blamer money monster is the trickiest task of all. Blamers can't accept responsibility for their problems. And paradoxically, without acknowledging a problem, it can't be fixed. The only way I've seen the Blamer be defeated is by a crushing blow to their egos. One so big they can't ignore it and pretend it is another's fault. When these people fall on their knees and beg for pity, maybe, just maybe, they can see the truth. May the Divine have sweet mercy on them when they do. It's a hard fall.

If you recognize the Blamer in yourself, then the best solution is radical responsibility. No one will ever care about your money more than you do, so accept the blame if you don't like where your life is at financially. Even if there *is* blame to share, how does that help you now? The past is over, and the only solution for a better future is to change yourself.

The Dreamer

The Dreamer is endearing but a little pathetic. They wish, hope, and pray for a big change in their financial life but still never act. They dream of winning the lottery, miraculously inheriting money, or getting rich quick. I've been there. A lot. The Dreamer archetype belongs to those with the double trouble of envy and self-doubt. Dreaming becomes a refuge in an unpleasant existence. Unfortunately, when the Dreamers come back to reality, it can hurt even worse since it's doubtful they saved very much or prepared themselves financially while waiting for their windfall. The Dreamers lack the courage to act and accept responsibility for their future. Dreaming, like praying, is great if it leads to action. But being stuck in a fantasy will waste your life away.

How to conquer the Dreamer demon? Realize you have a purpose to fulfill and a responsibility to act. You were put on Earth for a reason. What is it? What problem are you eager to solve and can devote your life to it? What actionable steps can you take right now to start making that a reality?

The Gambler

The Gambler is always looking for a way to get rich quick. They'll attend money-making seminars, buy Bitcoin, or day-trade. They are chasing the Next Big Thing. The problem with the Gambler is that they sometimes win, out of dumb luck, which reinforces their destructive behavior. The key is that they tend to overdramatize their wins and minimize their losses. Sometimes they are completely blind to their actual losses and will brag about how much they've won, when the reality is very different.

In finance, risk and return are correlated. The bigger the payoff, the bigger the risk. The only way to get rich quick is by taking huge, likely-to-blow-up-in-your-face risks. That is a "law" of finance, like gravity in physics. So most of the time they blow up in your face.

There are, of course, people who are truly addicted to gambling. The reasons for gambling addiction are varied and complex, and if this is you, get professional help *now*. Please call the twenty-four-hour National Problem Gambling Helpline (800-522-4700). Gambling addiction is a serious issue, and I won't try to tackle it here, but please get help if you have a gambling addiction. The pain won't stop until you get help. But not everyone who fits the Gambler archetype has a gambling addiction, which is why I include it here.

Let me tell you a quick story. When it comes to gambling, I learned a hard lesson early in life, thanks to my next-door neighbor, Mr. Deedee. He was a salty World War II veteran who was on the summit of Mount Suribachi during the famous flag raising in the Battle of Iwo Jima. The first flag raising.

When I was twelve, I had a yard service business and mowed

Mr. Deedee's lawn each week. One summer day, I was in our driveway washing my parents' car, and he walked over to pay me $60 for several weeks' worth of work. He looked down at the bucket of soapy water I was using and made me a deal. "Doug, I'll bet you sixty dollars that I can raise that bucket of water upside down over my head and not spill a drop." It was a tempting offer. How could I resist? No human being is going to violate the basic laws of physics. It was easy money. So I agreed.

Of course, if anyone ever offers you a bet, never take it. The game is rigged. That includes Las Vegas. So what happened? He picked up my bucket by the handle and gently began to rock it back and forth, back and forth, making larger and larger arcs, like a child on a swing. Then, when the momentum built up, he swung the bucket up over his head in a huge circle. He then gently slowed the bucket on the downswing, making smaller and smaller arcs until he set the bucket back down. He didn't spill a drop.

Without saying a word, he turned and walked away with my $60. I felt horrifically cheated. Why would a nice old man like Mr. Deedee take advantage of a kid?! It was a setup! Tears started to well in my eyes. He just cheated me out of what he owed me.

As Mr. Deedee walked down the block toward his house, I tried not to sob at this betrayal. Then he stopped, turned around, and slowly walked back. He put the $60 in my palm, giving it back, and held it there, sandwiching my hand between his gnarled arthritic ones. Then he looked me straight in the eyes, and, with heartbreaking sadness, said, "Kid, *never* bet something you aren't willing to lose."

It was one of the best life lessons I've ever received. It is good advice in finance, career moves, and relationships. Somehow I also understood his alcoholism a little bit better—some demons haunt us forever.

The Money Addict

The Money Addict is like the fictional character Gordon Gekko in the movie *Wall Street* who famously said, "Greed is good." That is *philargyria*, or avarice, not *agape-argyria*. Sometimes the Money Addict is just a workaholic who uses money and career as a distraction from internal discontent. Either way, it's a problem.

To put it in another context, there is a fitness instructor I know who has the most perfectly chiseled body I've ever seen. Every muscle is trained with meticulous care. He obsesses over every calorie, tracks and categorizes every bite of food, and maintains a grueling physical regimen. The results are impressive. However, this person's family and children are a mess. He spends so much time obsessing about his appearance that he has neglected the rest of his life and the people in it. That doesn't mean that working out is bad or that exercise is evil. This person just takes it too far. The same is true with money. You need to be financially fit and carefully build your wealth. But if money is all you think about, then your life is going to be a mess. Plus, you can hurt a lot of people in the process. You can be addicted to money, work, or working out—it is all a manifestation of egoism fed by our inner demons.

Money Addicts are self-obsessed and need to break out of their egoistic worldview. The world desperately needs our love, kindness, and care, not our selfishness, greed, and corruption.

It is okay to love money with *agape-argyria*—but not *philargyria*. *Philargyria* is a crisis of values. The best way out of our selfishness is through concrete acts of service to others. Start by spending a day volunteering at a homeless shelter, Habitat for Humanity, or your church. The only way to stop thinking obsessively about yourself is to think of others.

The TMI (Too Much Information)

The TMI blurts out every financial struggle to anyone who will listen. I'm a big fan of openness and honesty, and most of us need to talk about money more. One of the best ways to cope with any problem is by talking about it. But a few folks feel compelled to share all their gory details with everyone. After years of being closed lipped about money, I occasionally veer into this category, but I know not to share confidential information or let strangers into my current financial life.

A TMI is so anxious about money that they share money woes with coworkers and friends or anyone who will listen. The TMI is often oversharing in the hopes that someone will give them "the answer" to assuage their chronic nervousness. They open themselves to potential predators and can drive the people around them crazy.

The solution is simple but not easy. Take action. The TMI money monster will go away when the problems are solved, not before. They should be talking with a financial planner, financial adviser, or therapist, not their coworkers and casual friends.

If you are sharing your troubles just to vent and complain, like we all need to do at times, that's fine. If you are sharing your woes because you think the person you are talking to can help or give you advice, stop right there. Seek financial advice from reputable financial professionals only, just as you'd take health-care advice only from a medical professional. Most people you meet know little about money management because no one ever taught them; yet saying "I don't know" is one of the hardest phrases for humans to utter. If you ask people for advice, they will usually give it, even if they don't know what they are talking about.

Mindfulness is key. Openness is good, but so are sensible boundaries about with whom you share your intimate financial details. The best people to offer money advice are financial fiduciaries. Ignore the rest.

The Enmesher

The Enmesher pulls their children to an adult level, expecting their child to have the emotional strength to deal with a problem the parent can't handle. Divorced parents who use a child as a go-between to communicate messages or negotiate situations with the other parent are often Enmeshers. This is a perfect way to screw up kids.

For example, if you are divorced and can't talk with your ex, use a lawyer, family therapist, or older family member to mediate. Never make your kids do your dirty work for you. It makes you look like a coward, or worse, a bully. Your kids know what is going on, and it forces them to take a side.

A family will always face money issues, and it is good to be honest and factual with children about what is and isn't financially possible. Don't promise them the moon, but also don't bring them into your daily stress either. It is the parents' job to reassure their children, not the other way around. Don't overshare money stress with children and then expect them to comfort you. If you do, they'll start feeling responsible for your emotional well-being. They aren't therapists, and it is too big a burden for them, especially at a young age. Healthy boundaries are hard to set but essential with kids.

For example, if a child wants a new toy that you can't afford, it is helpful to tell them that, like most families, you are on a budget and a new toy isn't the highest priority. Food, housing, and school supplies are more essential than a toy right now, but you still love them very much. They don't need to hear about how your ex didn't pay child support or that you are worried about losing your job next week.

If every time your child asks for money, you tell them all the dreadful things happening in your life, they may associate dreadful things happening with their money requests. That can develop a hatred or fear of money in children.

You Can't Jump Over Yourself

Now that you've learned of some of the financial money archetypes out there and can begin identifying what you need to work on, I'm going to let you in on a secret. It is an ancient secret handed down in our monastery. Here it is: you can't jump over yourself.

What does that riddle mean? It means that your mind has blind spots and you'll never be able to see them or identify them on your own. It is impossible. Just like you can't jump over your own head since you take yourself with you wherever you go. Likewise, your mind can't diagnose your mind's flaws because the tool you are using to do the diagnosis is flawed in exactly the places you need help.

Your ego doesn't want you to see your worst attributes since it's painful. To see your worst attributes, you would need to remove or diminish your ego. And your ego will always find clever ways to fight back. The ego is like a multiheaded hydra. When you cut off one head, two more grow back. So what is the solution? Learn to seek out and accept critical feedback. Embrace it. It is your best friend in life. In fact, make a habit out of it. You'll be surprised by what you'll learn about yourself.

The best place to start is by having a mentor. Find someone you aspire to be like, build a relationship with them, and then ask them what you could be improving. It's free and often amazingly effective. You may even make a new lifelong friend. Ideally, your mentor should be someone you see on a regular basis, someone you want to emulate who has achieved the goals you want to achieve. If you can afford it, consider hiring a professional coach. I was skeptical of professional coaching until I tried it, and then I was delighted by the insights it provided. Coaching doesn't need to last forever; even just a few months can jump-start you in a new direction.

If your emotional struggles are too complex for a mentor or coach to handle, talk to a therapist or a counselor. It can be expensive but worth every penny. Your problems aren't really about money management but about letting your emotions around money hijack your life. Some churches and pastors even offer counseling services for free. Don't let your emotional fears stop you from getting help with them. If your arm were broken, you'd go to a doctor to get it fixed. If your mind has a glitch that is causing intense suffering, why not try to fix it? Ignoring it will only perpetuate your suffering.

Finally, get professional financial help. Hire a good fee-only financial planner or adviser who is a fiduciary to get you out of your rut. (We'll discuss how to find a good financial professional in chapter 14.) How will that help you tackle your money monsters? The problem is that if you fit one of the aforementioned archetypes, you are probably the last person to realize it. And chances are very good you fit at least one. The only way to find out which one(s) fits you is to complete a very difficult task: ask people you can trust, who know you well, for their opinion of your flaws. You have them. Trust me. We all have serious flaws.

Learning how to be wrong and accept your mistakes is the most powerful way to erode your ego. It also breeds humility and compassion toward others. It helps you move forward. It is also horrifically painful. You can discover the truth about yourself only by being humble. Being humble means clearly seeing your limitations. Which is why the meek, not the weak-willed, shall inherit the earth.

But beware. Don't ask toxic, negative, or abusive people for an opinion. If I've learned anything during my time as a monk it's this: *avoid those who try to fix others before they've fixed themselves!* They won't have a clue what they are doing but will do it with passionate intensity. Which is why we are admonished to "first take the plank out of your own eye, and then you will see clearly to remove the speck from your brother's eye" (Matt. 7:5). What people think about you is irrelevant. You want to concern yourself only with what good, competent people think of your strengths and weaknesses.

You can, and will, change. The question is, do you want to change for the better?

Regardless of whom you ask for help—a mentor, coach, minister, therapist, or financial planner—you need accountability partners. You can even have all the above. The best way to overcome your obstacles is to have someone hold you accountable for your behavior and call you out when your actions undermine your goals. This is a key step to climbing out of any economic hole in which you might find yourself.

CHAPTER 5

ASSESS YOUR TEAM

When playing the game of life, you need a good team. Many of our team members are provided by accident of birth, such as parents, siblings, and extended family. We do, however, get to choose some of our team members, such as our work and romantic partners or friends. Most people don't consider money values when they choose their spouses, but it is a crucial factor to ponder. An individual's attitude and habits with money can have a significant impact on the success of the whole team.

During my time as a mathematics department chair and business owner, I learned that a strong, balanced team is the most important part of running any successful venture. At the monastery I painfully discovered that an unbalanced team gets sunk, like a canoe with all the weight on one side. We didn't understand how to work together in a way that complemented our strengths, we had no team training and no coach, and we didn't understand the rules of the money game.

But you know what the biggest problem in the monastery was? Too much drama. I know that sounds weird, but it's true. Money drama pulled us apart.

We lost the ability to talk to one another openly, honestly, and without recriminations or guilt. And there was a lot of guilt. It prevented us from discussing the one thing—money—that drove every decision in our lives. In time, our values around money became too disparate. We were on opposite sides of a great chasm, and no matter how loud we shouted, our dear friends on the other side couldn't hear us.

Remember that the holy trinity in finance is earning, saving, and investing. Even when the monastery earned enough income, it didn't solve all our money problems. No one wanted to talk about saving, and investing was an evil spawned on another planet. Those beliefs aren't a recipe for financial success. Our team wasn't playing with the same goals.

Monks aren't supposed to get angry, but I did. I got angry because I felt alone, facing a seemingly impossible challenge. I couldn't talk to the other brothers about our money problems because they hated money. They didn't want to be bothered. (Who does?) It was okay for me to pay the bills, balance the books, and let them live in peace. Receiving support felt impossible. Our values were too different. And we were in a hermetically sealed environment. Finding a neutral voice to moderate difficult conversations wasn't possible.

I apologize for the discouraging tone, but I don't want to be a hypocrite and pretend like I've got all the answers to this one. One helpful cliché says, "When you lose, don't lose the lesson." At times I've lost at the money game. But here is the lesson: *money stress rips families apart—even rich families and monastic families.* Hiding from that truth won't help anyone.

What made the monastery situation even more tragic is that all the brothers were good, kind, holy people. But their lack of money skills disempowered them. They never had the wide impact on the world that the world desperately needs right now. Money is power—it gives us the power to do good deeds.

Throughout this book I'll share tricks and techniques for mastering your finances. But if you are married, you and your spouse are going to need to implement them *together*. That can't happen without the both of you sharing the same goals and objectives. If you have kids, at some point you'll need to teach them the rules of the game since they are on your team too. The earlier the better. As soon as your kids are old enough to make money requests, they are old enough to begin learning about the costs and benefits of those requests. (Since I don't have kids, I'm going to outsource this discussion to someone I trust. There is an outstanding book by Ron Lieber on kids and money, *The Opposite of Spoiled: Raising Kids Who Are Grounded, Generous, and Smart About Money*. I highly recommend it.)

If you want to create long-term financial stability for your family, then you need to agree on how to earn, save, and invest. Having a plan is the first step to becoming a little bit wealthy.

Before You Say "I Do"

Money is the leading cause of stress in relationships and a primary cause of divorce.[1] When selecting our romantic partners, we base our decisions on numerous criteria, but financial compatibility is rarely one of them. Same goes for business relationships. Before you enter a serious commitment with a financial partner, you need to make sure you share the same values and beliefs around money. If not, you are heading into tricky territory.

First, ask yourself these questions:

1. What would you do if you inherited $10 million?
2. How do you feel about debt? Do you have any debt? What is your plan to pay it off?
3. How important is saving money for you? How do you protect your savings? In a bank account, retirement account, or perhaps with an adviser?

4. What are your long-term life goals? When do you want to retire? How much money do you think you'll need to retire?
5. Do you ever check your credit score? Do you feel good about it?
6. How do you plan for financial emergencies?
7. Where are your financial weaknesses? Where might you need outside help? Are you good at budgeting or are you terrible at it? What's the first thing you do with your money after you get a paycheck?
8. And, most importantly: What is your form of selfless service? How do you give back?

Next, ask your potential spouse the same questions. How do your answers align?

While these are clearly important issues to have discussed before getting married, I suggest bringing them up early on. Talking about money, even with an intimate friend, can be very hard. The truth is that learning to talk about money with your spouse is a skill you need to master together, as a team, and it takes time, effort, and commitment. It won't happen overnight. So don't try to bring it up the night before the wedding and hope for the best. If you can't have these hard conversations, then there are communication or trust issues, and you should think twice before making a lifetime commitment. You can keep money conversations casual at first, and let the questions become more serious as your relationship progresses.

And here is another key habit of a successful relationship—talk about finances often. The more you talk about it lovingly, the better you'll become at it and the better prepared you will be when (not if) an emergency, tragedy, huge mistake, or some other unforeseen financial circumstance arises. Set up a weekly money meeting and put it on your calendar. If you'd like, it can even be a festive event. Bake some cookies or bring snacks! Have fun with it. After all, it is an opportunity to make your hopes and dreams a reality.

Money Is Every Member's Responsibility

If you are already in a relationship that is struggling from money stress, take heart. Even good people in excellent marriages have periods of money stress. Sometimes lots of money stress. That comes with the territory. You can get through it—most couples do. Just like you'll have struggles with children and periods of sickness. Money problems alone will not sink your marriage. If your team is strong, you can handle just about anything together.

The first thing you need to do is assess where your team has weaknesses. Hiding from them won't help. Do you struggle with overspending, underearning, budgeting, managing debt? Or perhaps there are addiction issues? Until you have a clear assessment of what the problems are, you won't be able to formulate a plan for dealing with them. Every team has flaws. That's okay. You can overcome them. But try to be clear-eyed about what they are. Then, tackle the hard part—formulating a plan to resolve them. While there are many first steps you can take on your own, you may need a professional therapist, financial planner, minister, or adviser to intervene.

The reason money problems are so difficult to solve in relationships is that they are a swirling vortex of power, values, communication, relationship timing, and money baggage. Untangling all that mess is like solving a Rubik's Cube while blindfolded. You'll probably need some help to guide you.

For example, one couple I worked with had a domineering partner, Steven, who was a Blamer. Everything was always someone else's fault. His wife, Maria, was a Poor Me, who assumed that terrible things always happened to her and that she couldn't do anything right. Every time money problems arose, Steven would attack Maria without taking responsibility for his overspending or unrealistic expectations. Maria accepted all the blame and incessantly apologized for all her "faults"—not managing the money more carefully, not making more money, not letting Steven have all the things he wanted, and so on.

These two money monsters tore at each other, creating a vicious circle. Steven egotistically wanted to deflect responsibility onto Maria, and Maria wanted to accept all the blame. This made Maria the center of all the attention—even negative attention. It feels better than being ignored.

In this case Steven couldn't accept responsibility for his money issues, and Maria couldn't let go of her perceived responsibility for Steven's problems. Maria enjoyed the illusion of power to control their shared destiny and also couldn't let go of the shame that Steven heaped on her.

Eventually they sought help but only after accumulating over $100,000 in debt. Before I could help them fix their financial problems, they had to resolve their communication issues, examine their different values around money, share responsibility evenly, and face their money baggage together. It also had to happen at the right time, when both were ready and willing to examine their faults. It was a big task. They could never do all that alone. They are now out of debt, and their relationship is stronger and happier than ever before.

In another situation John was a Gambler and Debbie was a Dreamer. John loved to chase get-rich-quick schemes and take wild financial risks in the hopes of hitting it big. Debbie sat on the sidelines and encouraged John to indulge in fantasies that were just delusions of grandeur. Debbie was continually sucked into John's promises of riches around the corner and enabled him to engage in risky behavior. Neither had the skills or self-control to solve their money problems unilaterally. With help, they've learned to spot their weaknesses and work together to build a real future, not a fantasy.

To add more complexity to these situations, many people have multiple money monsters. Suzan is a Big Blinger who is also a Weaponizer. She married Eddie, who is a Money Addict and a White

Knight. Watching that money drama unfold made the Kardashians seem boring. Their marriage didn't last long.

Your family is your team, but that doesn't mean everyone in your family is a good team player. Without a team approach, one person inevitably becomes the nag. Either that or you have a situation in which most of the family is on the same page, working hard to keep finances in check, until one person blows the whole thing apart with a single unbudgeted purchase. Either way, the results are the same: everyone is resentful. The nag hates being the one to say no all the time, and everyone else hates hearing no all the time. Or worse, the nag capitulates, and then you run up credit card debt. If it's the same person who regularly overspends, confronting or shaming that family member will make them feel singled out and vilified, and they'll be less likely to talk openly about their spending.

Many couples assume that money issues should be the sole responsibility of the person in the relationship who is "good at it." Some people take this responsibility on themselves, and some think that because they are "bad at dealing with money" or "don't know what I'm doing" that they should not get involved. But what if your spouse unilaterally decided that he or she wasn't going to do any childcare, ever, because you were better at it? How would that make you feel if they abandoned all parenting responsibilities? It would likely breed resentment and could blow the relationship apart. Parenting is a shared family responsibility—so are finances. When living in a family, even a monastic family, there is no opt out. Money is everyone's responsibility. Money dictates every decision, and if one person refuses to participate in money matters, they are excluding themselves from *all* decisions. That's not how a team works.

When businesses struggle, we often hire outside consultants to assess our teams, identify issues, and offer solutions. Marriages are similar. Having an outside, independent, neutral third party evaluate the situation can be the best remedy to complex problems. Just like when writing a book, I can't see the flaws I've created in my writing. That is why every writer needs a good editor. A relationship is similar. You can't jump over yourself, not individually or as a couple. You are building a team, and all great teams have great coaches. The New York Yankees don't win because of the dapper pinstripe uniforms. Who is your family coach? It may be a wise grandparent, a trusted friend, a therapist, or a clergy member, but reach out if you are struggling. Having a referee to moderate difficult conversations can produce breakthroughs if both husband and wife are open to the possibility.

No Easy Answers

If you and your spouse have different aptitudes for money management, let me share two extreme examples of what can, and cannot, work.

I have a friend, John, who is a famous artist. His art installations are at tourist sites around the world. John is brilliant, financially secure, and has a beautiful family. John is also severely dyslexic. Because of his dyslexia, he cannot read—John is functionally illiterate. His greatest regret in life is that he'll never be able to read a book. He certainly can't read his bank statement, pay his bills, or manage money on his own. Instead, his successful and talented wife, Karen, handles all money matters in their family.

Karen knew what she was getting into before they got married, and they both agreed on a solution. Karen does all the budgeting and bills, but John picks up the extra slack with dutiful childcare, cooking, cleaning, teaching art full time to keep their income steady, maintaining the family health insurance through his employer, and so on. They regularly talk through their budget and bills together, even if Karen does all the heavy lifting.

Although John can't manage money directly, he brings his best effort to the family team. He does the best he can with the skills he has. That's all anyone can ask of him. Karen still gets frustrated and sometimes resents having to manage all the household affairs, and they squabble over money like any couple. But after decades of marriage, they are still going strong. They love each other, support each other, and make it work even when it isn't easy. They've accurately assessed their collective strengths and weaknesses, built a game plan around them, and worked as a couple to reach their shared goals.

One key reason for their marital success is that John understands the burden Karen carries for their team and is grateful. And he regularly expresses his gratitude. That doesn't mean they both wouldn't prefer a different reality, but they are happy and financially secure.

In contrast, let me take you back to the monastery where, despite all their love and kindness, money remained a taboo subject with the brothers. The other monks were happy to delegate the work, but I had no authority to enforce a budget nor did we have a consensus on how to spend our money. Responsibility without authority stinks.

How did that turn out? Not well. Even though I made a vow, in a church—prostrate before God, a priest, my friends, and family—to remain a monk all the days of my life, I still left. Money stress tore our relationship apart. It was a problem I couldn't fix. Instead of two people with money baggage, we had a communal whirlpool of issues to overcome, including my own. It was just too much.

The monastery money problems didn't end after we declared bankruptcy; they just got started. Bankruptcy eliminated all our debts, but that still left us completely broke. Being broke felt great—at first. We were self-reliant, like any family, and had to work together and plan for the retirement of the other brothers who were already past middle age.

I wanted to leave the monastery years before I did; I just never had the heart to admit it. Why did I stay so long? I felt an obligation to put the monastery on a secure financial footing and make sure that neither it nor I would be financially devastated by my departure. The monastery operated on the assumption that it was the duty of the younger monks to support the older monks in retirement. Then when the younger monks are older, they are supported by the newbies. It is the earliest form of social security.

But what happens when no new monks are joining a monastery? I was the last brother to join the community in my twenty-year vocation, and I was decades younger than the other brothers. I was the only young monk left—the community was dying. If I quit, they would face an aging population, no savings, and no clear way to retire. So I stayed for a decade longer than I wanted to. I left when I knew that they could stop working with dignity and I could leave with some money in my pocket to start a new life. To depart earlier and condemn them to more financial suffering in their old age seemed cruel beyond measure. I did love them. I just couldn't live with them anymore.

The Money Talk

I'm not married, so I can't pretend to know all the answers to family issues. But I've learned a few things about resolving money conflicts that I wish I had known early on.

First, you need to give your spouse a fair chance. Money baggage is likely holding him or her back, and you need to find a way to break through and get him or her on board. It's also likely that you have issues that are contributing to the problem, and your spouse may have some hard truths to tell you as well. This means sharing your feelings and concerns thoughtfully and respectfully, asking questions, and listening. You need to have the Money Talk and bring things into the open. Here are a few suggestions on how to have that conversation:

1. **Meet in public.** Where you have the Talk matters. Restaurants or coffee shops are good, but any quiet public place where you and

your spouse cannot shout, run away, or storm out is helpful. A public location helps keep the tone civil and avoids emotional escalation. Just avoid a table where people can overhear your conversation.

2. Time it well. Try to schedule the Talk when you both are relaxed, rested, and at ease. A difficult conversation at the end of a long workday isn't likely to be productive. Don't ambush your spouse—let him or her know in advance what you want to discuss.

3. Share gratitude first. Before you jump into the hard stuff, what do you love about this person? What are you grateful for in the relationship? Have you told him or her lately? The Money Talk is challenging, so make it easier by reminding yourself and your spouse what you value and cherish about him or her. To quote the indomitable Mary Poppins, "A spoonful of sugar helps the medicine go down."

4. Watch your tone. One of the fastest ways to shut down your spouse is to go on the attack. The Money Talk needs to be a discussion, so try being kind, respectful, and compassionate. Otherwise, you'll be battling a money monster rather than a loving husband or wife. I've also found that it helps to be vulnerable and let your spouse see your suffering. He or she is certainly feeling vulnerable, so put your spouse at ease by sharing your feelings without judgment. Talk about yourself and your hopes, dreams, and fears. Dream about the future life you want together. This can create space for your spouse to share what he or she is thinking and feeling, which can help move the conversation forward.

5. Ask, don't assume. Asking good questions can produce breakthroughs. One of the most harmful things you can do when having the Talk is to assume you know why another person acts in a certain way, what he wants, how he feels. Instead, continually check in to make sure you understand each other, and ask questions about the other person's thoughts, feelings, and actions, even when you think you know the answers. When in doubt, circle back to questions about the future you hope to build together.

6. Stay on topic. You are looking to build a better financial future, so let go of the past. Focus on the goals you hope to achieve, and avoid blame for past mistakes. If you make it a barbecue where you roast your spouse, even if you are correct, don't expect him or her to come back to the table again. Do you want a team that works together, or do you want to be right about everything? You probably can't have both. Keep the conversation on the present and future, not the past. Most of all, have one or two key topics you want to address now and bring the conversation back to those topics if tension arises or you get offtrack with recriminations.

   7. Create action points. Have clear tasks and actionable goals where you hope to reach consensus. You are trying to strengthen your team, so you may need to start with team-building exercises by making it easy for your husband or wrife to participate. Look for baby steps you can both agree on to build trust. For example, can you agree to block out one hour each week to discuss the finances together and put it on your calendars? It's a start.

   8. Walk the talk. The only person you can change is you. You need to empower yourself to build the life you want, and with love and encouragement, your spouse may come along. The goal is to build a life together, so you need to work on your issues as well, not just cast blame or aspersions. Financial problems are often symptomatic of deeper relationship issues, not causative. Are you effectively communicating your hopes, fears, and dreams? Are you listening when your spouse expresses his or her hopes, fears, and dreams? If your husband or wife starts casting blame, accept criticism where it is valid. This is hard, I know. But try to lead by example and own your mistakes without drama or recriminations—*then quickly move on.* This can encourage your spouse to do the same. Model the behavior and attitude you'd like to see. Remember: forgiveness of mistakes is the heart of any spiritual practice—including your own.

   9. Share the power. The person who controls the money controls the power. One person in a relationship often feels entitled to too much power or feels completely disempowered, leading to myriad problems. It is helpful to remember that asking your spouse to limit spending means limiting his or her purchasing power, which is a blow to the ego and can trigger feelings of shame, anger, and resentment. Giving your spouse a voice and decision-making power can help, especially if one of you earns significantly more money. Ask your spouse for advice and his or her opinions. Let them know that you need them and their help. Are questions more helpful than making statements? I think so. When was the last time you enjoyed being lectured?

10. Provide a reality check. Be completely honest about the financial reality as you see it. Better to have a hard conversation now rather than a hard separation later.

11. Start over. If you get bogged down, start over and talk about your hopes and dreams once again. What do you want out of life and your relationship? Then transition to discussing how money will help you both reach your dreams. Try to build a game plan, together, to make those dreams a reality. Sometimes discussions get so emotional you need a time-out. That's normal. But before you step away from the conversation, commit to a specific time to reconvene. It could be five minutes or five days.

12. Never lie. Just don't go there. It doesn't end well.

13. Get help. Finally, if you are completely bogged down and can't see a way forward, find a counselor, adviser, or clergy member to help moderate difficult conversations. Having a neutral third party can provide you both the safety and space needed to be more open about what you feel. I'll discuss how to find good help in chapter 14.

The Money Talk may be one of the most difficult conversations you'll ever have. Even now I struggle to follow my own advice, so don't lose heart if the actual conversation veers wildly off script. The task of staying on script is itself a great team-building exercise. Money monsters are tricky and may disrupt your attempts at team building. Take a deep breath, refocus on your goals, and keep trying.

CHAPTER 6

BECOME FINANCIALLY LITERATE

Growing up rich, I should have learned a few things about money, but there was so much shame and secrecy around it that I went out into the world knowing nothing. No one taught me how to open a bank account, pay a bill, or balance a checkbook. My dad was a CEO, and my mom was a Certified Financial Planner (CFP), so the irony is palpable.

My story highlights a crucial problem—finance is a foreign language! We don't teach children the language of finance, and then we wonder why most adults struggle with money. We send young adults into the world financially illiterate, and then they fall into terrible predicaments because they've never been given the tools for success.

The world of finance has a unique vocabulary, set of rules, and etiquette. (Have you ever tried reading the fine print on a credit card application?) The world of finance is a bizarre parallel world, operating side by side your normal existence. It surrounds you but is often confusing. It's like being a kid and realizing, for the first time, what it's like to be an adult—there is a whole other way of being a human being, with new rules and expectations, which never occurs to you when you're eight years old.

Adding to the confusion are regional dialects—a real estate agent and a stockbroker may use the same words but in vastly different ways. Simple terms, such as *guarantee, safe, return, flexible*, and *long term*, all change meaning depending on the context in which they are used. In addition to vocabulary, professional etiquette changes by industry subset. Attend a convention of real estate agents and you'll see brighter, more casual clothing to convey warmth. Attend a meeting filled with stock brokers, and you'll face an ocean of dark suits. Go to a quarterly earnings call for a tech company in San Francisco, and you'll see hoodies and Allbirds. Get the etiquette wrong, and you'll feel like a pimply high school student in a frilly sky-blue tuxedo at prom.

To grow a little bit wealthy, you must learn and continually practice the language of finance and the dialects you interact with the most. Like mastering any language, fluency requires constant learning and practice. If you master the language of finance, or at least become conversationally fluent, then you'll have the power to improve your life and make the world a better place. That doesn't mean it will always be fun or easy, but it is worth it. Once, when in Rome, I sheepishly asked a waiter in English where the bathroom was. He rolled his eyes at me and pointed to the bathroom sign. I might have known I was standing right next to it, but I didn't speak the language.

Allow your desire to help yourself and others exceed your pride and shame in asking simple questions. Mastering the language of finance is difficult, but I don't mind admitting how complex it all is. I had to start at the very beginning, just like everyone else.

Learning is a lifelong endeavor, and how much you learn is up to you. I'll introduce financial terms in the pages to come, but for the purposes of this book, I want to focus on the two most foundational terms that will help you master the art of wealth.

Become a Capitalist, Not a Consumer

Before we dig further, I need to ask a small favor: please try to disregard any preconceived notions you have about the words *capitalist* and *consumer*. I'm reappropriating them for my purposes and ask that you let go of any negative connotations those words might conjure.

In the quest to grow wealthy, two categories separate the wealthy from the Desperate and Dispossessed. These are a bit simplistic, and most of us will wander between both categories throughout our lives, but they define the mind-set that builds wealth or destroys it.

The wealth-generating mind-set of the capitalist builds wealth; the wealth-destroying attitude of the consumer decimates it. Here's how.

What Is a Consumer?

When I talk about consumers, I am referring to people who spend all their income on stuff. We all need to buy stuff and are technically consumers with most purchases, but the wealth-destroying consumer works at a job and assumes that everything they earn is available to spend. They spend their hard-earned money on stuff that has no lasting value or declines in value over time. How much is a new pair of jeans worth after you've worn them? Unless you are Mick Jagger, not much.

Nonetheless, most consumer goods, like clothing, cars, yachts, and electronics, *depreciate* over time. Meaning they are worth less the longer you own them. Some things, like new cars, depreciate very quickly. The result is that consumers are always broke, in debt, and never able to accumulate wealth. Life for a consumer can also feel like a treadmill: work to make money, spend money, work some more, repeat ad nauseum. As a result, they are always trapped in a job or career and are required to work to sustain their lifestyle.

There is nothing wrong with stuff, but it is empirically obvious that having stuff doesn't make people happy. My rich parents struggled to find happiness—and they had lots and lots of stuff.

A consumer is also a pawn to advertisers. The media culture constantly manipulates our emotions to lure us into buying more and more. We are pushed to want the latest and greatest. It is the air we all breathe. The consumer treadmill makes corporations and capitalists rich, and consumers broke.

Not all consumer purchases are bad. You will always need to buy some consumer goods, like food and clothing, which are necessities. Buying new windshield wiper blades is a consumer good that depreciates but is important to have if your old ones are worn out. But do you need them to be gold-plated and shoot confetti? Anything that furthers your intellectual capital and helps you make more money, such as books on finance, can be very wise purchases. Just make sure your purchases serve a clear need and are not "comfort buys" to soothe your ego.

To become a little bit wealthy, you need to be hypervigilant about the intense amount of marketing that surrounds you. The media is always trying to get people aroused and excited about a new product or service. It is financial pornography—it teases or excites, manipulating consumers into a purchase.

The advertising message is sometimes subtle but always the same: "Your life will be better if you purchase X product or service. You suck without it." And everyone knows you suck if you have an older iPhone. Those are vicious lies. Your self-worth comes from your innate human dignity and lovingkindness toward others, not inanimate objects.

Somewhere along the way, as will inevitably happen, most consumers will have a crisis, a setback, or an irresistible and inexplicable desire to buy something called a Louis Vuitton. I still haven't figured out what a Louis Vuitton is. Is it a person, a place, or a thing? In any case, there is a tragedy, mistake, or Louis Vuitton that requires the consumer to spend more money than they make. But that isn't mathematically possible. You can't spend more than you have.

So what happens? The consumer uses a credit card to magically give them more purchasing power, which lands them in consumer debt, which starts the Debt Avalanche, which we will discuss in chapter 10. That never ends well.

The problem is that desires are infinite, and the amount of stuff you can buy is also infinite. But your money will always be finite, even if you're Warren Buffett—who is notoriously frugal. If you don't learn to control your impulses, shop sensibly, and put strong boundaries on your money, you will always be broke. I'll give you tips on how to do all that in chapter 9. For now, let's focus on the mind-set you need to build wealth.

What Is a Capitalist?

If you want to get off the treadmill of working to live, you'll need a way out of the consumer trap. For that, you need to become a capitalist. But what is a capitalist? If a consumer is someone who buys stuff that *depreciates* over time, a capitalist is someone who works to save and invest, buying as many assets as they can. Those investments grow in value and produce money. They *appreciate* and are *worth more and more over time.* That new money they create is reinvested to purchase more assets, which steadily compound until you are financially independent. That's wealth. Wealth isn't about how big your paycheck is or isn't; it's about how you use what money you have to create a lasting pot of cash that you can live off of indefinitely.

And here's the bonus round: if you avoid consumer goods that depreciate and focus on investments that appreciate, then you automatically reduce your consumption of disposable goods. Everything you buy that depreciates will, eventually, depreciate to nothing. Then it needs to be recycled, burned, or put in a trash heap. Usually it just ends up in a landfill. It also takes energy and pollution to produce every consumer good. Our overconsumption of disposable goods doesn't just destroy our wealth—it destroys the planet. On this point our financial best interest and Earth's best interest are perfectly aligned.

Eventually the capitalist's investments appreciate and generate independent income, without the capitalist having to work to sustain their lifestyle indefinitely. You know what's next? You can live a life of relative freedom. You'll certainly have less financial stress and can then focus on other priorities. Of course, there is no magic income number capitalists need to reach to be wealthy. Everyone has different income needs, and the amount of wealth required to sustain your lifestyle depends on your lifestyle. But the great news is that if you can lower your expectations and simplify your life, you'll need to accumulate less wealth. Some folks live beautifully free and happy lives with very modest incomes.

Sustainable wealth does not usually look like the images we see in the media. Real wealth is humble and has no correlation to fancy cars, lavish spending, or a huge home. You can't always see true wealth— appearances can be deceiving. Real wealth focuses on creating more free *time* and valuable *experiences* away from the rat race, not running harder to clutter life with more stuff, a longer to-do list, and a Mercedes-Benz.

To retire comfortably around age sixty-five, you'll need to save and invest at least five to ten times your annual income. For a median household with an income of $57,000, they'll need around $570,000 in wealth to retire comfortably. That's a big number. If you are retiring sooner, you'll need much more.

If you have other income sources, like a defined pension, inheritance, or equity in a home or business, you may need less. The goal is to replace at least 60 to 80 percent of your pre-retirement income. You can use a free calculator on my website (douglynam.com) to see if you are on track. It can even include an estimate of your Social Security benefits.

The great news is that technology has made it amazingly easy to buy investments. You can get started with just a few bucks in your pocket. You don't need millions in the bank or to be a venture capitalist to get rolling. Start small and eventually, with diligent effort, your investments will grow. Anyone can do it. You don't need to be a CEO to become a capitalist. A teacher, a janitor, and even a monk can do it. I'll show you how in chapter 12.

The secret to wealth is simple—be a capitalist, not a consumer. All personal finance hinges on this concept. Everything else is commentary. To be more accurate, everything else is the how-to part of the lesson. Knowing what to do is easy; knowing how to do it is hard.

How to Start Building Your Financial Lexicon

To tackle the hard part, you'll need to master the language of finance. I'll cover the basic terminology as we travel together, but there is no way to cover it all in one book. That will require on-the-job training. Here are a few tricks to help:

1. **Look up every financial word you don't know as you encounter it.** It helps me to remember that there is a huge difference between being ignorant and being stupid. I'm ignorant of many things—that doesn't mean I'm stupid.

For example, I'm completely ignorant about fixing car engines. That doesn't mean I'm too stupid to learn; it just isn't at the top of my to-do list. There is no shame in not knowing how to fix cars, but if I really needed that skill to survive a zombie apocalypse, I'd be willing to pick it up. To prevent, or survive, a personal financial apocalypse you are going to need to speak some finance. Even if it isn't on the top of your to-do list.

Learning to speak finance may be painfully slow going at first, and you'll find yourself looking up the same words multiple times, but if you stick to it, the process gets easier and easier. There will be a magical moment when you realize you don't need to look up words anymore, or at least rarely. Investopedia is one of the most popular Internet tools for financial vocabulary right now, and their free resources are often excellent. But be aware, they are also trying to sell you stuff. Don't get sucked into anything involving day trading, stock trading, or market timing.

2. Increase your exposure to the world of finance. There is no need to look up every new word you encounter if you never encounter new words. For that to happen, you must increase your exposure to new ideas and concepts. The best way to do that is to read—a lot. You will need to get out of your comfort zone. Sign up for investment newsletters, blog posts, and podcasts. Any list curated by a mainstream newspaper or magazine will likely give you a good place to start.

Subscribing to reputable financial blogs will give you a wide variety of tips and tricks each week. They will introduce you to novel words and ideas to help expand your financial literacy. It is okay if you don't understand everything you read. If you stick with it, in time you will.

To find out which blogs are reputable, simply search for the "best personal finance blogs." Also be curious as you read. Most articles will link to thought leaders, books, or other stories of interest. Follow those rabbit trails when you have time and see where they take you.

The Internet landscape is constantly changing, but here are a few of my favorite finance blogs right now:

- Get Rich Slowly (getrichslowly.org) is one of the most respected money blogs out there. It carefully examines all aspects of growing a little bit wealthy.
- The Penny Hoarder (thepennyhoarder.com) is one of the largest personal finance websites with great tips on earning and saving money.
- Your Money newsletter published by the *New York Times* is a classic and my personal favorite. You can sign up for it at nytimes.com/newsletters/signup/MY. The *New York Times*

allows only a few free articles each month; then you need a paid subscription to continue reading. It is worth the cost (around $8 per month), which includes full online access to the newspaper itself. If you want to take your financial literacy to the next level, also make a point to read the Business section of the paper. It may be confusing at first, but stick with it, look up those words you don't know, and you'll steadily master the language of finance.

- WiseBread (wisebread.com) is geared to those with big dreams and small budgets. Their tips on frugal living are particularly useful.
- BudgetsAreSexy (budgetsaresexy.com) makes personal finance fun, especially for newbies. It is a little edgy at times but entertaining.
- Shamelessly, my own blog (douglynam.com) is fun and light, bringing you financial concepts in the form of humorous cartoons. I try to digest complex concepts and deliver them in a picture. Why? Because I'm a visual learner. If I see a concept as a picture, I'll remember it. Hopefully, you will too. Subscribe and you can get my cartoons delivered to your inbox weekly.

The list of financial blogs is endless. These are just a few suggestions to get your feet wet. Try some to see what fits your style and interests.

Being a lifelong learner increases your intellectual capital, which is *the key* to all wealth creation. You can't grow wealthy and be financially illiterate. That would be like trying to diet and exercise without knowing anything about food or fitness. Even the best intentions and efforts will be frustrated if you lack the knowledge.

If you decide you want to learn more about economics than just personal finance, I strongly recommend *Naked Economics: Undressing the Dismal Science*, by Charles Wheelan. His engaging and thoughtful style helps decode the highly technical stuff and provides a strong foundation for understanding everything in the world of economics. If you want to take your financial literacy to the highest level, subscribe to *The Economist* magazine. It will show you the world from a global perspective. It's not everyone's cup of tea, but when you are ready to geek out, it's a great resource.

As a community service announcement, and a trick to building wealth, I ask you to please *make a point of paying for your news.* TV is great entertainment—investing is not. Getting your financial and business news only from TV or free Internet sources can cause serious problems and leave you excited or worried about the wrong things at the wrong times. You also want your news provider to work for you, not just for advertisers. One way to avoid this problem is to subscribe to your local newspaper or to a paper with a national focus, such as the *Wall Street Journal, New York Times,* or *Chicago Tribune.*

Once you master the language of finance, make an effort to give back. Share what you've learned with others to help make the world more financially literate. Start with family and friends, but also push for financial literacy classes in schools, work communities, and churches. It will make the world a better place.

PART 3

GET OUT OF THE RED AND INTO THE BLACK

CHAPTER 7

CONSIDER WHETHER TO FILE FOR BANKRUPTCY

Forgiveness of mistakes is the cornerstone of spirituality. That's what "redemption" is—clearing a debt you cannot pay. We are eager and willing to accept redemption for our moral mistakes but are sometimes horrified about accepting redemption for our money mistakes. Why?

In part because there are so many cultural taboos around money that bankruptcy feels like the ultimate personal catastrophe. It represents an admission of failure at the game of life. Having gone through bankruptcy myself, I can report that it isn't a picnic in the park, but it's not the end of the world either. In fact, it may be one of the greatest gifts you'll ever give yourself. It certainly isn't a millstone to hang around your neck for all eternity. If you are ankle deep in credit card bills, just imagine what your life would be like right now with no consumer debt.

Being bankrupt is one of the worst experiences to face. It's a punch in the gut—every day. Several times a day. Going through bankruptcy is an unpleasant but mostly tedious grind. Coming out the other side of bankruptcy debt free is glorious beyond imagination.

The monastery filed for bankruptcy after we started taking on credit card debt to pay credit card debt . . . then ran out of credit. The house of cards fell apart. Even if we made the minimum payments, it would have taken us about forty years to pay off our credit cards. We were guaranteed to be indentured servants to Visa for the rest of our lives. Just remembering that time fills me with anxiety as I recall the flood of phone calls from creditors and the pile of bills in the mail.

We should have filed for bankruptcy protection several years before we did, but shame, fear, and pride clouded our thinking. When we stepped back and looked at the situation more objectively, we realized that we had already paid back the money (or principal) we borrowed. The remaining debt was just a mountain of out-of-control interest that had compounded along the way. And that realization pushed us into motion.

What Is Bankruptcy?

If you can't pay all your debts, you can petition the court system to review your finances and forgive your financial mistakes. That's what bankruptcy is. It is an admission that your financial life went offtrack for reasons that are often beyond control. Not an admission of failure at life.

When confronting debt, the first step is to look at your emotions to try to see your situation clearly, without the painful cloud of shame and anxiety that debt produces. Easy to say, very hard to do. But essential.

Remember Rule #2 from the first chapter: bad things happen to good people.

A Harvard University study on the causes of bankruptcy found that

"62 percent of all bankruptcies have a medical cause."[1] Reduced income, job loss, credit debt, and divorce are the other top five reasons, in order, according to a separate article by the *Huffington Post*.[2] Bad budgeting and overspending are in the tenth spot down the list. While credit debt is one symptom of overspending, it is often necessary to cover basic needs during a personal crisis—not a symptom of luxury splurges.

For example, our monastic community amassed huge credit card debt over several years because its members faced chronic under-employment. We always worked, but there were lean years when one or more of us had to accept painfully low wages or intermittent income. There wasn't enough money coming in to cover our living expenses—the math didn't add up. So those expenses had to go on credit cards. It was a way of survival. Which isn't to say we never splurged on stupid things, but that wasn't the cause of our problem. Excessive materialism and binge shopping were never our weaknesses.

Going through bankruptcy isn't a good thing. But if that is where you are, that is where you are. And you are not alone. From 2006 to 2017, more than a million people per year filed for personal bankruptcy.[3]

People who borrow money should expect to pay it back, but both sides in a loan take a risk. The burden isn't entirely one sided. Remember, credit card companies loan money knowing that it is a high-risk gamble. That is why they charge insane interest rates—it is unsecured debt, and not everyone pays back the money they borrow on credit. And those insane rates and fees generated the credit card industry $163 billion in 2016.[4]

When to Consider Filing for Bankruptcy

If you see yourself in one or more of these bullet points, take a deep breath and tell yourself that you can, and will, get yourself out of this mess. One million people a year survive bankruptcy. You can too.

- You feel so much shame, fear, and anxiety about your debts that you become overwhelmed or start to panic just thinking about them.
- Debt is taking a toll on your physical and mental health. Perhaps you've developed depression, anxiety, or insomnia.
- You cut out or reduce necessary expenses, such as doctors' visits, prescription medications, or food, because of debt.
- You've stopped answering the phone or going through your mail to avoid debt collectors.
- You take on more debt to pay other debts.
- You are considering debt consolidation.
- Excluding a home mortgage, you can't pay off your debts within five years.

How to File for Bankruptcy

There are a few important steps that you'll need to take as you move through the process of filing bankruptcy.

Step One: Find Emotional Support

You are suffering and don't have to do this alone. The first step to getting past fear and shame is talking about it with someone you trust. Maybe it's a family member or friend. Talking with a priest, minister, or rabbi can be an excellent free resource. Therapy is also a worthwhile option. It may be expensive, but if you need help dealing with your emotions before you can face your crisis, do it. You will thank yourself later.

In your darkest nights of the soul remember—you are loved, eternally. Visa couldn't care less.

Step Two: Find Out If You Qualify

Not all debts can be forgiven—or discharged—in bankruptcy, and laws vary by state. But here is a rough guide:

Debts that *can* be forgiven in bankruptcy include

- credit cards
- medical bills
- personal loans
- collection agency accounts
- business debts
- money owed on lease agreements
- money owed on past-due utility bills.

Debts that *cannot* be forgiven in bankruptcy include

- student loans (except in rare circumstances)[5]
- child support
- alimony
- income taxes
- debts to government agencies
- debt for injuries caused while driving drunk
- court fines and penalties imposed as punishment
- any debt related to fraud.

There are a few gray areas:

- A home loan—Generally, you get to keep your home after bankruptcy because you need a place to live. But only if you can make the mortgage payments. Bankruptcy will stop foreclosure proceedings temporarily, but you must pay your mortgage, or the bank will repossess your home at some point. There are also limits on how extravagant your house can be and how much equity you can have in it. If your home value is less than a particular amount, you won't be forced to sell it. The rules vary by state and type of bankruptcy.
- A car loan—A car loan is treated much like your home loan.

You need a car for work, which allows you to pay your bills. As long as you can make your car payments, and you don't have a tricked-out luxury vehicle, you'll get to keep your car. It just depends on what the car is worth.

- Your stuff—Unless you have high-end art on your walls or tons of valuable jewelry, nobody wants your stuff, especially things with sentimental value. You get to keep your things if they aren't extravagantly expensive and could be sold to pay your debts.

Assets that can't be touched by bankruptcy include

- Social Security
- pension plans
- 401(k) or 403(b) retirement savings
- Individual Retirement Accounts (IRAs), up to $1.2 million
- disability benefits
- veteran's benefits
- alimony or support payments.

There are two types of bankruptcy. Your income level and debts determine which type of bankruptcy you can file.

Chapter 7. This is sometimes called "straight bankruptcy" and is the easiest. Chapter 7 eliminates all your eligible debts, and you get to start over with a clean slate. To qualify, you must pass the means test. *The means test requires you to earn less than the median income for your family size in your state.* It is designed to keep high-income earners who could repay some of their debt from filing under Chapter 7. You can do a quick back-of-the-napkin means test calculation by looking at this chart provided by the Department of Justice as of 2018[6]:

COMMONWEALTH OR U.S. TERRITORY	FAMILY SIZE			
	1 Earner	2 People	3 People	4 People*
Alabama	$43,476	$52,970	$60,367	$70,940
Alaska	$62,326	$85,281	$86,944	$97,831
Arizona	$46,779	$58,684	$62,227	$72,052
Arkansas	$39,265	$48,602	$55,175	$67,486
California	$52,416	$70,245	$75,160	$84,059
Colorado	$55,858	$72,037	$81,496	$95,117
Connecticut	$62,929	$80,974	$91,867	$113,409
Delaware	$51,703	$68,041	$77,862	$93,811
District of Columbia	$51,907	$99,046	$99,046	$113,478
Florida	$44,576	$55,344	$60,636	$72,382
Georgia	$43,274	$56,301	$62,483	$73,202
Hawaii	$61,057	$73,656	$85,099	$98,059
Idaho	$46,779	$55,532	$57,240	$71,195
Illinois	$50,765	$66,487	$76,406	$91,216
Indiana	$46,412	$57,558	$66,148	$77,566
Iowa	$47,147	$63,760	$70,989	$83,522
Kansas	$47,591	$63,327	$72,981	$83,528
Kentucky	$42,589	$51,524	$57,696	$72,863
Louisiana	$43,063	$53,080	$59,303	$71,957
Maine	$48,842	$60,398	$67,690	$81,950
Maryland	$63,401	$81,507	$92,819	$112,685
Massachusetts	$61,102	$76,414	$93,755	$113,651
Michigan	$47,088	$57,366	$68,192	$82,985
Minnesota	$52,785	$70,889	$85,033	$101,762
Mississippi	$37,051	$46,712	$50,614	$61,182
Missouri	$44,994	$57,288	$65,260	$81,172
Montana	$47,675	$58,348	$64,970	$79,929
Nebraska	$47,071	$66,165	$71,939	$83,719

COMMONWEALTH OR U.S. TERRITORY	FAMILY SIZE			
	1 Earner	2 People	3 People	4 People*
Nevada	$47,057	$61,609	$61,983	$72,918
New Hampshire	$62,357	$75,367	$89,188	$108,702
New Jersey	$62,933	$75,305	$93,656	$114,886
New Mexico	$43,104	$57,704	$57,704	$60,256
New York	$51,408	$66,056	$75,870	$91,998
North Carolina	$42,946	$55,722	$64,521	$72,830
North Dakota	$53,523	$71,100	$81,166	$96,473
Ohio	$46,242	$57,938	$68,361	$83,040
Oklahoma	$43,986	$56,532	$61,386	$69,061
Oregon	$50,333	$61,553	$70,877	$80,170
Pennsylvania	$51,138	$61,271	$75,018	$90,821
Rhode Island	$50,318	$68,303	$77,079	$100,468
South Carolina	$43,256	$55,598	$61,453	$71,876
South Dakota	$42,245	$63,684	$66,535	$81,509
Tennessee	$43,270	$53,887	$60,042	$69,160
Texas	$46,709	$61,704	$65,713	$76,842
Utah	$56,638	$62,903	$71,047	$79,710
Vermont	$54,121	$67,202	$80,415	$92,951
Virginia	$56,456	$71,871	$82,395	$97,731
Washington	$59,154	$72,460	$79,754	$92,727
West Virginia	$45,401	$48,325	$56,781	$71,399
Wisconsin	$48,407	$62,914	$76,179	$89,245
Wyoming	$59,974	$71,971	$80,219	$82,871
Guam	$40,152	$48,008	$54,708	$66,204
Northern Mariana Islands	$26,964	$26,964	$31,370	$46,139
Puerto Rico	$23,758	$23,758	$23,758	$29,502
Virgin Islands	$31,857	$38,288	$40,824	$44,725

* Add $8,400 for each individual in excess of 4.

If you pass this version of the means test, you're done. You get to file Chapter 7. However, if your household income is greater than your state median, the calculation gets complicated and is based on your disposable income. You'll want a lawyer to help. You can find the full version of the means test on the United States Courts website: http://www .uscourts.gov/forms/means-test-forms/chapter-7-means-test-calculation.

Chapter 13. This is more complex and sometimes known as "reorganization bankruptcy." It is for higher-income earners who can repay some of their creditors. For those with property that they want to keep, like a home, Chapter 13 may be a better option.

Chapter 13 reorganizes and reduces your debt to make it manageable so that it can be paid off in three to five years. It also requires supervision by the courts to ensure you maintain a strict budget. Not fun, but not as bad as being in debt forever.

Step Three: Contact a Lawyer

You can file for bankruptcy without a lawyer, but that is a ridiculous idea. Remember the proverb "He who represents himself has a fool for a client." Bankruptcy is a complex legal process, and a mistake can cost you dearly.

Finding a good bankruptcy lawyer is tricky because online searches can be unreliable, and you may not want to ask friends and family. That's awkward. So here are a few tips to finding the right person to represent you:

1. Ask a non-bankruptcy lawyer you trust whom they would use. Ask to speak with them in confidence, and they should keep your inquiry confidential, even if you aren't their client. It is simply good manners and professionalism. Hint: almost every church board has a lawyer on it.

2. Look on the website of your state bar association. There you can find a directory of local lawyers, and many states have a referral service. A typical referral service fee is $35. Also look on Avvo (avvo.com) and Martindale-Hubbell (martindale.com), which are credible rating services.

3. Make sure anyone you choose is a bankruptcy specialist. You don't hire a dermatologist to perform heart surgery. Law is as specialized a field as medicine. Get the right person for the job.

4. Interview your prospective lawyer. The first visit is often free, but don't be put off by a small consultation fee. It is a sign they are serious about their time. Most importantly, you should be speaking with your lawyer on each key visit—not a paralegal. If you meet a non-lawyer, then you've stumbled into a bankruptcy mill that churns out shoddy work. Bigger firms are more likely to be bankruptcy mills. It is important that one lawyer is your point of contact from start to finish.

There are three Cs in choosing a bankruptcy lawyer: compassion, competency, and cost.

Compassion: Stepping into a lawyer's office for the first time is, for most people, the hardest part of the process. It was for me. After you've hired a lawyer, they should hold your hand the rest of the way. There will be hard days ahead, but the worst is often behind you at that point. A good lawyer will let you cry yourself into a puddle on the first visit, and perhaps on every visit. They will need to hear your story, and should guide you through it, asking good questions and listening closely. It's okay if they try to keep the conversation focused and on point, since it is easy to get lost down rabbit holes, but they should always be exceedingly kind. They are in a helping profession and should care about people.

Competency: Before interviewing a lawyer, check their professional credentials. It is a good sign if they belong to the National Association of Consumer Bankruptcy Attorneys (nacba.org/find-an-attorney) and have a clean record with your state bar association. Belonging to the American Board of Certification (abcworld.org) is also an excellent sign. Be skeptical of any firm that advertises heavily, especially on billboards and TV.

Cost: Fees will vary by the complexity of your situation and geographic location. The range is between $1,000 and $3,000, with an average of around $1,500. You'll need to save some money to pay a lawyer to file for bankruptcy, which is an odd catch-22. You are filing for bankruptcy because you are broke, but it can be hard to pay the legal fees for bankruptcy because you are broke! However, this isn't the time to go with the cheapest service you can find. You are trying to reduce or eliminate an insane amount of debt, and it can be worth the extra cost to pay for a compassionate and competent lawyer.

For example, my bankruptcy lawyer had a sterling reputation in the local community and the court system. When my case appeared before the judge, she had worked with my lawyer routinely for years and trusted his professionalism. (And he brought her coffee each morning—read into that what you will.) As a result, she spent less than five minutes deliberating my case before discharging my bankruptcy. It was amazingly painless. That's worth something!

Your lawyer represents you. If your lawyer is shady, incompetent, or unkind, what will the judge think about your character?

What Is the Fallout?

In the short term, the first thing that will happen when you file for bankruptcy is that all debt collection efforts must stop at once. However, you still need to keep paying basic living expenses. Next, you'll be required to attend a court-approved credit-counseling class—which is a good thing.

In the long term you'll face a potentially trashed credit score for a few years, and your bankruptcy information is a public record. For most people, that's about it. And that doesn't mean you can't get credit or that your credit score will go down. By the time most people file for bankruptcy, their credit scores are already trashed, so *filing can cause your credit score to rise.* Before bankruptcy, we had so much debt we couldn't get more credit—believe me, we tried.

Massive debt you cannot pay is far more damaging to your creditworthiness than bankruptcy.

Ironically, credit card and car loan offers flooded our mailbox within a month of discharging our bankruptcies. Some of those offers were from the very companies to whom we'd previously owed money. Lenders troll the bankruptcy lists to look for customers because they know those folks have

- no consumer debts
- a history of taking on debt
- the inability (in most cases) to file for bankruptcy again for eight years.

They can also charge high interest rates. Those are their ideal customers.

Bankruptcy doesn't shut you out from consumer credit. Seven years after bankruptcy, we applied for, and received, a very reasonable thirty-year fixed home loan to purchase our monastic property. So how did bankruptcy hurt us personally or professionally? It didn't stop us from owning a home, getting a car loan (if we wanted one, which we didn't), or having credit cards. Furthermore, I'm now a professional money manager, responsible for millions of dollars of investments. It didn't shut me out of my dream job in finance. It made me much better at it. Nor does it make one ineligible to be the president of the United States. Presidents Jefferson, Madison, Monroe, Harrison, Lincoln, Grant, McKinley, Truman, and Trump have all filed some form of bankruptcy protection and/or faced insolvency.[7] So where is the reputational downside that is so terrifying?

That said, according to a survey done by CareerBuilder, 29 percent of employers do a credit check when interviewing candidates.[8]

You can check your credit score for free at AnnualCreditReport.com. (It is the only source authorized by federal law.) But remember, if you are considering bankruptcy, your credit score is likely a mess already. And bankruptcy is deleted from your records within seven to ten years, giving you a truly fresh start, whereas a large debt burden can keep your life stuck in neutral indefinitely.

A final word of warning: Never incur debt with the knowledge or assumption that you are going to file for bankruptcy. That is fraud and will create a mess-o'-trouble. For your bankruptcy to go smoothly, you need to avoid incurring any new debts before filing, paying off big debts (especially to friends or family), or engaging in money shuffling to hide assets.

A final word of encouragement: perhaps the greatest blessing of our bankruptcy was the realization of how little anyone cared. It was both a sad and a liberating epiphany—people are too busy with their mess to worry about yours. The horrific shame I experienced was mostly self-created.

CHAPTER 8

GET YOUR BUDGET IN GEAR

There is a cardinal rule of wise purchasing: if it isn't in your budget, you can't afford it. And if you don't have a budget, you'll never know what you can afford. Budgeting is just a fancy way of tracking all your money and creating a plan on how to spend it. Like in any game, if you don't have a plan, you are going to struggle. Since the money game is complex, you need a great game plan.

So how do you make a budget? It is a simple question with a complex answer. There is no perfect system, but if it works for you, then it works. If it doesn't, try something else. If you're starting to feel panicky about your own finances, take a deep breath—you're not the only one scrambling to learn the rules of the game. No one is born knowing how to budget; it's a skill that we all must learn, and trial and error is a part of the process. Because parents and schools don't teach it, most of us are stuck with on-the-job training.

When I first started teaching personal finance, I always made my students create a budget. It was the worst unit of the course. No matter how much I hounded them, no matter what punishment I devised, I rarely got any student to do a decent job budgeting. I could ask them to perform in a play, write a twenty-page essay, or solve complex math problems with aplomb, but budgeting never worked.

A third of the class never turned anything in, a third just spent their money until it ran out, and a third submitted beautifully detailed budgets that were complete works of fiction. How could I tell they were lies? The same way the IRS will flag tax fraud—the numbers were too good. If every item purchased and every category subtotal was a perfectly round number, the data had to be fake.

At one point, I had a realization: if my best and brightest students, those who consistently earned A grades on all assignments, were failing my budget project, maybe something was wrong with the assignment, not the kids! Budgeting is hard, and the less money you have, the harder it is. I realized I was giving them a near-impossible task. Budgeting requires several skills that few teenagers have:

- attention to detail
- long-term planning
- good impulse control
- consistent follow-through
- mastery of emotional money monsters

Many responsible, hard-working adults (like me) struggle with these skills as well.

The only way budgeting works for most people is if you can keep it simple. Otherwise, there is too much data to hold in your head and too many parts to manage. So here are the budgeting techniques I have found to work even for lazy teenagers. If you prefer to go fancy with the spreadsheets and workbooks, there are lots out there to choose from.

But remember: no system works if you don't use it.

Step One: Automate Everything!

And by "everything" I mean as much as you possibly can:

- Automatically deposit your income into your checking account.
- Automatically set aside your savings into a savings account.
- Automatically pay all your recurring bills.
- Pay all your expenses with a debit card so you automatically have a record of every transaction.
- Automatically download all your transactions into a good financial software program once a week.

Getting this set up will take time, but it is a critical investment of your energy that will reap huge rewards. It will save you hours of tedium with forms and checklists you probably won't complete anyway. It will make tracking your spending and paying bills infinitely easier for the rest of your life. And it will ensure that you never miss a payment if you keep enough money in your bank account.

There are several good software programs available, but I recommend the big names because you want to make sure the program syncs easily with all your bank and credit accounts. Mint.com is currently my favorite because it is powerful, easy to use, and free. Mint will also help you create and track financial goals and monitor your credit score. However, I personally use Quicken because it has more features, it is the industry workhorse, and I've already got years of data in it. But the Premier version costs about $60 per year, and Quicken takes time to master. Plenty of other options are available; just don't choose an obscure program no one has ever heard of because it may not integrate easily with your financial institutions. A quick online search of the best personal finance software will pull up the most current options. If you want help building a traditional budget, along with financial planning tutorials, I recommend You Need a Budget

(YNAB). It costs about $7 per month and is a great product to partner with Mint.

After you've automated all your income and bills, you'll be able to see where your money goes. The software will track your money for you, assuming you set it up correctly. It can be a little unnerving for some people to link their financial accounts to their financial software, but the most popular financial software programs have strong security features.

One of the most important steps is to make sure you accurately categorize every transaction downloaded into your financial software. After you download a transaction from a vendor, if you categorize it accurately, the software will automatically categorize every future transaction from that same vendor. If done incorrectly, you'll never get an accurate picture of where your money goes. It is tedious, but most programs have recently made it easier by including dropdown menus that allow you to select a predesignated category for each transaction and have gotten much better at autofilling categories for you. There are even premade categories for Not Sure and Miscellaneous for those oddball expenses. As a bonus this will make tax time a snap. You'll be able to hit a button in your financial software and run one report to help complete your taxes.

Many folks hate budgeting and money because they hate math. For me, as a financial professional, having good number intuition is important, but the amount of math I do by hand is minimal. Computers do all the hard work for us now, so don't let a fear of numbers get in the way of your goals. Saying "I'm bad at math" is your ego looking for an excuse.

Step Two: Carefully Track All Your Expenses

Many people try looking into the future to plan their budgets. If that works for you, great. I haven't seen that be very successful in most cases because the future always brings unexpected surprises. But if you carefully track all your expenditures as you spend, you'll have a detailed and accurate record of what you've spent in the past. Then you can use the past data to help predict what the future will look like. This method is much more manageable psychologically than guessing what you might spend.

Here is a simple exercise for tracking your expenses and building a budget. In my economics class we called it the AB/CD technique, and my students adopted the AC/DC song "Back in Black" as the soundtrack:

A. Automate.

Then carefully record and categorize all your expenses for at least two months.

B. Break it down.

Once you have two months or more of data, break it down into two categories: fixed expenses and flexible expenses. Your fixed expenses are things like the mortgage or rent, utilities, gas, and minimum debt payments. These shouldn't change radically from month to month, except for heating bills in the winter or air-conditioning in the summer.

C. Comb through your expenses.

Look for leaks in your wallet: small, recurring charges for things you can do without and might have even forgotten you signed up for in the first place. These can include extra services tacked on to your cell service or Internet bill, apps on your phone that charge you $0.50 a month but that you rarely use, and online subscriptions you've forgotten about. Do you have Netflix, Hulu, and Amazon Prime? And cable TV? Choose one. Slim down.

D. Do the math.

What does your household bring in? Subtract your fixed

expenses from your monthly income. This is what you have left for everything else—your flexible expenses. Flexible expenses are food, clothing, dining out, entertainment, gifts, and so on. Now take your flexible expense total and divide it by thirty days in a month. This is your daily budget. Ta da! Budget accomplished.

If you have $1,000 in flexible spending each month, then you can spend approximately $33 a day or $250 a week, whichever number is easier for you to work with. If you have $1,500 in flexible spending, your budget is $50 a day or $350 a week. Some days you'll go way over budget, like when you go grocery shopping, and then you need to reduce your daily budget accordingly for the week. If you are a frugal and conscientious shopper, you can even include your weekly food budget into your fixed expenses to make your daily budget easier to track. But you'll need to stick to a rigorous food budget, which is tricky.

The key is to hold as few numbers in your head as possible. Once you have the numbers, though, it becomes a game to see how many days you can go without spending anything so you can build more flexibility in your budget or save up for larger purchases. If your daily budget is $30, and you go three days without spending anything, you have banked $90 you can use, save, or splurge on larger purchases.

We'll get to debt, savings, and investing soon enough, but your daily budget is the place to start.

Step Three: Play Lava

Did you ever play "Lava" as a kid? We would throw the couch pillows around our living room when we were small, and then try to jump from each piece of furniture or pillow to the next without touching the floor. The floor was lava. Anyone who hit the floor burned up in a fiery blaze of imaginary agony. The game was to circle the room while siblings pushed and jostled for furniture space. It was like King of the Hill for rainy days.

I do the same thing with my checking account. I set an imaginary lava point I cannot hit. For me it is $1,000. I will never, ever, ever let my balance fall below $1,000. If I do, a fiery financial death awaits. Have I ever crossed my lava point? Of course. Just like in the childhood game when my brother would throw me off the couch onto the floor, unexpected things will throw your budget to the ground all the time. You'll hit lava.

But what happens next? You scream, you panic, and you scramble until you get back on solid ground. Your world stops until you get out of the lava.

Why is this important? Because the real lava point is zero. No money. Broke. But if you hit zero, what happens? You start to bounce checks, or worse, you start taking on credit card debt. You can *never* go there. So your fake lava point of $1,000 is your new zero. If you accidently, from some twist of fate, fall below your new zero point, life is still okay. You need to scream, panic, and scramble until you get back above $1,000, but you won't fall into credit card debt.

The secret to winning at Lava is to check your account balance regularly. Make it a ritual. You need to know exactly what your account balance is so you never fall below your lava point. Smartphones make this easy, no math required. You can even have your bank send you text alerts when you approach your lava point.

You can set your lava point at any dollar amount that works for you. Some folks go as high as $5,000 or $10,000. You may need to go lower, even to $100. But you need a lava point that you never cross under pain of imaginary death. It's a mind trick to help you reframe your expectations.

Without a budget and spending goals, you are likely to burn in a molten pit of financial torture for the rest of your life. However, if you automatically pay all your bills, set a budget, and play Lava daily, you've started down the path to becoming a little bit wealthy.

CHAPTER 9

LIVE BELOW YOUR MEANS

Many people dream of becoming rich, but they don't think carefully about what that really means. They incorrectly assume that being rich means having a large income. How much money you make is meaningless. It's how much money you keep that matters.

Rich people make lots of money. Wealthy people save lots of money. Which would you rather be? Okay, that doesn't need to be either-or. Best of all is to be rich and wealthy. But I've met many high-income earners who don't save, which means they're poor. And I've met many low-income earners who are frugal savers and have significant wealth.

One of my clients is a cafeteria worker in a private school who makes about $30,000 a year. She is married to a man who works in construction, and she has two children. She immigrated to America as a young woman and is intimately familiar with the pain of poverty. She doesn't want that life anymore, especially for her children, so she budgets, saves, and invests carefully. At thirty-five years old, she already has a solid six-figure retirement account balance. On her current trajectory, she will likely reach $1 million in savings.

My father is a good example of what not to do. As a former CEO and high-income earner extraordinaire, he made a lot of money, but he didn't save much of it. With each promotion and pay raise, his lifestyle became increasingly lavish. He started out in a small efficiency apartment, then traded up to a stylish ranch home, and then to a three-story mansion on fifteen acres at the height of his career. He had a black luxury car for work, a red sports car for the weekend, and two motorcycles—one black and one red—for random fun.

Where is he now? Back in a small efficiency apartment living off Social Security. He lost it all. Watching him suffer through that transition has been heartrending. Especially because it didn't have to be this way.

My role as a financial adviser is a little unique because I work with entire institutions, not just wealthy clients. When working with educational plans, I serve the retirement needs of everyone in the school, from the college president to the maintenance staff. When first analyzing account balances, I expected the administrators with the biggest salaries to have the most wealth, and that the teachers and then maintenance staff should have the least savings. Much to my surprise, that isn't always the case.

A philosophy professor showed me a happy, healthy way to build a small fortune. Laura is a classic "Earth mother." She drives a beat-up blue truck, grows much of her own food in a vibrant organic garden, and hangs her clothes out to dry to protect the environment. She waltzes across campus in hand-knit hippie dresses and sandals, with a wild mane of frizzy black hair.

When we first met, I expected a financial train wreck. However, after decades of living below her means, taking joy and gratitude in the blessings of each day, and not giving a flying fig about what other people thought, Laura has more money in her retirement account, by far, than any other employee in her school. The college president has a fancy car, nice suits, and a vacation home, but Laura has two times as much money saved. She is solidly in the seven digits in her retirement account. Yet she only has a five-digit salary. She also raised two fabulous children and sent them to excellent private schools.

It can be done, but the key is a healthy relationship to your money and to stop caring so much about status symbols.

How to Spend Less Than You Make

If you want to be a little bit wealthy, then your lifestyle must lag your income. To be wealthy, you need to spend less than you make, save your extra money, and invest it. Here are a few tricks to help you live below your means. This isn't an exhaustive list, but it's a good place to begin the journey.

Start by categorizing your frugality into three categories: Income, Core Expenses, and Entertainment, or ICEE. Analyze each aspect of your financial life, carefully looking for ways to save money and put an ICEE-y freeze on money mistakes.

Income

Odds are good that you are going to struggle to make ends meet when you start your first job or career, but as you become more established in life, you need to save a portion of every pay raise. This is where most of your savings will come from. Save all of your pay raises if you can, but inflation will make that a challenge, so try to save at least half of each raise. As your income increases, your savings must increase proportionally.

Getting a raise is a wonderful blessing. Celebrate it. But your income is not an allowance. Please don't assume that because someone hands you money you should spend it all. That is one road to poverty. Instead, use the first month's pay raise for a special treat, like a nice dinner out with friends and family, or maybe splurge on a one-time house-cleaning service. Save the rest.

With luck, most workers will get a 2–3 percent pay raise each year. Here is my favorite strategy: try to increase your retirement savings by 1 percent per year, every year. It is a gift to yourself that will help you become a little bit wealthy. Don't stop until you are saving at least 15–20 percent of your income. It will take a decade or more, but it works. It's better than waiting for "someday" when you have the money, a point that rarely arrives. Saving 1 percent more at each raise allows you to increase your savings rate and not feel the sting of a reduced paycheck. The best employer retirement plans will do this for you by auto-escalating your retirement savings each year. And since retirement savings are tax deferred, if you are in the 25-percent tax bracket, you are missing out on only 0.75 percent of your paycheck. You'll likely never feel the loss, but the money will accumulate surprisingly fast.

Start where you can—it may be at 1 percent or 5 percent—then work your way up. Anything is better than nothing. And it needs to be automatic so that you don't have to think about it. Thinking about money causes stress, worry, and fatigue. Instead, make one good decision so you can avoid worrying and having to make countless more each month. The best employer retirement plans will also auto-enroll their employees to ensure they take this key step.

One of the secrets to growing a little bit wealthy is to understand how *your* mind works. We are all different, but there are "hacks" we can use to trick ourselves into good behavior. For me, making one or two good decisions is hard, but possible. Making thousands of good decisions each day is a real struggle. So I look for good, simple, and big decisions I can make that will allow me to avoid having to make lots of smaller, but exhausting, decisions each day. Automatically increasing your retirement savings rate by 1 percent each year is an example of one good, big decision.

Another good big decision is to increase the amount of federal tax your employer withholds each month. On your Form W-4 that you complete for your employer, line 6 lets you select any additional amount you want withheld from each paycheck. Have your employer withhold *more* money from your paycheck and send it to Uncle Sam each month. Crazy, right!? It violates the wisdom of every financial planner I know, but hear me out.

You'll get the extra withholding back at tax time in a nice big lump. Yes, you are giving the government an interest-free short-term loan, but then you get a fat check in April that you can use to pay down debt or invest. But here is the catch: You need to make *two* good decisions for this to work. The first is to save the money; the second is not to spend the refund in a silly way. It is not vacation money—it is for reducing debt, investing, or building up your emergency fund.

The good part about this strategy is that the money is out of sight, out of mind, and untouchable until you get your refund. You can't make a bad decision with money you don't have access to. Which makes saving your money inside a retirement account or with Uncle Sam a good idea if you struggle to live below your means.

If you are self-employed, these tricks don't work so well, but try to keep the concept in mind. Look for simple, big decisions that help control your behavior. Set up a SEP IRA and automatically contribute to it each month and increase your savings as your income rises. When starting a business, it is common for entrepreneurs to plow all their income back into their venture to help it survive and grow. However, once business is steady, be sure to make retirement savings a fixed expense each month, or you'll never be able to stop working.

Impulse control is hard, and having your money within easy reach requires constant self-control. Lock it up so you can't mess it up.

Core Expenses

Living below your means requires you to cut the fat out of your living expenses and challenge every budget item. Start with fixed expenses, then look at flexible expenses. Examine each core category and try to keep your spending to a minimum.

A key trick is to know exactly how much you earn per hour, then convert each purchase into units of time rather than money. For example, if you make $20 per hour, and a steak costs $15, then it will cost you forty-five minutes of work to earn that steak. Money is often too abstract a concept for the human brain, so convert all costs into units of time and then you can see how much time, effort, and freedom you need to sacrifice for each item you buy. It may radically change how you view the world. Do you really want a $600 jacket if you'll need to work thirty hours to pay for it?

Here are a few tips to help you lower your core expenses and stick to your budget in the essential categories of housing, food, clothing, and other life necessities.

1. Housing. This is the big budget killer for most. Here are a few key tricks to keep your housing costs reasonable.

- If you struggle to make rent, you can share the rent instead. Two can live cheaper than one.
- When buying or renting a home, go smaller than you can afford. Owning a big house comes with a laundry list of extra expenses, including the attendant taxes and upkeep. Besides, most people spend time in only three rooms of the house: the bedroom, the kitchen, and the living room. (My father rarely left the main floor of his McMansion.)
- Owning a home for the long term can help reduce your living expenses if you have a fixed-rate mortgage. Your mortgage payment will stay the same, but your property value and salary will hopefully increase over time. Your mortgage payment then becomes a smaller and smaller percentage of your income each year, giving you more disposable income. Rent payments, on the other hand, tend to continually rise. You

can find a free Home Rent vs. Buy calculator on my website at douglynam.com.

- Reduce your utilities. The full list of utility-saving tips is long, but here are a few quick ideas to consider: Ditch your landline. Cut the cable and just use the Internet, which you can now stream over your TV. Put low-flow aerators on all faucets and install low-flow showerheads. Put milk cartons or soda bottles filled with rocks and water in your toilet tank to reduce water consumption. Install LED lights. Keep your air vents clean and open. Wash clothing in cold water. Use a programmable thermostat to reduce the heat at night. Make sure your home is properly insulated. Always purchase energy-efficient appliances.

2. Food, Clothing, and Necessities. I'll confess. I hate shopping. It may just be a midwestern guy thing, but for me, walking into a huge store creates information overload and then decision paralysis. I've gotten stuck in the cereal aisle for forty-five minutes trying to pick out breakfast. Don't get me near the pasta sauces—I'll be trapped there till closing time. And do we really need 127 different brands of shampoo and conditioner? I can't process that much information. So I need to make shopping as simple, painless, and cost-effective as possible.

For those who enjoy shopping or have a hard time resisting shoes and nice clothing, this tip comes from my former student and current intern: Never buy an expensive item right away. If you walk into a store and see a fabulous jacket that you must have, walk out again immediately. If you still want it just as badly a week later, reconsider if you can afford the splurge. If it's no longer available, then it's a sign from the universe that you didn't need it anyway. (That's good advice. Thanks, Leah.)

Here are a few of my favorite shopping tips:

- Shopping is *not* entertainment. Shopping is to purchase the stuff you need to run your life. Don't get caught up in consumerism.

If shopping is something you do to let off steam, carefully consider the impact that will have on your finances. I suggest other hobbies.

- Buy in bulk when you can. It is cheaper and it also saves time, gas, and mileage on your car.

- If you can, purchase groceries online. It will allow you to review your order before checkout and reconsider after you see the total bill. It is easy to order nonperishables via Amazon, and some grocery stores like Walmart and Sam's Club let you shop online for fresh foods and will deliver to your car in the parking lot.

- When you do go into a store, always arrive armed with a shopping list and a budget. Then stick to the budget.

- When shopping for groceries, eat something beforehand. Grocery shopping on an empty stomach guarantees impulse buying, and probably some junk food too.

- Consider reducing your meat consumption. It is better for your wallet and better for the planet. Cows, for example, release an absurd amount of methane gas, which contributes to global warming. A new study concluded that the world's top five dairy and meat producers combined produce more greenhouse gases than either ExxonMobil, Shell, or BP alone.[1] That said, I still love a good steak. I just try to indulge in beef as I do anything else—in moderation.

- Clothing shop at thrift stores and consignment stores. Buy things that are gently used if you can.

- Plan and cook your own food. Make a meal plan for the week and stick to it.

- Pack your lunch.

- Avoid prepackaged food. You are paying an upcharge for someone to prepare your meals for you.

- Use coupons and look for sales, but remember that there is an "opportunity cost" when saving money. If you spend two hours to save $10, and you make $20 per hour, you've "lost" $30. Make sure that any savings are worth the time and effort required, or you are better off working more hours.

3. Entertainment. Everyone needs to cut loose and have some fun. But when we relax and play, it is easy to let our guard down and spend money on indulgences we would normally avoid. Especially when in a group. And especially if alcohol is involved. Peer pressure is always hard to resist, no matter how old you get. But if you are struggling on a tight budget, think of entertainment as a "luxury item" that you'll need to manage carefully. Instead of heading out to fancy restaurants, bars, or amusement parks, here are a few simple entertainment ideas that don't cost much.

- Get romantic. You don't need to buy flowers to snuggle, and you get a nice boost of oxytocin for free. Close relationships are also one of the key predictors of overall happiness.
- Exercise as entertainment. Work out in the gym with friends, take a hike, or go ride your bike. You'll save money, get fit, and control your waistline. It will also help you live longer.
- Skip the movie theater and make your own popcorn. All those films show up on Netflix or Amazon eventually.
- Use your local library. They have lots of terrific books, movies, and music you can borrow for free.
- Attend free events. Check out street fairs, farmer's markets, concerts in the park, and festivals. If you live near a college campus, pay attention to their weekly newsletter or website for interesting events.
- Young kids can have fun just about anywhere. Disney World is great, but a trip to the park and an ice cream cone can be magical too. Memorable experiences don't need to be expensive. Some of

my favorite childhood memories are playing in the woods and picking wild raspberries, not taking ski trips to Aspen.

- Play games. Board games or card games are inexpensive and provide countless hours of entertainment. The recent proliferation of board games for adults is amazing, and some of them are hysterically funny—especially with a group of friends.
- Make music. Play instruments together, perform your own rap songs, or have a karaoke night.

Set Good Boundaries

A mental trick for healing your relationship to money is to give it a pet name. I know it sounds a little silly, but it works. I call my money KP. KP is the nickname for Kitty-Puss-Rex, the huge Russian blue cat who lived in our monastery for over twenty-two years. He was the most loving, affectionate, and attentive pet I've ever had. When I'd come home from work, KP would be at the door waiting for me every day. He wouldn't leave me alone until he got a serious snuggle. His favorite trick was to jump up on my shoulders, drape himself around my neck, and nuzzle my ear while purring loudly.

He passed away several years ago, but I named my money after him. KP is the name I gave my primary checking account. Can I neglect KP? Can I be angry at KP? Can I hate KP? Never. He may claw the furniture and cough up a hairball on my pillow, but that's just how KP rolls. With KP, there is no anger. No judgment. No shame.

We're old friends, KP and I, and we take care of each other. I look after KP, and he looks after me. Having a good friend is a blessing, and when you build a healthy, friendly relationship with your money, you'll be happier, healthier, and more in tune with all the other blessings in your life. But you must set clear boundaries with both your money and your pets. Let me show you an example from KP, the cat.

Have you ever heard a rabbit scream? Here in Santa Fe, we have coyotes. And big jackrabbits. When the coyote packs travel through the arroyos, you'll sometimes hear them catch a rabbit. That's when a rabbit screams—as it becomes a coyote snack. It is a loud, ear-splitting, and bloodcurdling cry. The haunting sound of a rabbit scream is unforgettable.

The real KP was a master escape artist. He always wanted to run outside and play in the arroyo. It was hard to tell him no and drag him back inside when he'd sneak out—which he tried to do every day. I know he just wanted to play, but I had a duty. Cats can't live outdoors here, or they become coyote snacks. We also have fleas that carry the bubonic plague. (Yes, the plague still exists.) A friend lost both his legs from amputation when his dog brought plague-ridden fleas into the house.

KP desperately wanted to run wild every day. I get it. But it was my job, out of love, to say no. I set boundaries and made KP live by them, especially when he didn't want to. If I didn't, this extraordinary joy and blessing in my life would either disappear or literally bring in the plague and destroy our family. That's an excellent analogy for money.

You can't let your money run wild. You must give it love by setting strong boundaries. The most important boundary is that you live below your means. Always spend less than you earn. Always save your raises.

And remember—the coyotes are hungry.

CHAPTER 10

RUN FROM CREDIT

It all started with a couch. That was my first big credit card mistake—a stupid couch. We made our old one last as long as humanly possible, even throwing a sheet over it to hide the Jackson Pollock–like stains. One evening while watching a rerun of the comedy *The Lady Eve*, the wooden spine cracked, sending us backward onto the floor. The timing was perfect. As Barbara Stanwyck deviously tripped Henry Fonda in the movie, we took a coordinated pratfall. Monks tumbling across the living room is a funny sight.

However, with no emergency fund and living paycheck to paycheck, we didn't have a way to replace the couch. At the end of a long workday, curling up on the couch is sometimes necessary. Spending an evening in a hard chair from the kitchen table was wildly uncomfortable.

The next weekend, we piled into the car and drove to Albuquerque, about an hour away, to a discount furniture outlet. A group of monks cruising a furniture store is also comical. We spent an impossible length of time deciding on price, style, and options. Decisions by committee are always a hassle, but in the end we chose a sturdy, practical design in brown that would hide stains well. We had guests, and frequent spills, plus a cat. Stain removal and durability were the key features.

The price tag was $1,200. Expensive, but not a bad deal for an industrial-size, industrial-strength, multipiece furniture set. We made a group decision to put it on a credit card. None of us, however, understood how credit cards worked. Yes, it was debt, with some interest, but the minimum monthly payments were manageable. The only thing we understood was that we would have a minimum payment of $30 a month. Not a problem, right?

Wrong. Oh my, was that wrong.

First, let's look at the interest payments. Interest is the extra money that must be repaid for the privilege of borrowing money. At 19 percent annual interest, we paid an extra $659 for that stupid couch. That's a 60-percent price increase. Ouch. That's a horrible deal. What's the point of shopping all day for the best bargain to save an extra $100 to $200 only to pay an extra $659 in interest?

Debt Avalanches Will Bury You

If that was the only thing we ever put on a credit card and paid it off on schedule, it would still be unfortunate. However, it was simply the beginning of the Debt Avalanche. That wasn't the last "emergency" that needed a credit card. Even when the balance on the card dropped, there was always another purchase close behind, leaving a constant balance that, little by little, grew and grew.

Here is how debt avalanches out of control. It's called the time value of money. It explains how investing will grow your wealth and debt will destroy it.

Money, like people, has an earning capacity. If you go to work at a job you might make $15 an hour. Your time and effort are worth something; in this example, $15 per hour. Money, when put to work, also has an earning capacity. Like that of people, the earning capacity of money changes wildly depending on what job you give it. The minimum wage for money is what you'd get if you sent your money to work at a traditional bank by depositing it in a money market account or certificate of deposit (CD). Between 1.0 and 2.0 percent right now. Not great.

However, higher-risk jobs pay much better. Higher risk means higher expected pay or returns. If you put your money to work in the stock market, the historical wage you can expect is around 10 percent per year, every year. If you sent $100 to work in the stock market, you'd expect to earn $10 per year (more or less, depending on how the market is doing).

The magic happens in the second year. Now you'd have $110 working for you—the original $100 and the $10 earned for one year of work. By the end of the second year, you could expect to make 10 percent on $110, or $11 in wages, for a total of $121. In the third year you'd make $12.10 in wages for the work your money performed. This is called compound growth. If you kept reinvesting all your earnings, your money should grow exponentially. If you did this for forty years, not adding any extra money, you'd have a total of $4,525.93.

Money, invested over time, grows. That is the time value of money.

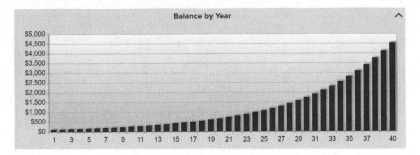

The growth of $100 invested at 10 percent for forty years.

Now let's get back to the other direction—growing debt. How does a credit card company work? They could invest their money in the stock market, so why are they giving it to you or me?

They've found a very high-risk, high-paying job, like a stunt performer. The work is dangerous because people like you and me might go bankrupt or fail to pay our debts. Therefore, the credit card companies charge a very high fee to let us use their money. We are borrowing their money and using their employees' labor, so we need to pay for it.

The monastery was paying around 19 percent interest on our credit cards, only making minimum payments, and adding small charges each month that exceeded the minimum payments. As a result, the total balance kept growing and growing.

Here is what 19 percent interest looks like on $1,200 over forty years without paying down the balance. It compounds to $1,262,001.01. That isn't a typo. That's a Debt Avalanche.

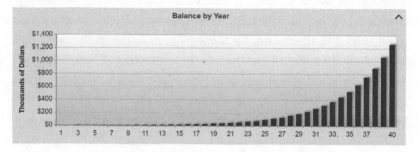

The growth of $1,200 invested at 19 percent for forty years.
Compound interest graphs provided by dinkytown.net financial calculators.

In time, we had to take on debt to make the minimum payments on the old debt. Credit cards love it when you get stuck in the Debt Avalanche. That is their business model. Then you are trapped under a mountain of debt. It is like signing up to become an indentured servant for life.

Get Out of Debt with a Debt Snowball

If you are already deep in debt, I'm sorry. That sucks. Getting out of debt is an entire book unto itself, but please avoid all the credit consolidation and credit repair companies. They aren't there to help, just to prey on your suffering. They are selling a dubious financial service, and that service comes with a price. Which means you are taking on high-priced debt when drowning in debt. Their products are, at best, a convenience, like prepackaged food that you can cook better and cheaper yourself.

A credit counseling service is different. They are nonprofit (or should be) and are like a financial coach to help you get out of debt. But they aren't free either. Make sure that any credit counseling agency is a member of the National Foundation for Credit Counseling (www .nfcc.org). Services provided vary widely in both cost and scope. If you feel lost and unable to organize your finances alone, a credit counselor can be a lifeline. Just do your homework first and make sure they are nonprofit, accredited, and your best choice. I suggest talking with a local bankruptcy lawyer first (which we discussed in chapter 7). If you don't qualify for bankruptcy, then look for a credit counselor if you can't manage your debt alone.

If bankruptcy isn't an option, the best way to reverse the Debt Avalanche is with the Debt Snowball. It is a simple system proposed by many other financial advisers. There are a lot of other techniques, and they all work if you consistently pay down your debt and stop using credit cards, but I like the Debt Snowball because it is simple to understand and psychologically rewarding. You can see your progress with the greatest ease. Here's a checklist to keep you on track:

- Start by listing your credit cards by total balance. Pick the one with the lowest amount. Then use every financial resource available (except more debt) to pay it off. Ignore all savings, investing, and other goals. Nothing else matters until you pay that sucker off. I suggest starting with the smallest balance because it is the easiest to pay off and you can see your progress. Progress creates hope. Hope keeps you going.
- Once the first card is paid off, torn up, and closed out, turn

all your attention to the card with the remaining lowest balance. Attack it with everything you've got. When that card is paid off, keep going. Move to the next lowest card. Repeat until debt free. There are more mathematically efficient techniques, like starting with the card that has the highest interest rate, but starting with the lowest balance and working up is the most psychologically rewarding. It keeps you focused, and it feels great every time a credit card is paid off. With each card you pay off, you'll have fewer minimum payments to make and more income available to pay off the next card. The process goes faster and faster, snowballing until you are liberated. There is a free Snowball Debt Elimination Calculator on my website (douglynam.com) that can help make the process easier.

- In the meantime, call each credit card and try to negotiate a lower interest rate. Move balances around if you can to put the most money on the lowest interest rate card(s). If your situation is bad, then be honest and transparent with your credit card companies. They may work with you and provide a temporary payment reduction, lower interest rate, long-term payment plan, or forbearance with no payments for a short time, or they may offer a lump sum payment. You never know what you can get. It may be the most frustrating and humbling thing you ever do, and it may not work, but persistence can pay.

- However, be ready for them to cut off your remaining credit and close your account. I think this is a very good thing, though your credit score will be hurt. As you'll soon see, I don't think much of credit scores, and I'd rather have a lower credit score for a few years than be a slave to credit for life.

Take Responsibility for
That Piece of Plastic

Close all but one of your credit cards. Why risk the temptation of ever using them again? If you have a balance on your card when you close it, you'll still need to pay all that money back, and you'll take a hit to your credit score, but so what? In time those credit hits will fade and disappear, your debt will get paid off, and you'll be free.

I recommend having one credit card for some purchases, like dubious online sites, rental cars, and extreme emergencies. Just be sure to pay off the balance every month. (I'll discuss the nature of true emergencies in the next chapter.)

Here is the truth about credit: Why would you spend someone else's money for living expenses and luxury items? If you don't have the money to afford that stuff now, what makes you think you can afford it later? Why would your financial situation improve in the future when you now have credit card debt that you'll need to pay? Your future just got worse by taking on consumer debt, so paying it back in full, with interest, is going to suck.

Instead of vetting who can responsibly use a credit card or subprime home loan, some institutions give out money carelessly. Doing this on a massive scale caused the 2008 economic crisis. Lenders got bailed out when they made stupid loans, but consumers got crucified for taking on stupid loans. Heads the banks win—tails the consumer loses. Don't let them intimidate you.

The Mob was much kinder than credit card companies are now. If the Mob offered to lend you $5,000 to pay for a vacation, would you take it? You know they will break your kneecaps if you don't pay it back with interest. It's a horrible idea. And yet credit card companies are worse. The Mob might ask for 50 percent straight interest, so if you borrow $5,000, you'll pay $7,500 from your future earnings. Ouch. But Visa can charge you 19 percent *compound* interest, which can have no end to it if you keep using the card. You can pay that debt down for the rest of your life and never have it go away.

Here's my best advice about keeping a credit card in your wallet:

1. **Get one card, pay it in full each month, and to heck with your credit score.** The credit bureaus don't work for you and are not your friend. They work for the banks and the credit industry. They want you to borrow more money and obsess over your credit score. They try to force you to borrow money to prove your "creditworthiness." Instead of worrying endlessly about credit scores and free airline miles, focus on building up your wealth instead. Then your credit score doesn't mean a darn thing because you can pay in cash.

Remember that there is no interest charged on a credit card until after your monthly billing cycle. If you pay the balance in full each month, you'll never incur an interest charge.

I also recommend that you ignore all rewards and airline miles. I've never earned more back from my credit card company in free miles or rewards than I paid in interest and fees. How could you? If that happened regularly, the credit card companies would go out of business. As I've mentioned, in 2016 credit card interest and fee payments reached $163 billion. Who is winning the free-rewards game? Probably not you.

2. **Remember your debit card.** With a debit card, I can take all my wealth with me anywhere on the planet, without actually taking my money with me. That is a super power. I can live in Rome, park my money in a bank in America, and access all my wealth as needed with little risk of losing it all. I love modern inventions.

Debit cards are amazing because you truly can't spend more than what you have. Trust me—paying with your own cash, although less flashy than using a fancy new credit card, is still the best way to go. Debit cards are also just as secure as credit cards and carry the same fraud protection. I've been the victim of identity theft, and my bank quickly and painlessly reimbursed me for the losses on my debit card. Just like credit cards, be sure to report any losses promptly.

3. Don't buy things that depreciate on credit. Consumer debt comes from buying things you *consume*, use, and no longer have. To build wealth, pay with cash or a debit card rather than borrow and spend money you don't have, especially on things that lose value over time.

New cars are generally a very poor purchase decision and significantly depreciate the second you sign on the dotted line. What do you do if you want to buy a new car? Most people take out a loan. However, car loans and leases are generally bad deals. Stay far away. Again, spending someone else's money never works out well. Buy in cash if you can. And buy a reliable used car until you are a multimillionaire.

Most of the private clients at my firm are considered high net worth, with an average balance of $1 million or more. I'm always intrigued to see what cars pull into the parking lot. Yes, there are some nice luxury vehicles but not that many. Most drive reliable nondescript sedans that are at least five to ten years old.

Conversely, our office shares employee parking with two restaurants. The restaurant staff make close to minimum wage, but some drive beautifully tricked-out muscle cars. Most high-net-worth clients would never buy such expensive vehicles. They don't think they can afford it—and they're probably right. Millionaires are millionaires for a reason. This phenomenon was documented in a famous book mentioned earlier called *The Millionaire Next Door*. Frugality is a key habit of most high-net-worth individuals.

Oddly, many of the people who buy luxury items aren't wealthy. They are just average people trying to appear wealthy. The hard truth is that most of us are faced with a choice: try to be wealthy or try to look rich. You can't have both. Save the luxury items until you are truly wealthy. By then, you might not care about status symbols anyway.

The way to build wealth is to buy investments. The way to be poor is to buy stuff. The way to bankruptcy is to buy stuff on credit.

4. Most debt is a bad idea but not always. Carefully used—again, *carefully used*—some debt can be beneficial, like a home mortgage, modest student loans, or a small business loan. With luck, a home will appreciate, a college degree will increase your lifetime earning potential, and a business loan can launch your career when used wisely. However, if you can buy a home, pay for college, or start a business without debt, that is an infinitely preferable option, though not always possible. That doesn't mean you have permission to take on stupid amounts of student loan debt, use mortgages to try flipping houses, or get a loan to start a cat-walking service.

The Bottom Line: Unpaid Credit Card Debt Makes You Poor

As a math teacher, I would often give students math puzzles or riddles to play with for the first few minutes of class. One of my favorites is this: Imagine you have a circular petri dish for growing bacteria. You place a small sample of magical fast-growing bacteria in the dish, and the bacteria doubles in volume every minute. If you put the first sample of bacteria in the dish at 1:00 p.m., and the petri dish is full at exactly 2:00 p.m., at what time was the dish half full?

Think about it for just a moment before looking up the answer. No, stop. Try again. Anyone can do this; you just need to try. If you are doing crazy calculations or complex math, diagramming a word problem, or counting on your fingers as I do, then you are doing it wrong. If you don't know, take a break. Make a cup of tea and think for a few minutes. It is a riddle, so the answer must be simple.

Have you got it? Okay, here is a hint. The bacteria doubles in volume every minute. If the dish is full at 2:00 p.m., when was it half full? Got it now? Yes?! The dish is half full one minute before 2:00 p.m.

What does this have to do with debt and investing? Everything. Bacteria grows exponentially. So does money. This is one reason the rich get richer and the poor stay poor. Wealthy people have money that, if invested wisely, grows exponentially. You need to make sure the same is happening for you. The problem is that this exponential growth is most effective over a long period of time. Instead of doubling in volume every minute, like bacteria, money invested at a rate of 10 percent would double every 7.2 years. If your bank account is "full" when you reach $5 million, when will your account be half full? 7.2 years before then. If your account is "full" at age 50, then you were likely halfway to your goal at 42.8 years of age.

But it works in reverse with credit cards! It is the same phenomena when you take on debt, only now you are paying out compound interest and the time value of money is working against you. And at a much higher interest rate. With unpaid credit card debt, you are getting exponentially poorer and poorer, no matter how much money you make.

Wealthy people use the time value of money to their advantage while the poor are taken advantage of. Which side of that game do you want to be on?

Stay out of consumer debt at all costs!

Student loans can be especially devastating. The average college student with a bachelor's degree graduates with $28,400 of debt. If invested over forty years, that's $798,914.13 in lost wealth. I'm a fierce advocate for education, but remember that a student loan is just a small business loan in disguise. What is your business plan for taking on $28,400 in debt? Will it help you establish a solid career or teach you how to think deeply and critically? Don't take on a business loan to play beer pong. I often meet clients who struggle under $100,000 to $200,000 in student debt—and it cripples their lives.

The time value of money principle shows that the longer the time horizon you have to invest, the more money you are likely to make. And the longer you stay in debt, the more money you lose. If you wait and don't start fixing your finances immediately, things are only going to get worse. (You can quickly and easily do a time value of money calculation for both debt and investments using a free online calculator on my website: douglynam.com.)

This is why so many people end up delaying retirement—they run down the clock. They are trying to make up for lost time early in their careers while also lowering the number of years their retirement money needs to last, meaning they need to work harder and longer than they'd like. A rather morbid calculation but one that too many must face.

Don't Sell Your Soul

The most intriguing, humorous, and possibly immoral experiment I conducted in my economics class was when I asked if there were any atheists in the classroom—then I offered to buy their souls. I told the class that I was willing to buy only one soul that day, and if more than one student was willing, I would accept the lowest offer. After a bidding war to the lowest price, a student sold me their immortal soul for $1. We even used red pen in the contract to make it a little creepier.

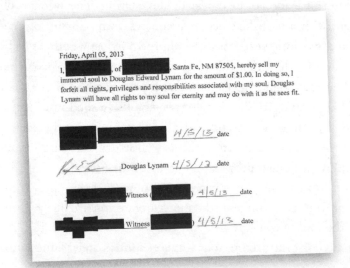

Friday, April 05, 2013

I, ▮▮▮▮, of ▮▮▮▮, Santa Fe, NM 87505, hereby sell my immortal soul to Douglas Edward Lynam for the amount of $1.00. In doing so, I forfeit all rights, privileges and responsibilities associated with my soul. Douglas Lynam will have all rights to my soul for eternity and may do with it as he sees fit.

_____ 4/5/13 date

_____ Douglas Lynam 4/5/13 date

_____ Witness ( ) 4/5/13 date

_____ Witness ( ) 4/5/13 date

Of course, I don't believe you can ever sell your soul because it isn't transferable property. You can't abdicate responsibility for some things. The contract we wrote isn't legally binding. But let's assume it is transferable. Who is better equipped to care for and tend to a soul? A reasonably reliable middle-aged monk or a reckless atheist teenager? Wouldn't I be a better steward of this valuable property? Shouldn't every young person sell their soul to be cared for by a religious professional?

Now, you're probably wondering what this story has to do with debt and investing. A lot. When people are young, they have so much life ahead of them that death doesn't feel like a pressing issue. There aren't many ninety-year-olds who would sell me their soul at any price. The same is true with taking on debt—it's one of the worst things you can do.

The hard truth: Forgiveness and redemption are possible at any age, but that doesn't mean there is still time to fix your life. The longer you wait, the more difficult it gets.

Like money borrowed or spent in our youth, a soul isn't always perceived for its true value. Money that you have when you're younger is more valuable than money accrued when you're older. Why? You have time to invest it and let it grow using compound interest, allowing you to leverage it into more money. A younger person can spend $50 for a pair of shoes without seeing the true worth of their money. Fifty dollars spent now is potentially worth $1,407 in forty years if invested wisely. Charged to a credit card, that same $50 could potentially cost $52,584 after forty years.[1] That doesn't mean you should never buy shoes, but you sure as heck shouldn't buy them on credit. It is important to understand the true cost-to-benefit analysis of your money decisions.

Remember: Credit is cruel. It is the fastest way to sell your financial soul to the devil.

If my former student ever wants his soul back, I'll gladly return it. I'm busy enough dealing with my own. But he'd better hurry; at 8.7 percent interest, the price is going up. If he waits for all eternity, he'll owe me the whole world.

Beat that investment, Warren Buffett.

CHAPTER 11

PAY YOURSELF FIRST

Which bill do you hate the most? The credit card? The rent? The student loans? Are there any bills you like to pay? If you are normal and sane, you probably hate all your bills. But I'd like to challenge that.

As a former broke person, I can attest to the fact that *our monastery's problems with money weren't about money; they were about priorities.* If you don't set your priorities, eliminate debt, and put your savings first, then there will always be another crisis you can't afford to deal with. Money problems will never stop until you get your financial house in order. Financial freedom requires money, and you'll probably never have any money unless you pay yourself first.

If you are financially wise, you'll learn to love the first bill you pay each month. The trick is to pick the right place to start: with paying *yourself.* Paying yourself first is a concept that helps set your priorities. It means that the first dollar of every paycheck gets spent on you. More specifically, the future you, by saving a healthy portion of everything you earn. (For those who tithe, I'll discuss charitable giving more extensively in chapter 20.)

In your budget you have fixed expenses and flexible expenses.

Once you are debt free, the first fixed expense must be your savings. Decide what your savings goal is, then save that first. *It must be a fixed expense.* Automatically pay yourself at the start of each week or month by scheduling payments to a savings or investment account. Make it happen before you spend a single penny. Then focus on staying inside your budget, keeping other fixed expenses to a minimum, and the rest is your flexible spending to use any way you like. Easy. (Well, easy to say, hard to do.) If savings are a flexible expense, they will typically fall below your lava point and rarely happen. Your money will disappear faster than donuts in a teachers' lounge. The demands of the world will eat up your income before you save any of it.

Your Savings Paycheck

Once you decide to pay yourself first, your next decision is how much. As discussed in chapter 9, my suggestion is to work toward the goal of saving 15 percent of your money automatically when you get paid. Make that your priority on every single penny you make.

Make it a habit. Habits are hard to break. Paying yourself first will be insanely difficult at the beginning; then over time, maintaining this good habit gets easier and easier. Eventually it just happens. You'll hardly notice you are automatically saving—until you wake up several years from now with a small fortune.

What things are you willing to sacrifice now to have a big pile of money in the future? Can you reduce your consumption in the present to have financial freedom later? Save first, spend second.

After you decide how much to pay yourself, the next question will be what to do with the money you save. Thankfully, that's an easy one. Start by building your emergency fund. Put your money into a regular savings or money market account. You won't be making any money on what you put away, but you won't be risking it either. It must be available, almost instantly, when an emergency hits. Second, you'll want to put your money into a retirement account. Third, an investment or college savings account.

Your Emergency Fund

Ideally, your emergency fund covers three to six months' living expenses. It needs to pay for the random and horrible crises that can hit at the worst possible times, like a job layoff or serious accident for you or a loved one. (A cousin's wedding in Paris is not your emergency, no matter how socially awkward your absence might be.) When your emergency fund is in solid shape, you can deal with the crisis, and not the money problems that are the result. Should you ever deplete your emergency fund because of a real emergency, this becomes your first savings priority again.

For example, when my grandfather was dying of lung cancer (thank you, Philip Morris), I took time off to be his primary caregiver. It was an excruciatingly painful time for our whole family, but it was one of the most valuable experiences I've ever had. It brought me closer to my extended family and helped me forge a bond with my grandfather before he died. Fortunately, I had the financial resources to cover my living expenses while I took several months off from work. Where was that money going to come from? I couldn't have done it without an emergency fund, and in the end, it turned out to be worth every penny. Caring for him was a master class in dying with grace. My fear of death diminished significantly after that.

When I was about fifteen, my mother called me into her home office. She pulled open a drawer in her large file cabinet and showed me an innocuous file buried deep inside labeled "School." It was an odd choice for a file name. She then pulled out the file and showed me the contents. Inside the file was an envelope and inside the envelope was several thousand dollars in cash (this was before debit cards existed). She then told me this was her "run money." She explained:

Sometimes life gets really, really bad. When that happens, you can't always fight; you can only flee. Then you need money to run. And you need it fast. This was her run money in case of extreme emergencies, and she wanted me to know where it was in case anything happened to her. If things got so bad that she wasn't around, or able to use it herself, it was my responsibility to take it. What terrified me the most is that she made me promise not to tell anyone about her secret file, especially other members of my family. The implication was clear: there were reasons we might need to run.

The gravity of what she was trying to teach me at fifteen was frightening but essential. I've never forgotten that lesson. I've always tried to keep some run money (an emergency fund) for extreme personal emergencies. I've had to use my run money more than once. But it saved me. Without it I would have been trapped in horrible situations and suffered untold amounts of extra pain. I regularly see abused spouses and children trapped in appalling situations because they have no way out. They have no run money, no backup plan, no resources to call upon as a lifeline out of a personal hell. So please, fix your finances. Build your wealth and guard a portion of it carefully. You'll need it for an emergency someday, and when you do, you'll be infinitely grateful that it is there.

Your Retirement Fund

After establishing your emergency fund, the next thing you should try to do is put your 15 percent savings into a retirement fund. It can be through your employer, or you may need to open an IRA. Make this your second savings priority . . . if you've already paid off all credit card debt. Hopefully, you get an employer match on your retirement savings, which can instantly double your money. *That's a great deal; don't pass up an employer match—ever.* No other investment is this good. If you make an annual return of 30 percent in the stock market, the world will think you are a genius. In one second, you can make a 100-percent return, or double your money, just by getting your employer match. And it's sheltered from taxes. That should make you grin like the Cheshire cat.

To find out if you are on track with your retirement savings, a free and easy-to-use calculator available on my website will provide a good back-of-the-napkin assessment of your retirement readiness.[1] It will also factor in Social Security for you. Playing with it for ten minutes might be the most helpful retirement planning exercise you'll ever do.

When you have a strong emergency fund, have paid off all credit card debt, and are contributing at least 15 percent to your retirement account, that's when you can start saving for bigger things like cars (always used), college tuition for kids, and that vacation to a tropical resort.

Your Investment or College Savings Account

If saving for college is a priority, that's a lengthy and complex topic I'm going to sidestep for now. Besides, someone else has already done that work in a free, easy-to-use format. Check out SavingForCollege.com for unbiased information, tools, and calculators to help you navigate the crazy world of college savings.

Once that to-do list is checked off, which is a massive accomplishment, you're ready for bigger investment goals. We'll get to that soon in part 4.

For now, focus on this step-by-step approach to saving what you need:

- Make saving 15 percent of your income a long-term goal. Then make a plan to get there. Start by saving what you can, even 1 percent, then steadily increase your savings rate each year as your income increases.

- Automatically pay yourself from all money you make.
- Establish an emergency fund that will allow you to weather a major crisis. Three months of living expenses is a great start, $4,000 at a minimum.
- Next, switch to saving for retirement. Always put enough into your plan to get the full employer match, but 15 percent overall is highly recommended. If you are nearing retirement and haven't saved much, you'll need to contribute more aggressively.
- Assess your retirement readiness by using a free calculator on my website: douglynam.com.
- After saving for retirement, open an investment account for future goals, such as buying a home, sending your kids to college, or starting a business.
- Finally, start buying more investments to grow a little bit wealthier. (More on how to do that in part 4.)
- If you ever deplete your emergency fund, make that your top savings priority once again.

Don't Put Yourself in Harm's Way

As you can imagine, paying ourselves first wasn't a high priority during my early years at the monastery. Instead, we scrambled to pay all the bills each month, with nothing left to save. Yet there were still meals out, gifts for holidays, and periodic retreats. We even gave money away or spent it to help others, which was a nice thing to do. However, we had our priorities mixed up.

For example, there were several friends of the community who lived out of state and were unable to travel but still needed spiritual and emotional help. So what did we do? We packed up and went to them. Most vacations were spent helping other people in crisis. Those were noble gestures, born out of love, compassion, and kindness. Even if we couldn't afford it, we went anyway. It was a form of service. Saying no didn't feel like an option, especially for monks, when someone was suffering spiritually.

We were drowning financially and let other people use us as a life raft. That didn't turn out well. To effectively help others, especially with money, you need to operate from a position of strength. It is one key reason you need a little bit of wealth.

For this discussion, we need to make a clear distinction between a money rescue and a money emergency. A money emergency is why you need an emergency fund, like if someone you love is sick or injured. Or your dog gets mauled by a pit bull and needs surgery. Then the rules of love override the rules of finance—you do what you have to do. A money rescue is when you take pity on someone or perform an act of charity out of generosity. Sometimes that generosity is overzealous, and we start behaving like a White Knight or Angel of Mercy. In those situations, it can be helpful to remember that giving people your time is sometimes more important, and more generous, than giving money.

When doing search and rescue work, I trained for water rescues. The first rule of basic water rescue: don't jump into the water. You need to avoid putting yourself in a dangerous position where you can become a victim as well. And never place yourself close enough to be grabbed by a panicked victim.

Helping people is a wonderful thing, but here is another hard truth: sometimes life gives you bad choices and worse choices. Just like in a water rescue, you can't help if you aren't on solid ground. It may feel noble to risk your life to save someone else, but if you become a victim, then someone else must put themselves at risk to save you. In theory, that could create an infinite chain reaction where everybody in the world drowns.

If someone is in financial distress and needs your help, give it if you can. Give lots of it. But don't destabilize your financial future, and don't ever expect to see any of that money back again. Give money out of love, kindness, and selflessness. Then let it go.

For example, a student of mine lost her mother and was the oldest child in the family. Then, near the end of high school, her father was suddenly deported. But she and her four siblings are US citizens. At eighteen years old, she instantly became the parent and sole provider for her family. She ran her father's business at night, attended school during the day, and tried to hold the family together. Helping her financially was a no-brainer. And we weren't alone in our efforts. Others did far more to help. It was a gift, and we never once expected to see a penny of that money back. No strings attached. Fortunately, at that time we had the money to give without depleting our emergency fund, taking on debt, or compromising our long-term financial health. Giving freely is one of the greatest joys of being a little bit wealthy.

In extreme contrast, one friend keeps bailing out his daughter after every money mistake. This is still going on after decades. The result is that he is broke and his daughter is a permanent adolescent who never learned to take responsibility for her life.

The hard truth: a financial house in order tends to stay in order, and a financial house in distress tends to stay in distress. When a person needs help because they can't get their money situation under control, there is a good chance that even with your help things are going to stay the same. Chronic money problems are often similar to drug problems—the person you are trying to help must first decide to help themselves before you can make a difference. If you toss money into a burning building, don't expect to see that money again.

When someone wants to borrow money, either make it a gift or walk away. If the loan doesn't get paid back in full, and on time, the relationship can be permanently ruined. Is that a risk you want to take with the people you love most?

Building Good Habits Takes Practice

You now know how to prioritize your money. However, you're not going to get it right every time. It helps to remember that failure is the first step to success. How many times do you need to practice with a basketball before you can hit a three-pointer? Can you do crow pose in your first yoga class? You are going to fail a lot at anything you try to accomplish. But keep trying and you get better at it. Eventually you become a pro. *Managing your money is like anything else: it takes a lot of mindful practice!*

Don't let your money failures shame you. You are going to screw up sometimes. I still do. It is tax time as I'm writing this, and I made a miscalculation in my taxes. The result: an unexpectedly large tax bill. Ugh! But what happens now? I get upset, kick myself mentally for a few days, then forgive myself and move on. It's like when my cat KP would get sick on the carpet—super annoying but fixable with some industrial stain remover.

But here's a key point: my tax problem is fixable because I have a strong practice of saving money so that when an unexpected bill hits, it's fine. I planned for the unexpected, so when the unexpected happens, I have a plan. I clean up the mess gracefully and move on. Minimal stress.

And just to clarify, paying yourself first is not the same as splurging. That comes at the very, very end when you've earned it. When all your bills are paid, all your debt is gone, and you've saved a portion of your income, then you can splurge a little. Until then, you can't afford it. Sorry.

Constant self-denial is impossible, and saying no all the time drains your mental fortitude. So I prefer to reframe my desires, not deny them. I choose the reward of a large bank account and of accumulating investments over the reward of accumulating stuff that depreciates. Both provide pleasure and enjoyment, but I get a *much greater* sense of pleasure and delight at having wealth than spending money.

The real question to ask is, what do I value? Do you value being wealthy? How much? Can you do the hard work necessary to build lasting wealth? If the answer is yes, then you should start by setting your priorities and paying yourself first.

PART 4

IT'S TIME TO BECOME A LITTLE BIT WEALTHY

CHAPTER 12

GRASP THE BASICS OF INVESTING

Now the fun part—becoming a little bit wealthy. The catch is that most people can't earn their way to wealth. You can't get there by saving either. You'll only get there by investing. It will take time, but it will happen if you stay focused.

The only way to invest is to have money available to invest. Which means that saving money comes first and investing comes second. If you haven't solved your debt and savings problems yet, that's okay. Read on. This chapter may help motivate you to work harder on your debt and savings issues. Knowing the destination can make the journey easier.

According to the US Census Bureau, the median American household income is around $57,000 a year. If the median household saved 15 percent of their income for 30 years by either stuffing cash in a mattress or opening a savings account in a bank, how much would they have? Since your brain just froze at being asked a random math question, here's the answer: $256,500. That's a lot of money by any standard, but not enough to retire on. Retirement needs to last 10 to

40 years. If you retire at 65 and live to 95, $256,000 would give you about $712.50 a month to spend. That's going to be tight, even with Social Security. Especially since most people won't save consistently for 30 years. And inflation is going to decrease the spending power of all savings significantly.

According to the Economic Policy Institute, the average retirement savings of working-age families headed by someone between the ages of 56 and 61 is just $163,577.[1] However, wealthy people skew the average. The median (the number in the middle) for families headed by someone between those ages is only $17,000. Almost half of working-age families have no retirement savings of any kind. According to Fidelity Investments, a 65-year-old couple retiring in 2018 will need $280,000 *just to cover health-care and medical expenses throughout their retirement.*[2] And that doesn't include everyday expenses, fun trips, or slipping $40 into your grandkid's birthday card.

To avoid being on the wrong side of those statistics, you must invest your money—wisely. It needs to grow steadily over time, compounding over the years. The historical rate of return for a balanced portfolio of stocks and bonds is 8.7 percent.[3] If you took that same 15 percent savings from an income of $57,000 a year, for 30 years, and invested in a balanced portfolio, how much would you have? (Sorry for the flashback to high school math.) The answer to the question is . . . *a staggering $1,154,230.*

The world of investing is vast and complex, and trying to explain all of it is an impossible task. So I'm going to cheat a little. I'm just going to share the best of what I've learned as a money manager, without trying to justify all of it. If you want to dig deeper, the data and research to support my conclusions is plentiful and easily accessible online. I didn't invent any of this. For data freaks who want to research and verify my suggestions—go crazy. But I'm not going to swamp you with charts, formulas, and lingo you might not care about or remember.

Seven Basic Principles of Investing

To succeed and invest wisely, you'll need to follow a few principles. An adviser can help, but you still need to know what is happening. Never outsource responsibility for your money. Only outsource the hard work.

Here are seven basic principles that are important to remember when investing. We'll go through them one at a time to be sure you have a strong foundation of understanding before you ever walk into an investment adviser's office.

1. Allocate your assets according to your age and goals. Asset allocation is the ratio of stocks and bonds in your portfolio. When you are younger, your portfolio should be mostly stocks, and as you get older, it should favor bonds. Break it down by age and it will look something like this:

Age Bracket	Stock/Bond Ratio
20 to 30	95/5
30 to 40	90/10
40 to 50	80/20
50 to 60	70/30
60 to 70	50/50
70+	30/70

What are stocks and bonds? Stocks represent ownership in companies. When you purchase a stock, you become a partial owner in the profits and losses of that company. (That doesn't mean you can buy stock in Starbucks and expect free drinks.) The stock market is the place where people buy and sell stocks, just like a fish market or a flower market. It used to be a physical place, but it is now mostly online. The purpose of a for-profit company is to make money, and stocks let you buy ownership in those profits. Historically, stocks have outperformed all other investment options—by a lot. Stocks are where most of your money belongs, most of the time. Investing in a company is the most effective legal way to make money because making money is a for-profit company's reason for existence.

Bonds are different from stocks. They are debt that companies or governments take on, like a line of credit. You give your money to an institution, on loan, with the promise that they will pay it back with interest. When you buy bonds, you own part of the debt sold by a company or government. You get periodic interest payments, then they give your money back when the loan is due.

Bonds are safer than stocks because governments and companies are legally required to pay back debt. Stocks are riskier, but they also have a higher historical rate of return (they make more money) than bonds. This is one of the fundamental "laws" of investing: Risk is correlated to reward. The riskier an investment, the higher the expected returns must be to entice anyone to invest. When the risk is low, the return is also likely to be low. Stocks are higher risk, higher return, while bonds are lower risk, lower return.

Long-term investments belong in stocks. Short-term investments, where you might need your money soon, should be mostly in bonds. Money you could need right away doesn't belong in any investment, so use a savings account. Savings accounts are FDIC (Federal Deposit Insurance Corporation) insured up to $250,000, so even if your bank goes under you have no risk.

Investing always involves the risk of volatility. If you can't afford to see your portfolio drop in value during a market crash and then wait for the recovery, avoid stocks. However, just because stocks have risk doesn't mean you should be afraid of them. Time is your ally. If you buy and hold stocks for the long term, your risk goes down exponentially. The market is unpredictable in the short term, but over the long term it has delivered annualized returns of roughly 10 percent. The longer you remain invested, the more likely you are to capture these returns, and the less important the day-to-day fluctuations become.

I regularly meet clients who are terrified of stocks because they hate the idea of a potential loss. While I sympathize with their anxiety, not investing in stocks is an even riskier route in the long term. You'll never lose money in investments you don't have, but then you have no investments—and we know what that looks like. Investing is the engine that drives wealth. Not investing, especially in stocks, is like refusing to drive a car, ride a train, or fly because you're scared of an accident. You'll never get into a car accident if you never go anywhere, but then you must live with the reality of never going anywhere— ever. That is guaranteed failure in life. Not investing for the long term guarantees failure in becoming a little bit wealthy.

There is also the problem of inflation. Inflation is the steady rise in the price of things over time. You know how a Coke used to cost a few cents and now costs more than a dollar? Inflation erodes the purchasing power of money. It causes the value of a dollar to decline, so a dollar buys less stuff each year. If you stuff your money under a mattress, you don't get any interest, which means inflation steadily destroys your money. Like termites in the walls slowly destroying your house, inflation guarantees money loss and diminished wealth if you don't invest.

As you age, you need to move more money into bonds to protect your assets. Stocks are your offensive game; bonds are defense. Just playing offense isn't a great idea. In fact, it's a really bad idea. With a purely offensive game, you'll likely score a lot of points, while taking a lot of hits. And, to put it bluntly, as you age you have less time and fortitude to recover from the hits you're guaranteed to take.

On the other hand, if you play only defense, it's game over from the start. You'll never reach your goals and the points never accu- mulate. I've seen far too many people invest entirely in "defensive" low-risk investments for decades, then retire with inadequate net worth. They didn't lose much, but they certainly didn't gain much either. (And all investments have some risk, including bonds.) The best path is a healthy mix of offense and defense, just as it is for a good soccer team. Offense grows your money and defense protects your money after you've accumulated a big pile.

With that in mind, the subject of annuities comes up. The word *annuity* shouldn't be on your lips until after age sixty; then hire a professional investment adviser for conflict-of-interest–free advice on annuities. They are tricky, tricky beasts. Many annuity salespeople are coyotes looking for a big snack and can destroy your retirement savings with the stroke of a pen. Never purchase an annuity without an independent review. Like a root canal, it may be something you really need, but this is not a do-it-yourself project. Annuities can serve a useful function providing steady income during retirement, but like any powerful tool, they can be easily misused.

I'll say it again: *most people cannot save their way to retirement—* they must save *and* invest. Investing takes time to work, so start saving early and invest aggressively at the beginning. Remember the time value of money.

Notice what else is missing from this conversation? Real estate, gold, hedge funds, cryptocurrencies, and so on. For the average investor, all that is noise. Ignore it. If you want to add in 5 to 10 percent of alternative investments like gold or real estate for further diversification, fine. But don't overindulge on them. Your core investments should be in stocks and bonds.

2. Diversify. Diversification is simply investing your money in a lot of different businesses, sectors, and countries, rather than concentrating your money in just a few companies. The more broadly you invest, the more diverse, and thus diversified, your portfolio is.

Diversification reduces your market risk by combining a mix of investments that move in different directions at different times. The more diversified your portfolio, the more likely you are to have steady returns. Returns will vary, of course, depending on the portfolio investment mix and market conditions.

If you are a professional investor, there are times when concentrating your portfolio in just a few great investments can have outstanding results. However, the risk is high. Don't go there until you are truly an expert in investing.

The research is clear. *For the average investor, picking individual stocks is a losing game.* You are wasting time and money and will never diversify your portfolio adequately. Besides, buying and selling individual stocks is zero-sum. For each winner there is a loser, and you'll be playing against all of Wall Street. Do you really think you can outsmart the entire financial services industry while trading stocks in your free time? And do you think that subscribing to a newsletter or watching TV shows on investing is going to help? I tried that a long time ago. It doesn't work. Those are get-rich-quick schemes for the person selling you the newsletter or hawking a TV show. All that stuff is investment porn. Stay away!

Instead, buy and hold index-based mutual funds, which we'll cover soon. (A mutual fund is a pool of money from lots of investors that a professional money manager invests on their behalf.)

3. Protect the future you are saving for. Just as there are good and bad people in the world, there are great companies and some that cause serious harm to our communities and planet. You need to avoid the bad apples if you want to help make the world a better place.

Money is power, and how we invest our money is a clear expression of our values. If we give our power to bad people or unjust causes, we are responsible for increasing the suffering of the world. Ignoring or creating suffering to grow wealthy is *philargyria* and zero-sum thinking. It is a problem we must face with clarity and wisdom. *Agape-argyria* allows us to be deeply concerned with personal profit, which is self-care, but we also need to love our neighbors, our country, and the global community.

One way to protect the future is to invest in environmentally and socially responsible funds. The good news is that there are excellent funds that apply rigorous environmental, social, and governance (ESG) screens to their investments. The more exciting news is that some of these funds have performed as well as or better than their conventional peers.

This topic is so important that I've devoted all of chapter 13 to it. But for now, let me just say that we can't turn our ethics off when investing.

4. Simplify your investing with passive index funds. "The market" is a common expression for the stock market. There are lots of complex ways to measure the performance of the market, and there are fancy names for these measuring sticks, like the S&P 500, the Dow, NASDAQ, and so on. You don't need to worry about that stuff right now. What you need to know is that the annualized return of the market has been better than almost any other investment option—around 10 percent, depending on who you ask and how you do the calculation. How do you get the average return of the market? By investing in index funds and holding on to them for the long term. An index is a basket, or pool, of investments that covers an entire sector or the entire market. Instant diversification.

When you put $100 into a total market index fund, it spreads out that money over almost all the investable stocks in the US stock market. If you invest in a total market index fund, you can now expect to earn the rate of return of the stock market. Investing made simple.

There is a bonus: index funds don't require high-salary fund managers to run. Computers do most of the work, so investing in index funds is inexpensive as well as efficient.

In any diversified portfolio, you'll want a US market index, a developed markets index (Europe, Japan, et al.), and an emerging markets index (China, India, Brazil, et al.). As a rough guideline, of your money invested in stocks, I recommend 60 percent in the US market, 30 percent in developed markets, and 10 percent in emerging markets. But remember, stocks are just one part of your portfolio, alongside bonds.

You can also choose a total world stock market index fund if you want to be super simple, which will give you roughly the percentages I suggest. However, I strongly recommend adding additional environmental and social screens beyond just a total world market index, which we'll discuss soon.

A bond index fund works the same way as a stock index fund, except it is investing in a diversified mix of government, corporate, and municipal bonds. The bond portion of your portfolio can be easily handled with a total bond market index fund.

If this is as much investing knowledge as your brain can handle right now, it's not a bad place to end up.

Here's the easiest investing option: use a "target date" fund. If you don't have the time or expertise to learn more about retirement investing, stick with an index-based target date fund from companies like Vanguard, Fidelity, Schwab, Dimensional Fund Advisers (DFA), or TIAA. It will serve you well. Target date funds are a one-stop shop for retirement savings. They automatically set your asset allocation according to your age, and rebalance, or shift, the proportions of stocks and bonds as you approach retirement. They are customized to your expected target date for retirement. There are even ESG target date funds and portfolios now available.

If you are investing for something other than retirement, most large mutual fund companies like Vanguard and Fidelity also have all-in-one "target goal" portfolios for things such as an emergency fund, a house, a wedding, a baby, college, or a car. These are excellent choices for other investment goals because they build the portfolio for you based on that goal.

The alternative to index funds are actively managed funds. Indexing is called "passive" investing because no thought goes into picking stocks. Index funds buy them all and get the average return of the market. Actively managed funds try to research who the winners and losers will be and invest in the presumed winners. Not surprisingly, that often doesn't turn out well. According to the S&P Dow Jones Indices, "Over the 15-year investment horizon, 92.33 percent of large-cap managers, 94.81 percent of mid-cap managers, and 95.73 percent of small-cap managers failed to outperform [their respective benchmarks] on a relative basis."[4] These active funds are run by smart people with advanced degrees in finance who still can't consistently outperform the market.

That said, I'm loath to be a purist about anything in economics. There are always exceptions, and I've seen some active fund managers produce consistent, strong returns. However, it is hard to know in advance who those active fund managers are. It is a full-time job to research and pick the best active managers and investments. It is a task for a professional.

Unless you are a highly trained investment ninja, trying to beat the market through active management will likely get you beat up. Stick to environmentally and socially responsible index-based funds.

5. Pay attention to fees! To be a successful investor you need to be mindful of fees. Fees are tricky. They can sneak up on you without you noticing. Excessively high fees can eat up one-third to one-half of your investments over a lifetime! An extra 2 percent in fees could reduce your fund balance by 40 percent over 25 years. The biggest problem with fees is context. It is hard to know what fees are reasonable and what are excessive.

Worse, in managed accounts or retirement plans, like 401(k)s, there can be layers of fees. Sorting through them all is sometimes a nightmare. Many investment books talk about fund fees, which are critical. But they aren't the whole story. There are also adviser fees and plan fees for employer-sponsored retirement plans.

Here is a quick breakdown of fees you might encounter. Each is based on assets under management (AUM). If you invest $100 and incur a 1 percent AUM fee, then you'll pay $1 per year.

Fund Fees:

0–0.30 percent: Low cost and reasonable. All your core index-based funds should be in this range.

0.30–0.60 percent: Moderate cost and sometimes okay. Not great for your primary holdings, but for specialty funds or emerging market funds, this is acceptable.

0.60–1.00 percent: High fee and questionable. There should be a very special reason for any fund to be in this range. I can think of only a few exceptions where I'd be willing to pay this much.

1.00 percent or more: Extremely high for the average investor. In a professionally managed portfolio, some specialty funds could fall into this range, but I'd generally avoid them.

Adviser Fees:

1.00 percent or less for a human adviser, 0.25–0.50 percent for a robo adviser.

The percent charged typically decreases as the account value increases. Good advisers can help with a wide range of financial planning needs, not just selecting investments. We'll discuss how to find a good adviser in chapter 14, *but my advice is to never work with anyone who is not a fiduciary.* (This will exclude most brokerage firms.) A fiduciary is legally required to act in your best interest at all times. Generally, the rest are coyotes waiting to snack on your hard-earned money.

There are lots of other hidden fees you should never pay, like sales load fees, and redemption fees that a good adviser will help you avoid.

Employer Sponsored Retirement Plans:

Your total fees for funds, plan adviser, and plan administration should rarely total more than 1 percent and should be much lower for large firms. As a rule, the bigger the plan, the bigger the volume, the bigger the discount.

You wouldn't shop for a car without looking closely at the price. The same is true for your investments. High-priced funds will decimate your expected returns, just like an overpriced car will break your wallet. That said, you also don't want the cheapest car on the lot.

The most important consideration with any purchase is value. I've lost bids on retirement plans to lower-priced competitors. That's life in business. But sometimes you get what you pay for. The prices I've listed above are acceptable ranges. Anything higher than these is not in your best interests—stay away. But the bottom prices in these ranges aren't always better choices either. There is no fixed formula on price, so do your homework, be discerning, and look for great value. The most important criteria, above all else, is that the company running your plan be a fiduciary, working solely in your best interests. If they are not, put the minimum necessary in to get your employer match, if you have one. Then open an IRA.

6. Ignore the stock market. Unlike some pundits, I can predict with 100 percent accuracy what will happen in the stock market next week. I know for certain—the market will go up, or it will go down. Neither outcome matters to me in the least. It won't change my investment strategy, and it shouldn't change yours. Index-based investing is wildly liberating because then you can go back to Netflix with a little less guilt.

The evidence is clear: the average investor will get the best results from a buy-and-hold index-based strategy. The best way to torpedo the hold part of buy-and-hold is to get caught up in the daily fluctuations of the stock market.

No, I don't follow Bitcoin. Approximately two hundred stocks outperformed Bitcoin during its height. Why focus on one asset and get caught up in a market bubble and the inevitable crash? I don't care if Elon Musk launched his grandmother into orbit. How would any of that change my investing strategy? Gossip and the catastrophe of the hour aren't relevant to me, so I ignore them.

I love to watch TV. I'm not anti-TV. A good binge is a wonderful way to decompress after a long week, but please turn off the investing shows. TV is entertainment. Investing is not. Good investing practices are boring. TV shows on money are often just financial pornography. They are inappropriate and will hurt your chances of having a healthy financial life and growing your wealth. TV must grab your attention by making investing enthralling and get you to take action now. The best way to grab your attention is by preying on your fear and greed, two emotions that can quickly derail the best-laid financial plan.

Money and emotions do not mix. TV shows will rile up your emotions, captivating your attention, which drives up ratings. Change the channel.

7. Don't lose sight of the forest or the trees. Building wealth through investing requires attention to detail—seeing the individual trees in the forest of finance. Things like fund fees, asset allocation, keeping a budget, avoiding debt, and so on are trees and big landmarks. You can't navigate your way to wealth without them.

You also need to have big-picture thinking—seeing the whole forest. That means having a clear goal and staying focused on it. Problems can arise quickly when investors focus only on the small details, getting stuck along the journey, or focus only on the big picture and charge blindly through the forest.

In the Marines, some of the field exercises involved compass navigation, at night, with no flashlights allowed (the compass needle glows faintly in the dark). To navigate with a compass successfully, you need a goal: a heading and a distance. But in the dark woods, you can't see very far, so instead of shooting for your goal, you pick a nearby tree or rock that you can see along your compass heading and aim for that, counting your steps. Once you land at your nearby objective, sometimes only a few feet away, you take a new compass reading, course correct, find a new destination you can see along your heading, and count your paces to that objective. The trick is to break the journey into small pieces and continually course correct. Otherwise, in the dark, over uneven terrain, you'll just get lost. Moreover, additional information might be available farther along the journey . . . like gunfire, a cliff, or a friend's cry for help. Then you process that new information and course correct again.

There are lots of paths through a forest. You don't just pick one heading and charge forward blindly. Success requires continual feedback and openness as new data, priorities, and possibilities unfold.

While hope and courage are good, too many self-help books on money devolve into the Cult of Confidence. They give readers an ego boost of self-esteem, convincing them they can accomplish any goal with enough sacrifice and motivation. This kind of advice makes people feel great and sells books but can also do serious harm. It causes people to lose sight of the trees while in the forest.

I've seen several people destroy their lives and relationships by consuming too many motivational books and videos. They become convinced the world is destined to go their way, so they take reckless risks, turning off reason and common sense. The results can be disastrous when it comes to investing and building wealth.

One friend spent over $120,000 on motivational seminars, workshops, and business development courses. All on credit cards. She had found the "keys" to success and believed she was unstoppable. No risk was too great to fulfill her dreams. She really went for it . . . until all the business development courses turned out to be get-rich-quick schemes that took her money and failed to produce any personal income.

Another friend wrecked her marriage and traumatized her son by incessantly consuming motivational materials and chasing the "next big thing." Ironically, all the confidence training heightened her anxiety and lack of self-worth because she was continually comparing her success to others. She developed a chronic sense of failure and a need to push for bigger and bigger goals. She risked more and more, until she lost everything. Her marriage fell apart, her son needs serious therapy, and the last time we spoke she was being evicted from her home for not paying rent for three months.

Yes, you need to get motivated. Without motivation you are going to fail at any goal. But just because you have confidence doesn't mean you should run headlong through the woods in the dark. You'll either get lost or kill yourself.

Even if you go for it with everything you have, failure is an option. Knowing you can succeed gives you hope—knowing you might fail gives you drive and wisdom.

There is no easy balance between wisdom and courage. It is a razor's edge. Sometimes you need to take big risks in life to earn big rewards. But don't ignore the risks or stop paying attention to the small details. Minimize risks where you can. And constantly course correct if you see dangers in the way.

The biggest source of confusion around building wealth involves investing. Unless you have an extraordinarily high income, you'll never become wealthy through earning and saving. It will only happen through investing the hard-earned money you've saved, so invest wisely. Stick to ESG index-based stock and bond mutual funds.

CHAPTER 13

INVEST
SUSTAINABLY

I suspect most of you would not expect a book on personal finance to include a discussion about climate change. Here's why I can't avoid it: Our climate *is* changing. These rapid changes will negatively impact everyone on Earth, regardless of political and religious belief. And some of the harshest effects will be economic.

If we continue to ignore climate change, it will devastate the lives of billions of people worldwide, and you will be in very good (and desperate) company as you watch your hopes for future prosperity evaporate like rain in the desert.

Yet, somehow, climate change has morphed into a political left-versus-right wedge issue that divides us along party lines, with vegan, tree-hugging, PETA-loving, save-the-whales champions on one side, and coal-loving, oil-drilling, MAGA supporters on the other. Both extremes are mistaken. The real problem is that climate change will impact *every* facet of our lives, including our investment portfolios. It will also devastate our economy, our communities, and God's creation.

If we can all take a step back from politics, it becomes clear that climate change is primarily an economic and moral issue, and that if we want to remain a prosperous society, we must deal with the issue *now*.

But because this book is about money and building your wealth, I'm going to focus on how you can invest while also being part of the solution to climate change. And as it turns out, helping mitigate climate change through your investment choices could be extremely profitable.

You Can't Invest for the Future While Destroying the Future

When investing, your first goal is typically to maximize your rate of return with the least amount of risk. In a cage fight between profit motive and altruism, profit motive often wins even when we wish it didn't. It is why both tobacco companies and energy companies have lied about the risks associated with their products, even funding false research to protect their bottom lines.

In the past, environmentally and socially responsible investing was framed as a feel-good issue. Like a day trip to a spa, it felt wonderful but was expensive. Responsible investing often required a sacrifice of accepting lower returns in exchange for avoiding the bad apples that also made a lot of money from things like child labor, pornography, and rampant pollution and things that kill people, such as weapons, cigarettes, and alcohol.

That isn't the case anymore. If nothing else, one reason you should care about sustainable investing is that it can produce competitive returns with less risk. Environmentally and socially responsible investing is rapidly becoming the new normal—it's just good business.

It makes sense that environmentally and socially responsible funds may outperform their peers in the long run. Why? Because unsustainable companies are . . . unsustainable. They sell products that may kill their customers. They operate in ways that ultimately destroy what they claim to serve, meaning they will eventually die. That's a bad long-term business model even when it produces short-term profits.

We can either restructure our economy to reduce greenhouse gases, and fight for love and justice, or we can create a dystopian future where our economy collapses and civilization is upended. I'm not being melodramatic. All life is sacred. We don't get to pick and choose, or else we create a philosophical inconsistency that we could drive a truck through. Protecting the environment means protecting life and the source of all life.

Investing for the future while destroying the future makes no sense.

But here is the good news: We all need to save for retirement and grow a little wealthy. We also need to save the planet. We want the highest possible returns on our investments while being good people. Investing responsibly can do it all.

The terms *environmental, social, and governance* (ESG) *investing*; *socially responsible investing* (SRI); and *sustainable investing* are often used interchangeably, and the differences among them are more historical than anything else. I prefer to lump them together under the term *ESG*. It's simpler. The world doesn't need more investing jargon.

Make Money and Save the World

In an era of the Great Political Divide, let's try to make environmental considerations a political middle ground upon which we can all meet. It is in our individual and collective best interests to do so.

In 2015, Oxford University conducted a meta study of more than two hundred independent investigations into environmentally and socially responsible investing. Their findings were remarkable:

> 90% of the studies on the cost of capital show that sound sustainability standards lower the cost of capital of companies; 88% of the

research shows that solid ESG practices result in better operational performance of firms; and 80% of the studies show that stock price performance of companies is positively influenced by good sustainability practices. Based on the economic impact, it is in the best interest of investors and corporate managers to incorporate sustainability considerations into their decision making processes.[1]

That is a complex way of saying that firms that operate with strong ESG principles are often better run and better investments.

Following is a fancy chart that further supports that conclusion. It's called the MSCI World SRI Index. MSCI (Morgan Stanley Capital International) is a respected company that provides impartial research for institutional investors. Again, SRI stands for *socially responsible investing.* The MSCI World Index tracks all the prominent stocks in the world across twenty-three countries. The MSCI World SRI Index does the same but favors companies with outstanding ESG ratings and excludes companies whose products have negative social or environmental impacts.

The annualized return of the MSCI World SRI Index from September 2007 to August 2018 is 5.90 percent. The MSCI World Index (non-SRI) returned 5.40 percent. *The SRI Index produced higher returns.*

It also earned those higher returns while taking slightly less risk. The way economists compare risk to return is with a fancy term called the Sharpe Ratio. The higher the Sharpe Ratio, the better. For that same period, the MSCI World SRI Index had a Sharpe Ratio of 0.39. The MSCI World Index (non-SRI) had a Sharpe Ratio of 0.36. The SRI Index made more money with less risk. That is something investors can cheer.

Remember the most fundamental law of investing? Risk and return go hand in hand. Higher risk is accompanied by higher expected returns. Over the past fifteen years, ESG investing has

MSCI WORLD SRI INDEX (USD)

The MSCI World SRI Index includes large and mid-cap stocks across 23 Developed Markets (DM) countries*. The index is a capitalization weighted index that provides exposure to companies with outstanding Environmental, Social and Governance (ESG) ratings and excludes companies whose products have negative social or environmental impacts. The Index is designed for investors seeking a diversified Socially Responsible Investment (SRI) benchmark comprised of companies with strong sustainability profiles while avoiding companies incompatible with values screens. Constituent selection is based on research provided by MSCI ESG Research.

CUMULATIVE INDEX PERFORMANCE - GROSS RETURNS (USD) (SEP 2007 – AUG 2018)

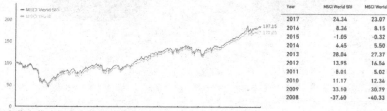

ANNUAL PERFORMANCE (%)

Year	MSCI World SRI	MSCI World
2017	24.34	23.07
2016	8.36	8.15
2015	-1.05	-0.32
2014	4.45	5.50
2013	28.04	27.37
2012	13.95	16.54
2011	5.01	5.02
2010	11.17	12.34
2009	33.10	30.79
2008	-37.60	-40.33

INDEX PERFORMANCE — GROSS RETURNS (%) (AUG 31, 2018)

	1 Mo	3 Mo	1 Yr	YTD	3 Yr	5 Yr	10 Yr	Since Sep 28, 2007
					ANNUALIZED			
MSCI World SRI	0.93	4.59	15.12	6.01	13.35	10.78	7.95	5.90
MSCI World	1.28	4.46	13.71	5.26	12.56	10.84	7.74	5.41

FUNDAMENTALS (AUG 31, 2018)

Div Yld (%)	P/E	P/E Fwd	P/BV
2.40	19.41	16.35	2.81
2.35	19.45	15.58	2.47

INDEX RISK AND RETURN CHARACTERISTICS (SEP 28, 2007 – AUG 31, 2018)

	Beta	Tracking Error (%)	Turnover (%)[1]	3 Yr	5 Yr	10 Yr	3 Yr	5 Yr	10 Yr	Since Sep 28, 2007	(%)	Period YYYY-MM-DD
				ANNUALIZED STD DEV (%)[2]			SHARPE RATIO [2,3]				MAXIMUM DRAWDOWN	
MSCI World SRI	0.98	1.79	15.77	9.57	9.82	15.88	1.26	1.03	0.53	0.39	55.57	2007-10-31—2009-03-09
MSCI World	1.00	0.00	2.33	9.56	9.80	15.96	1.19	1.04	0.51	0.36	57.46	2007-10-31—2009-03-09

[1] Last 12 months   [2] Based on monthly gross returns data   [3] Based on ICE LIBOR 1M

The MSCI ESG Indexes use ratings and other data supplied by MSCI ESG Research Inc., a subsidiary of MSCI Inc.

The MSCI World SRI Index was launched on Jun 28, 2011. Data prior to the launch date is back-tested data (i.e. calculations of how the index might have performed over that time period had the index existed). There are frequently material differences between back-tested performance and actual results. Past performance — whether actual or back-tested — is no indication or guarantee of future performance.

Source: MSCI[2]

INDEX CHARACTERISTICS

	MSCI World SRI	MSCI World
Number of Constituents	397	1,642
	Weight (%)	
Largest	8.01	2.78
Smallest	0.02	0.00
Average	0.25	0.06
Median	0.13	0.03

TOP 10 CONSTITUENTS

	Country	Index Wt. (%)	Parent Index Wt. (%)	Sector
MICROSOFT CORP	US	8.01	1.97	Info Tech
INTEL CORP	US	2.21	0.54	Info Tech
PROCTER & GAMBLE CO	US	2.04	0.50	Cons Staples
ROCHE HOLDING GENUSS	CH	1.71	0.42	Health Care
DISNEY (WALT)	US	1.64	0.40	Cons Discr
NVIDIA	US	1.58	0.39	Info Tech
PEPSICO	US	1.55	0.38	Cons Staples
TOTAL	FR	1.47	0.36	Energy
IBM CORP	US	1.32	0.32	Info Tech
MCDONALD'S CORP	US	1.26	0.31	Cons Discr
Total		22.77	5.61	

SECTOR WEIGHTS

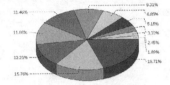

● Information Technology 19.71% ● Financials 15.76% ● Health Care 12.23%
● Industrials 11.86% ● Consumer Discretionary 11.46% ● Consumer Staples 9.31%
● Energy 6.85% ● Materials 5.15% ● Real Estate 3.33% ● Utilities 2.45%
● Telecommunication Services 1.89%

COUNTRY WEIGHTS

● United States 58.34% ● Japan 8.36% ● France 6.00% ● Germany 4.89%
● Canada 4.33% ● Other 18.10%

INDEX METHODOLOGY

MSCI SRI Indexes are constructed by applying a combination of values based exclusions and a Best-in-Class selection process to companies in the regional indexes that make up MSCI World, an index consisting of developed countries. After securities of companies involved in Nuclear Power, Tobacco, Alcohol, Gambling, Military Weapons, Civilian Firearms, GMOs and Adult Entertainment are excluded, MSCI's Best-in-Class selection process is applied to the remaining eligible securities in the selection universe. The MSCI SRI Indexes target sector and region weights consistent with those of the underlying indexes to limit the systematic risk introduced by the ESG selection process. The methodology aims to include the securities of companies with the highest ESG ratings making up 25% of the market capitalization in each sector and region of the parent indexes. Companies that are not existing constituents of the MSCI SRI Indexes must have an MSCI ESG Rating above BBB and the MSCI ESG Controversies score above 3 to be eligible. Current constituents of the MSCI SRI Indexes must have an MSCI ESG Rating above 0 and the MSCI ESG Controversies score above 0 to be eligible. The selection universe for the MSCI SRI Indexes is the constituents of the MSCI Global Investable Market Indexes. The Index is float-adjusted market capitalization weighted.

ABOUT MSCI

proved to be an exception to the rule. Finding higher returns with less risk is like seeing a leprechaun riding a unicorn while dancing to Louis Armstrong's "What a Wonderful World." It's awesome.

This information isn't an isolated data point. From May 1994 through March 2018, the MSCI KLD 400 Social Index had an annualized return of 9.94 percent, versus a 9.86 percent return in its benchmark. It also had a higher ten-year Sharpe Ratio of 0.66 compared to its benchmark of 0.64. The MSCI KLD 400 Social Index is an index of four hundred US stocks with outstanding ESG ratings.

Consistently beating the market or outperforming a benchmark is hard to do. Most active funds fail to beat their benchmark in the long run. But just by adding an ESG filter to the entire index of stocks, we can get potentially higher returns.

While stocks get most of the attention among investors, the bond side of your portfolio is just as important. Adding ESG criteria works very well there too. For example, as of May 2018, the TIAA-CREF Social Choice Bond Fund beat its benchmark by 1.18 percent over the past five years.

As ESG investing evolves, I believe it will continue to outperform traditional investing. It just makes sense. ESG practices often result in better operational performance at firms because they are forced to be more mindful about how they operate, leading to greater efficiency. ESG-based firms also tend to have lower market volatility and are less likely to be involved with fraud, corruption, or bribery, making them prudent investments.[3] Long-term growth requires long-term thinking. Who does that better than ESG-minded companies?

I can't promise anything about future returns in the stock market, but my money is on ESG investing. If we are going down, I'm not going down without a fight.

Types of Investing Screens

We can apply five different types of filters, or screens, to align our investments with our values. Many funds use a combination of these.

1. **Negative Screens.** These are the most common type but vary widely depending on the causes you care about most. Negative screens

exclude companies or entire industries. For example, the MSCI World SRI Index discussed earlier starts by excluding companies involved in nuclear power, tobacco, alcohol, gambling, military weapons, genetically modified organisms (GMO), and adult entertainment. (Notice that fossil fuel companies are not in this list, although plenty of other funds screen them out.)

2. Positive Screens. Positive screens allow investors to go one step further by investing in companies that have a strong record in one or more areas, such as social or environmental performance, investing more heavily or exclusively in the good guys and gals.

After rating each company, some positive screens apply a "tilt," or "weight." It skews the portfolio more heavily, or tilts it, toward the companies that received the best ratings during the positive screening process. Other funds invest in only those companies with the highest positive ratings.

3. Best in Class. Best-in-class funds invest in only the most forward-thinking companies in *every industry*.

For example, the MSCI World SRI Index applies a complicated rating process to the stocks remaining after the initial negative screen has been applied. Within each industry, it evaluates each company according to thirty-seven key ESG issues, such as climate change, human capital and labor management, corporate governance, gender diversity, privacy, and data security, among others. After rating all companies, it includes only those in the top 25 percent of their sector or region of the index—the best in class.

This approach would appeal to my father, who was an oil company executive, because no industry is excluded, including oil. It may seem ironic that an ESG fund would invest in oil companies, but we don't want to destroy the energy industry—we need to transform it. Best-in-class investing supports the industry leaders who are moving in the right direction—toward renewable energy.

4. Impact Investing. Impact investing takes positive screening even further. Impact funds invest in companies and organizations whose positive effect on the environment and society is specific and measurable. Sometimes the return is expected to be below market rate, which means that impact investing is often a form of philanthropy. For example, providing microloans in poor communities around the world has a strong positive social impact. However, the rate of return may not be competitive compared to other investment options. The primary goal is a measurable impact on a problem, with profit as a secondary consideration.

For those who feel comfortable with the basics and want to take their ethical financial strategy one step further, impact investing opens up a whole new world of possibilities. It is a terrific form of philanthropy and can be an exciting part of your charitable efforts. Just don't make these your core investments. And for those who consider themselves spiritual but not religious or who don't tithe to a church, committing 10 percent of your income to impact investing could be a great tithing alternative.

5. ESG Shareholder Activism. When you buy shares of a company, you are a shareholder, which means you have the right to show up at annual shareholder meetings to discuss company policy. This is too much to ask of most individual investors, especially if you own thousands of different stocks in each mutual fund. However, you can invest in funds that do it for you. This is called shareholder activism.

Funds or individuals that engage in ESG shareholder activism will intentionally buy stocks of companies that engage in bad behavior. They become insiders who try to elect new members to the board of directors and file shareholder resolutions with the intention of putting socially and environmentally responsible business practices in place.

Shareholder activism can be a very effective method of using personal investments to change the world for the better. It can expose company malpractice and bring media attention to the dreadful things that companies are trying to get away with. By putting their agenda on the table, shareholder activists can sometimes change the way a company is run.

To combine sustainable investing with lower-cost index funds, you'll need to do a little homework. You can find excellent resources by looking at companies like Vanguard, Pax World, Nuveen, State Street, BlackRock, and Dimensional Fund Advisers (DFA).

We're All in This Together

A strong portfolio requires a cold-eyed look at the truth, evidence, and facts. There are few universal truths in life, but there is one truth that all people of faith, all people of science, and all economists can share. It is the central truth of life, morality, and ethics: we all are interconnected. There is no escaping this reality. No man or woman is an island. At the simplest level, we cannot survive without the air we breathe, the water we drink, and the food we eat.

In one of the most intellectually vigorous and thoughtful defenses of the planet, Pope Francis is unequivocal in his encyclical *Laudato Si'* on climate change. "We need to strengthen the conviction that we are one single human family. There are no frontiers or barriers, political or social, behind which we can hide, still less is there room for the globalization of indifference."

If we recklessly pollute our air, poison our water, and destroy the complex ecosystems necessary for sustainable food production, the world will fall apart. Communities will disintegrate, global economic and political systems will collapse, and countless souls will be cast into dire poverty, starvation, mass migration, and even death. There is no greater moral or economic imperative than to stop climate change.

Climate change is also our gravest national security threat. Imagine if the oceans continue to rise. What will happen? Our naval bases will be underwater. How effective will our military be without reliable naval bases? And that is but one example. Most trade and commerce move through coastal cities. If those cities become uninhabitable or subject to chronic flooding, what will the economic and social impact be? It is incomprehensible and incalculable.

The Department of Defense and CIA take climate change very seriously. In a report to Congress, the Department of Defense made this statement in the opening paragraph:

> DoD recognizes the reality of climate change and the significant risk it poses to U.S. interests globally. The National Security Strategy, issued in February 2015, is clear that climate change is an urgent and growing threat to our national security, contributing to increased natural disasters, refugee flows, and conflicts over basic resources such as food and water. These impacts are already occurring, and the scope, scale, and intensity of these impacts are projected to increase over time.[4]

The CIA even launched a separate unit, the Center on Climate Change and National Security, to study the "national security impact of phenomena such as desertification, rising sea levels, population shifts, and heightened competition for natural resources."[5]

In personal finance, climate change transcends politics and religion because it destroys wealth and personal property regardless of affiliation. Just ask those hit by storms in New Orleans, Puerto Rico, Florida, and New York. It disrupts the global food supply chain and creates immeasurable suffering around the world. We don't need to debate this one. This is a problem where opinions don't matter. The hard truth is that your opinion about climate change doesn't mean a darn thing. It is already happening, so how do we face it together?

There is another rule of finance to remember: the stock market loves certainty. Investors are happy when they feel safe and the future looks bright. Climate change is the mother of all wild cards. All our data calculations, predictions, and investing patterns are based on historical data. However, we've never seen anything like the chaos climate change may bring. What will that do to all our investment models, projections, and strategies? No one knows. We must minimize this systemic risk.

What is the solution? Use the most powerful tool in the history of civilization at our disposal—capitalism—to help change our investing patterns and our economy. Best of all, we can remake the world while making strong profits. In time, perhaps very soon, we'll make renewable energy cheaper than fossil fuels, which is like a *huge* tax cut for the entire world, generating even more wealth!

Free markets, when combined with good governance, can function as a collective wish-granting machine. Sometimes with unintended consequences. For example, we all were hungry, and we wished for food. Now we all are overweight and at risk for type 2 diabetes because the food industry delivers us so much amazing food. We wished for longevity, and the medical industry doubled our average life expectancy.[6] Now we can't fund Social Security. We grew tired of playing with balls and sticks, and the entertainment industry gave us Netflix, and now we have *Game of Thrones*. (Which, God help me, I absolutely love.) We all were cold and tired and wished for warmth as we huddled in the dark. So the energy industry lit up the world and kept us all from freezing to death. Now the planet is overheating.

If we all demand a solution to climate change, in time the market will deliver whatever we ask of it. But we need enough people pulling together in the same direction, at the same time, before it is too late. The best news of all: whoever does solve the problems of renewable energy could be the *next richest person in the world*. And that's what makes human beings great. We see a big problem, we pull our heads out of the sand, and then we work together to save the world.

Or we can ignore climate change and protect industries that need to disappear.

We face several questions: Will we make the transition fast enough to hold off the worst effects of climate change? Will America dominate in the renewable market, or will we let other countries beat us? Will we support innovations that protect the world and its people even if that means some old industries must change or die?

Pope Francis stated in his encyclical *Laudato Si'*: "Obstructionist attitudes, even on the part of believers, can range from denial of the problem to indifference, nonchalant resignation or blind confidence in technical solutions. We require a new and universal solidarity."

One new solidarity is to harness the power of free markets and good governance by aligning our economic interests with our moral convictions. Free markets are the most powerful instruments for change our society has access to. But, right now, they are the problem. For example, capitalism rewards polluters with lower production costs. This is especially true of companies that manufacture in developing countries with weak regulations and corrupt oversight. Even in the United States rural areas and the poorest corners of urban society become the dumping ground for toxic waste and trash. We can change that by punishing the polluters and the bad apples by withdrawing our investments in their companies and sending that money to their competitors or through shareholder activism.

Adopting a New Normal

Before entering the monastery, I spent some time traveling the world. Those were glorious adventures. The poverty I saw was heartbreaking, but the landscapes were majestic. Now, when I visit developing countries, I'm shocked by the vast amount of environmental deterioration that occurred in just a few decades. Trash is rampant, pollution is noxious, vast ecologies are dying, and countless species are fading from existence. Water insecurity is growing as clean water is harder and harder to find, while soil degradation and weather changes threaten the most vulnerable.

The slums of Nairobi, Kenya, have burst into a full-blown humanitarian crisis, in part from droughts that left millions in dire need of humanitarian aid. The air in Mumbai, India, is so polluted that spending one day in the city is often equivalent to smoking five packs of cigarettes. You can imagine what that does to infants and the elderly.

One morning in Mumbai I woke up and took a stroll on the rooftop patio of my hotel. At dawn I could see sunlight glimmer on the ocean to my left and reflect in pink hues off a range of hills to my right. Then the morning began. Traffic picked up with blaring horns, smoke from cooking and trash fires snaked into the air, and factories came to life. Within thirty minutes, I couldn't see the hills, and the ocean was a muddy haze from the pollution. That cannot be the economy of the future.

Both science and religion agree: our planet is the most precious gift of the universe. *All life* is dependent upon the earth. And all life is both religiously sacred and scientifically necessary for a healthy ecosystem. Any ethical system, especially religion, must address climate change.

The Interfaith Center on Corporate Responsibility, which represents over 330 faith communities, asset management companies, labor unions, pension funds, NGOs, and college and university endowment funds, made this statement in a letter to Congress:

> Our diverse faith traditions are guided by principles of compassion, justice, dialogue, and stewardship. We believe that it is the moral responsibility of our nation—and our sacred task as people of faith—to act to address climate change. We feel a special calling to pray and work to overcome the divisions and fears that have prevented action to address one of the greatest threats to current and future generations.[7]

With climate change, like it or not, we all are on the same team. We are in one boat and need to row in the same direction to survive. That requires people of all political persuasions to stop demonizing one another and unite. We must find a way to talk with one another and cooperate inside our respective nations and around the globe. If we can learn to speak with integrity and decency while having hard political conversations, then the process of solving climate change may be one of the greatest gifts the world has ever received.

The good news is that we've invented a way to talk to everyone on the planet at the same time. It's called the Internet. But we're also going to need to use all our advertising and marketing skills to get the message out in a palatable way. Ironically, Don Draper may be the very hero we need right now.[8] The same genius who created the Marlboro Man cigarette ads, wedded to *agape-argyria*, could make sustainable investing the coolest thing on the planet.

Earth is one of God's most defenseless children. We need to become like Saint Francis of Assisi and know the earth as our sister, our kin. Then Jesus' words become a powerful pro-earth statement: "Truly I tell you, whatever you did for one of the least of these brothers and sisters of mine, you did for me" (Matt. 25:40). Here our communal economic, religious, and scientific interests align. With good hearts and good minds working together, it is a problem we can and must solve.

Now go fix your investments, make some money, and help save the world. The future is watching.

CHAPTER 14

GET GOOD HELP

Now that you know the basics of investing, let's talk about how to find someone to help you navigate this unique world that has not only its own laws but also its own language. As I mentioned in chapter 6, the world of finance includes a bewildering array of strange vocabulary words. Even people in the finance industry can't keep them all straight. Reading some technical reports and industry white papers requires a PhD in mathematics, the Rosetta stone, and a cereal box decoder ring.

The only way people give you their money is if they trust you. One of the quickest ways to establish trust is to have a fancy title, work in an impressive-looking office, and use big words no one understands.

The list of titles people can put before or after their name is staggering, and there are huge differences in training and expertise from title to title. There are 183 professional designations listed on the Financial Industry Regulatory Authority (FINRA) website. Here are just a few:

Accredited Financial Counselor
Accredited Wealth Management Adviser
Asset Protection Planner
Behavioral Financial Adviser
Certified Credit Counselor

Certified Estate Adviser
Certified Financial Consultant
Certified Financial Fiduciary
Certified Financial Planner
Certified Portfolio Specialist
Certified Private Wealth Adviser
Certified Annuity Specialist
Certified Retirement Planner
Chartered Financial Analyst
Chartered Financial Consultant
Chartered Financial Engineer
Chartered Retirement Plans Specialist
Financial Paraplanner Qualified Professional
Financial Services Specialist Certified
Global Financial Steward
Master Financial Planner
Personal Financial Specialist
Qualified Financial Planner
Registered Financial Consultant
Registered Financial Planner
Registered Financial Specialist
Wealth Management Specialist
Private Wealth Adviser
Certified Wealth Strategist
Certified Estate Planner
Certified Exit Planner

And those are just some of the *officially recognized* certifications and designations.

The list of titles that some people put before or after their names can be deceiving, titles such as Wealth Manager, Financial Coach, Financial Consultant, or Life Coach.

I met a smart and ambitious financial adviser at a conference who is about half my age. After sharing career war stories, we exchanged business cards and promised to keep in touch. When I looked down at his card, my eyes bugged out. Then a hot wave of jealousy flashed through my body. He was a vice president at Morgan Stanley! How did this kid become a vice president of one of the largest financial services firms in the world when he could barely shave? Was he a child prodigy? Was his family well connected?

The moment I got home, I looked him up online. I quickly learned he was vice president of a local branch affiliated with Morgan Stanley, that his branch had only four people in it, and the lowest-ranking title in that branch was associate vice president. Titles can be deceiving.

Financial titles can be like first-grade achievement medals: everyone gets one.

I'm no exception. Nobody is. When hired at LongView Asset Management, I received the title Director of Educator Retirement Services. I was the director of one person: me. That's how the game works. I also have fancy initials after my name. I'm a Chartered Retirement Plans Specialist (CRPS). The training I underwent to earn those initials was helpful and rigorous, but it doesn't guarantee anything. It just proves I can take tests well.

So how do you find good financial advice?

The Most Important Term
You Need to Know

If you understand very little about finance, there is one term you must know. Everything else depends on it. The most important term is *fiduciary*. A fiduciary is a person who is legally required to act in your best interests at all times. Fiduciaries come in many forms, but as you navigate the world of finance, be sure that every person providing you with financial advice is a fiduciary.

As an extra precaution, make sure they put their fiduciary commitment to you in writing. This makes them legally bound by the courts to uphold that commitment. If they significantly violate that commitment, you can legally nuke them, which can include compensatory damages, punitive damages, and disbarment from their profession. According to the Law Dictionary, "There is no legal standard of care higher than fiduciary duty."[1]

Many money managers, advisers, planners, and retirement plan companies are not fiduciaries. They have no legal obligation to act in your best interests or provide you with the best advice possible. They are just salespeople in disguise. So guess what happens? They sell products, funds, and services that make themselves rich and you poor.

Or, as explained in the book *Where Are the Customers' Yachts?* by Fred Schwed, the Wall Street game is rigged to make brokers and sellers of stocks rich while keeping average investors poor. Many brokers and advisers have yachts while their clients don't. If they were great at their jobs, shouldn't it be the other way around?

Given the scandals and corruption we see daily, the trust most of us have in the financial industry is near zero. This breeds cynicism and, worse, paralysis. People who need help are scared to ask for it because they don't know who the good people are.

The hopeful news is that amazing people do work in finance. As a monk who previously hated money, I assumed that the entire industry was a corrupt cesspool filled with slime. There is plenty of that. But there is an equal measure of wonderful people with good hearts and minds who truly desire to help and serve others.

The hard part is sorting the wheat from the chaff. The best way to find out if someone is a fiduciary is to ask. If the conversation becomes uncomfortable, you have your answer. Even scoundrels avoid making false fiduciary claims. They prey on the "buyer beware" loophole of capitalism, which puts the burden of due diligence on the customer. This keeps them out of jail. Fiduciary duty puts the burden of due diligence on the financial professional.

You'd think that everyone providing financial advice would be a fiduciary, just as doctors take the Hippocratic oath, vowing to put patients' well-being first. Sadly, that isn't the case. Would you work with a lawyer who didn't care about winning your case, only racking up as many billable hours as possible? Don't work with an adviser who isn't concerned first and foremost with your best interests and prudently making you money. That is their job.

Fiduciaries want to make money, just like everyone, but they must be transparent in the fees they charge and make sure they have no conflicts of interest when providing you advice. You pay them up front for their hard work and good service to you on a fee-only basis. Almost everything else is a con job.

The alternative is to work with someone who works on commissions or hidden fees. Commissions and hidden fees are a disaster because then the wealth adviser or annuity peddler makes their money by pushing you into investments or products that make the salesperson the most money. They aren't working for your best interests—they are working for *their* best interests. The tricks they can play on you are too numerous to list.

Ask right away if the person you are working with will sign a fiduciary pledge. If not, take your money elsewhere. Good fiduciaries are eager to sign a pledge. They love it, embrace it! It lets them prove they have your best interests at heart. If someone waffles or if they "have to check with their supervisor and get back to you," run for the exit.

You can find fiduciary pledge templates online with ease. Here is a short and simple one we use at LongView Asset Management. You can find it on my website (douglynam.com); put this into your phone and ask any financial professional you encounter to sign it. It ensures they are legally bound to represent your best interests, not just talk a big game.

The Fiduciary Pledge

• I promise to act in the best interests of my clients and operate in good faith as a fiduciary at all times.
• I will disclose of any potential conflicts of interest between myself or my firm, and our clients, and will always place my clients' best interests first.
• I will act prudently, with the skill, care, and conscientiousness of a licensed financial professional.
• I will not mislead my clients in any way.
• I will not pay or provide compensation for client referrals.
• I will not receive incentives or rewards that impair my ability to act in a fair and impartial manner or that compromise the integrity and impartiality of the advice I provide to clients.

This fiduciary pledge covers all services provided by
_____ (name of firm).

Printed Name: _____

Signature: _____

Date: _____

If you look carefully, you'll notice that the fiduciary pledge doesn't prevent a financial professional from making a profit. They just can't make a profit to the detriment of their client.

Next, do a background check. A quick search on the Securities and Exchange Commission (SEC) website will at least tell you if

there are any criminal or regulatory issues with an adviser: www
.adviserinfo.sec.gov. Then review their credentials. One of the top
credentials is a CFP, or Certified Financial Planner. This doesn't
guarantee anything, but it helps a lot, and you still need to make sure
they are a fiduciary. I'm not a CFP, and many great advisers aren't.
Requiring every financial planner to be a CFP is a bit like requiring
every lawyer to attend an Ivy League school. It's nice to have but
expensive and hard to find in some cities. Many CFPs are so busy they
can't take on new clients. Frustrating, I know.

Finally, like dating, you want some chemistry between you and
your adviser. You don't have to be best pals, but you should be able
to listen and communicate effectively on both sides. Friendliness is
great; competency is better. Find both and you have a keeper.

Financial Planners and Investment Advisers

There are two forms of financial help that you may need. The first is
a basic financial planner. The second is an investment adviser. Some
investment advisers are also financial planners. If you don't have any
money yet, or not much, then find a good fee-only, independent
financial planner first. They are your coach, battle buddy, and wise
counsel to get you on track toward your financial goals.

Financial planners aren't cheap, but they are worth every penny.
Think of it as a major appliance purchase, such as a new refrigerator,
dishwasher, or perhaps a big car repair. It is one of those events in
life where spending money can make you money, save you time, and
significantly reduce your stress.

A typical flat fee is around $1,000 to $3,000 for a financial plan
or an hourly rate of $200 to $400. I'd suggest a complete financial
plan to start, then switch to an hourly rate if you have only specific

questions down the road. If you'd prefer more consistency and have the money, some financial planners work on a retainer of $2,000 to $8,000 per year.

Once you have some money saved and are looking to invest, find an investment adviser. An adviser will invest and manage your money for you. A planner only gives structure, coaching, and expert advice. An adviser helps lead the way and does the heavy lifting for you.

Most in-person fiduciary financial advisers have a minimum investment amount, often $250,000 or more. They act as a financial planner and do the work of investing and managing your money for you. They are expensive and a luxury service, charging a hefty fee of around 1 percent of assets per year. There are strong opinions about a 1 percent fee, but a good adviser is worth it.

I'm not impartial on this issue; I'm an adviser, so I can't claim objectivity. I do know from academic research and personal experience that most people who invest on their own mess it up in ways that cost far more than a 1 percent annual fee, so in my opinion it is well worth the cost.

If you can't afford an in-person adviser or are just starting to invest, a robo-adviser (online automated investing platform) is a good option. They usually have no minimum balance and are much cheaper but provide limited personalized service. Fees range from 0.25 percent to 0.75 percent of assets per year. They tend to be low cost and easy to use.

People will pay thousands of dollars for a motivational workshop or a week relaxing on vacation. But hiring a financial adviser and getting your house in order may have a greater impact on your stress level and quality of life. A service that can provide that much value is going to cost something. A study from the *Journal of Consumer Research* in 2017 demonstrated that perceived financial well-being is a key predictor of overall well-being. The quality of your financial life has as much impact on overall mental health as job satisfaction, relationship stability, and physical health combined![2]

Fee-only services are important but so is independence. For example, if a financial planner or adviser works for Hogwarts Financial Services and they recommend only Hogwarts Mutual Funds, Hogwarts Annuities, and Hogwarts Insurance, they are not independent. They are going to push you into (okay, here is a complex term) *proprietary products*. Proprietary products are created by the firm an adviser works for. Advisers should be independent and offer the best products, not only the ones with which they are affiliated.

Independent, fee-only advisers who are fiduciaries are legally obligated to provide you with the most prudent, low-cost investment vehicles to suit your needs. They don't take a commission or cut from embedded fees. *Nonindependent* advisers are salespeople working on commission. They make absurd amounts of money through high product fees. (This is especially true in teacher retirement plans.)

There are several online networks of fee-only, independent financial planners, and more growing every day. A few places to start looking for a financial planner/adviser are the Garrett Planning Network, the Alliance of Comprehensive Planners, the XY Planning Network, NAPFA (National Association of Personal Financial Advisors), Financial Planning Association, and 403(b)wise for nonprofit professionals. (Disclaimer: I'm associated with 403(b)wise and friends with the founder, Dan Otter.)

Does everyone need a financial adviser? Absolutely not. It's just a solid idea. I'm a professional adviser, and I have a financial adviser. You can't see past your blind spots, and we all have them. Your adviser is one-third financial expert, one-third therapist, and one-third battle buddy who can save you from the dumb stuff you are likely to do.

Humility is a much-forgotten virtue.

Remember the proverb "A man who is his own lawyer has a fool for a client." No decent lawyer represents themselves in court, and no doctor performs surgery on themselves. Olympic athletes always have a coach, especially when they are at the top of their game. Likewise, few people should manage their money all alone. A good financial adviser keeps you honest with yourself and on track with your goals.

To be fair, my adviser is also my business partner, so I get his services free of charge. But still, I run my personal investment decisions past him. It is easy to be objective with other people's money—I don't do as well with my own. That's just human nature. Everyone has money-monster archetypes lurking within. For example, I have a bad habit of keeping too much money in cash. Why? I've been broke, and the idea of investing most of my money is hard. I prefer to keep a big cash reserve for emergencies, and sometimes I go too far. To fix the problem, I make my brain override my gut when my emotions start messing with my money. Having an expert adviser validate these decisions lets me sleep well at night.

I've learned that good advisers are measured not only by what they do for you but also by what they don't let you do. They don't let you do stupid things with your money. This alone can save you a fortune. Preventing one tragic mistake can make a lifetime of reasonable fees worthwhile.

While anyone *can* manage their own money, most people who try mess it up. And they mess it up in catastrophic ways. Why? Because our brains get hijacked by our emotions, fears, and anxieties. They also get derailed by investment-news porn, market crashes, and speculative bubbles. Or worse, our money monsters haunt us, leading us astray (see chapter 4).

Investing is a bit like plumbing. When something breaks, the results can be horrifying. Hiring a good plumber who is licensed and insured can save you time, frustration, and catastrophic mistakes—I should know. The plumbing in the monastery broke, a lot. Especially the drip system I built for our garden. However, we were often short on cash, so I did it myself. In retrospect, that was a poor decision. I lacked the tools, time, or knowledge to do it right. I wasted countless weekends fixing pipes. Every time I solved one problem, I mistakenly created another. Even the problems I did fix didn't stay fixed.

After years of duct-tape solutions, extensive water damage, and outrageous water bills from undetected leaks, I gave up. I retreated and hired a real plumber. Could I have done it all myself? In theory, yes. But not with my brain. In all, it cost three or four times more than if I'd just gotten a plumber in the first place. After including the cost for tools and avoidable water damages, not to mention the cost of my time, I'd have saved money, stress, and anxiety if I'd just paid to have a professional do it right.

The fancy economic term for this is *specialization*. Professionals are specialists in one complex task. It means they are much better at that task than you'll ever be. That is why you pay them. Finance isn't different. If you need assistance with money management, plenty of good, kind, decent people are ready to help. To avoid the financial predators, make sure everyone you work with is a fiduciary who eagerly signs a fiduciary pledge.

One Piece of the Climate Puzzle

Preventing radical climate change will require multiple solutions on many fronts, but fiduciary duty could play a crucial role. Under ERISA law (the Employee Retirement Income Security Act of 1974) that governs many retirement plans, a fiduciary must act only in the best interests of clients and their beneficiaries. Every retirement plan has a fiduciary even if it is simply the employer offering the plan. Traditionally this has meant that only three criteria are used to select investment choices offered to employees: performance, price, and risk. The expected returns for investments should be competitive, the overall price of the plan should be reasonable, and the investor risk should be minimized through appropriate fund selection and diversification.

The rapid growth and sophistication of ESG investment options, as well as the increasing adoption of ESG practices and reporting in the corporate world, have opened a new chapter in the field of ESG investing. ESG-based funds were judged historically to underperform their conventional peers, be too expensive to manage, and be potentially riskier for investors because they eliminated certain industries. For these reasons, ESG-based funds were rare in institutional retirement plans, and many still avoid them completely.

However, with the growth of ESG investing, these concerns have become obsolete. The evidence of the past two decades demonstrates (as shown in chapter 13) that investors do not need to sacrifice expected returns or take on extra risk to align their investments with their values. The Department of Labor (DOL) has responded to the growing interest in sustainable investing by clarifying the old definitions of fiduciary duty. In 2016, the DOL released guidelines on fiduciary practices that made more room for ESG considerations. Their ruling noted that if positive economic impact to investors can be demonstrated, or that "all things being equal," a fiduciary may prefer ESG-based investments to more conventional choices.[3]

Then in April 2018, the DOL released a new bulletin. This ruling strongly cautions fiduciaries from basing investment policy solely on ESG principles. Instead, it reaffirms that economic performance should be considered ahead of any potential social impact that investments may have. While it does not exclude ESG investments, it has created some confusion about the appropriate role ESG practices should have in retirement and pension plans. It affirms the right of fiduciaries to include prudent ESG-based investment options in an institutional retirement plan as long as they are secondary to a conventional lineup of fund choices.[4]

This new DOL bulletin suggests that ESG investing remains a sideshow because ESG investing may not be competitive compared to more conventional options. As a result, many institutional retirement plans either don't have any ESG funds available to employees or the funds are niche investments. They certainly don't funnel employee money by default into ESG funds, and we know from behavioral economics that most employees will stick with a default investment option if you give them one. Well-designed retirement plans now auto-enroll all employees (with the option of opting out) because it significantly increases employee participation. This helps ensure that senior employees can retire on time rather than linger because they can't afford to retire. The default investment option in such plans is typically a target date fund.

The technical term for a prudent default investment is a qualified default investment alternative (QDIA). In regard to a QDIA the most recent DOL bulletin states,

> the selection of a ESG-themed target date fund as a QDIA would not be prudent if the fund would provide a lower expected rate of return than available non-ESG alternative target date funds with commensurate degrees of risk, or if the fund would be riskier than non-ESG alternative available target date funds with commensurate rates of return.[5]

In other words, an ESG-based QDIA is not recommended unless it is both appropriate for the plan population and has a commensurate rate of return and comparable risk to a non-ESG alternative. For these reasons, defaulting all employees into ESG investments was previously unheard of.

Hewing closely to this ruling, LongView Asset Management recently built an institutional retirement plan and QDIA for United World College USA that adheres to the traditional fiduciary standards of performance, price, and risk. In addition, the plan vigorously embraces the United World College goal of a peaceful and sustainable global future by investing according to ESG practices. This is the first ESG-themed QDIA for a school to be built and implemented while adhering to all the fiduciary criteria set forth by the DOL. A new precedent has been set that other companies could follow.

This is news. Geeky news but important. It could permanently change the interpretation of fiduciary duty for the better. I believe many more institutions will follow the lead of United World College and adopt ESG investments as the default choice in their retirement plans, pension plans, and endowments. Companies such as TIAA and Vanguard now allow advisers to build customized portfolios that behave similar to a target date fund. Advisers can then fill these portfolios with the ESG investments of their choice.

I strongly believe that fiduciary duty requires thoughtful consideration of ESG issues. I'll say it again: investing for the future while destroying that very future makes no sense. Fiduciary duty requires all investment decisions to be in the best interest of employees *and their beneficiaries*, and beneficiaries include multiple generations. In my opinion that means ESG considerations, in combination with traditional standards of fiduciary duty, should be a *requirement* of all fiduciaries. Reinterpreting the definition of fiduciary duty in this manner could have positive, far-reaching implications throughout the financial-services industry. It would force every retirement plan, pension plan, and many endowments to consider ESG criteria in their investment selections.

As of June 2018, there were approximately $15.8 trillion dollars invested in employer-sponsored retirement plans of all types in the United States.[6] Shift all that money into ESG-based investments, and we can move the world. And we don't need to get too legalistic about it. ESG investing should be loosely defined in the same manner as other fiduciary criteria. Expected performance should be competitive, fees should be reasonable, investment options should be broadly diversified to minimize risk, and ESG considerations should be *thoughtful*. This still gives fiduciaries and investors wide latitude to invest in every sector and industry and invest according to *their* values. We need to agree on what "the best interests of beneficiaries" means in broad terms. I don't see how destroying the ecosystem our children's economy depends on is defensible behavior or is in their best interests.

If consumers demand that every financial service providers is an ESG Fiduciary—a term I've just developed and trademarked—then that could fix things quickly across the board. The positive ripple effect is hard to predict, but it has the potential to solve numerous problems. It also produces the greatest possible good for the greatest number of people with as little downside as possible. Yes, some people in the finance industry may resist this change, but they will be on the wrong side of history.

The best news is that there is something practical and actionable for you, me, and everyone else to do in a time of uncertainty: insist that every financial service provider you work with is an ESG Fiduciary. Instructions on how advisers can register as an ESG Fiduciary are available at esgfiduciary.org. I've tried to make the process as easy and affordable as possible. The ESG Fiduciary designation will be administered as a nonprofit with the goal of spreading this new standard of stewardship throughout the investing industry.

It is important to remember that the economy is a result of our choices. The economy doesn't lead the way but collectively reflects our individual actions. We vote with our money. Each financial decision we make is accounted for by the economy and signals where we want it to go. If we each insist that all our financial service providers are committed to our best interests by being ESG Fiduciary advisers, then everyone wins. We grow wealthier than we would by hiring a self-interested salesperson, the ESG Fiduciary advisers win because customers will prefer them over less scrupulous competitors, and we help make the world a better place by protecting the miraculous blessing that is our planet for a few more generations.

We've reached the tipping point, and we no longer have the luxury of letting anyone opt out of the communal problem that is climate change. We all have skin in the game. The hard truth: our planet has already seen five mass extinction events. Let's not delude ourselves into thinking we can't create another.

The baton of civilization was handed down to us from our ancestors. Let's not betray those who struggled and suffered to make a reasonably free and prosperous society possible by squandering it on narcissistic self-delusions and avaricious greed. That is *philargyria* and is the root of the greatest evil I can imagine—throwing the gift of all human life back in the face of God.

CHAPTER 15

PAY ATTENTION TO TAXES

Taxes are one of the best inventions in the history of human civilization. I may be the only person who thinks that, but without taxes, civilization would collapse. How else do we pay for our military, roads, emergency services, schools, hospitals, and social programs? Liberals tend to hate military spending, conservatives tend to hate entitlement and social programs, and we all can argue those issues ad nauseum. But without taxes, government doesn't function. Without a functioning government, life begins to look like a *Mad Max* movie.

I'll watch a postapocalypse movie—I don't want to live in one.

With the understanding that taxes are good, taxes are patriotic, and taxes are essential to civilization, I concede they also destroy wealth. Taxes are a wood-rotting fungus on the tree of personal finance. If you don't pay attention to taxes, they will eat away at your income, savings, and investment returns. The median household income is around $57,000 in the United States, and the effective median tax rate is around 30 percent, including federal and state taxes, while ignoring sales taxes, property taxes, or any other miscellaneous local taxes. State taxes vary, but this is a ballpark number we can play with.

A 30 percent tax rate on $57,000 is $17,100 per year. If you live to be eighty years old, don't pay taxes for the first twenty years of your life, and pay taxes for sixty years total, that is $1,026,000 in lifetime tax payments. Ouch!

But remember the time value of money?

Instead of giving your money to the government, pretend you invested $17,100 per year at a rate of 8.7 percent in a balanced portfolio for sixty years. How much would you have? No tricks here, I promise. The answer: $30,484,450.

Are you interested in tax policy now? It can be a dry topic until you realize what it does to your net worth.

Wealthy people pay attention to taxes—it's like a giant pay raise if you play the game well. One friend, Tony, is a professor at a prestigious university. He never pays income taxes—*ever*. Tony legally games the system by obsessing over his tax bill. His aggressive avoidance tactics led to two IRS audits, but he stayed within the bounds of the law and passed both audits with no taxes due.

To be fair, he *obsesses* over taxes. That's his sport of choice.

As a tenured professor, Tony carefully selects his classes and teaching assignments so he can maximize his deductions. Every movie he watches or fancy electronic gizmo is deductible for a film class. A mini production studio in a spare bedroom became a home office expense.

He also has a side business as a photographer and takes pictures everywhere he goes. Traveling to random festivals and photographing them allows him access to the world, making his vacations deductible. He once traveled cross-country to Pageland, South Carolina, a town of 2,700 people, to get a handful of photos of their annual watermelon festival. The seed-spitting contest was a highlight.

There is one excellent photo of a young girl in an elegant watermelon-print dress, holding a watermelon slice, and expertly spitting seeds across a green lawn. But, to be honest, none of his photos are going to end up in the Met anytime soon. However, artistic skill isn't one of the IRS criteria. Auditors aren't trained to determine what art is and certainly not what defines good art. I don't know how much of his work Tony ever sold, but his business is a great tax shelter.

He plays the corporation game with gusto and owns several rental properties managed by his own small real estate company. Every rental upgrade project is tax deductible while his property values increase. Since he owns the house next door, is the privacy fence he built that straddles both properties a home improvement or rental-property improvement? Who can say? He took it as a tax-deductible business expense.

Like Quakers and Mennonites, who are historically pacifists and refuse to fight in wars, even under pain of death, Tony is a tax pacifist. He refuses to pay taxes. Why? He hates how the government spends money and has found a way to legally opt out of the system without running away to the woods and living off the land.

I disagree with his worldview and would hate to live my entire life around my tax bill, but that's his choice. It's a part-time job, and it saves him a fortune.

How to Avoid the Hard Lessons

I learned my hardest lesson in the high cost of taxes by working part time for a wealthy couple as a recent college grad. I was their computer guy, research assistant, and jack-of-all-trades. They knew the tax game; I didn't.

To say that I was financially illiterate when I left college would be an understatement. I didn't know when, how, or where to file my taxes. No one ever talked honestly about money when I was growing up. Each parent tried to hide their real net worth from the other, and that meant shielding the truth from their children was well. This made all money talk dangerous territory, so where would I have learned that stuff? My parents didn't teach it, and schools don't teach it. The result—my first few years out of college I didn't file my taxes. I assumed they were being paid by my employers, and I just ignored them. Absurd, I know.

In truth, I was afraid of taxes. I was scared I would file them the wrong way and get audited. I was scared I would owe money I didn't have. Paying rent was hard—how was I going to afford an accountant or pay a tax bill? I did what many folks do when faced with a seemingly unsolvable problem—I ignored it.

Denial is the last refuge of the terrified.

The truth is that taxes are terrifying for most people, which is why half of Americans pay someone else to do their taxes for them—even when they don't need to.

After several years of not filing my taxes, panic set in. The fear of not filing steadily exceeded the fear of filing, year by year, until I was completely petrified. I finally got my act together and sheepishly found a tax preparer to help get my financial house in order. This was pre-Internet, so I looked in the phone book (remember those?) and picked the most professional-looking ad for tax help, then made an appointment.

I nervously packed up my meager folder of tax documents and chaotic pile of miscellaneous receipts and headed to visit my tax pro. Would this person shame or scold me for my negligence? Would they talk over my head? I was embarrassed to admit how little I knew about taxes, something everyone else seemed to have under control. My ignorance and shame were about to be exposed.

When I got to her office, I was surprised. The office was just the converted living room in her home. The brown shag carpeting (a holdout from the '70s), dusty bookshelves, and tired furniture spoke of quiet indifference. She sat me down in front of her huge steel desk, the kind you might find in a military fallout shelter, and started riffling through my bookkeeping nightmare. She bypassed the mess of receipts, grabbed all the official documentation, such as W-2s and 1099s, and with only minimal conversation, started typing my data into her computer.

My tax pro was a former school bus driver with only a high school education and little training. Arthritis made driving a bus difficult, so she switched careers. She prepared five years of tax returns in about an hour. The only thing she did was enter my data into a computer program and hit print. Her knowledge of tax law was minimal, and she couldn't add her way out of a wet paper bag.

Then came the shocker. My bus driver turned tax pro explained that I was working as an independent contractor for my wealthy part-time employer, not as a regular employee. I was an entrepreneur and didn't know it. Self-employed people are responsible for paying their own federal and state income taxes, along with all Social Security and Medicare taxes. My wealthy employer withheld nothing.

My tax debt: $17,000, not including fines and interest payments. Some of that money I'd have been responsible for anyway, but my wealthy employer had sneakily shifted their tax burden onto me.

This is just one example of how the rich get richer, the poor stay poor. What a mess.

If you think credit card debt is bad, the IRS is worse. They want their money, and they aren't messing around. They charge a late-payment penalty *and* interest. Getting my kneecaps broken would have been more fun. The IRS customer service representatives, however, were very kind and helped me set up a payment plan. No yelling, scolding, or nastiness. No jail and no threats, but they were firm about getting their money. One way or the other.

The lesson learned—don't mess with the IRS. Here are the most important things I can pass on to you to help you avoid this school of hard knocks.

1. Always file your taxes. Do it by April 15 of each year, even if you don't have the money to pay them. Not filing will always end badly.

If you do owe back taxes, they have a Fresh Start program that can help set up a payment plan while possibly reducing the amount owed.

2. Never, ever lie. If you make a mistake, you can face penalties and fines, but not jail. If you lie, that gets ugly. It is what sent Al Capone to prison—tax fraud. You can stretch and bend the law, but don't break it. That is both unethical and illegal.

3. Document everything. The hardest part about taxes is keeping good records and categorizing all expenses properly. The more you document, the more you can deduct. As a rule, if you can't document it, you shouldn't claim it. Incorrectly claiming a deduction may get you a slap on the wrist with a fine and, only if egregious, into serious trouble. Claiming a deduction you don't deserve is fraud. That is a world of hurt. If you can't afford a professional bookkeeper/accountant, then schedule an hour each week for bookkeeping. Don't try to do it all during tax time, which is a nightmare inside a migraine.

4. Don't buy something you don't need just for a tax deduction. Generally, a deduction costs more than it saves. Especially a house. The home mortgage interest deduction is potentially huge, but if that's your main reason for doing it, you probably shouldn't.

5. You really can prepare your taxes yourself. Like investing and bookkeeping, they are complex, but if your situation is simple, then a good software program will do all the hard work for you. Just let the software guide you, step-by-baby-step, and you'll get it done. If you run your own business, have a zillion different deductions, or just prefer the convenience, then a good tax preparer can be a lifesaver. Even in those situations there is good tax software available for all but the most extreme situations.

Having someone do your taxes for you is often reassuring, but you are still the one liable if they make a mistake. Your tax return is only as accurate as the data entered. If you give the "tax pro" bad data, then it doesn't matter if they are an expert or not, the tax return will be incorrect. Bad data in, bad results out.

The IRS audits less than 1 percent of all tax returns, and most audits are of high-income or complex low-income returns with lots of deductions. The chances of getting audited when using the standard deduction are slim, and roughly 70 percent of Americans use the standard deduction (a number that is likely to increase with the new tax bill passed by Congress). If you ever get audited, it's not as frightening as you might expect; most questions are handled by mail.

Tips and Tricks to Avoid Overpaying

There are plenty of ways to legally minimize your taxes and maximize the income you keep. Almost everyone can use a retirement account as a tax shelter. Money goes in pre-tax, which shelters it from the taxes until withdrawn. If you put $1,000 into a retirement fund, it could save you $330 in taxes, and that extra $330 grows according to the time value of money. If you saved an extra $330 per month and invested it at 8.7 percent for 40 years, you'd have an additional $1,292,373. Not bad.

You may have a retirement plan with your employer, but if not, setting up an IRA is relatively easy. If you don't have a retirement account, set one up now. The simplest way is to contact a major mutual fund company like Vanguard, Fidelity, or Charles Schwab. Please stop making excuses and procrastinating. You might not have any money to contribute yet, but you will. It gives you something to dream about and aim for.

Numerous companies offer IRA accounts with no minimum balance requirement. The hard part is deciding between a Roth and a traditional IRA. There is no simple answer to this question because it depends on your income level in retirement, a near impossible calculation for most of us to figure out when retirement is decades away. You'll need an adviser to help answer that question for you. But to get a current tax deduction, go with the traditional IRA.

Most financial planners will warn you that consistently getting a refund check at tax time is a bad idea. It means that you are withholding too much in taxes from your paycheck and need to reduce your exemptions. Mathematically, they are correct. Getting a refund check means that you've loaned your money to the government all year and they didn't pay you any interest for it.

While that math makes sense, the psychology doesn't. Understanding how your emotions work is one of the best life hacks to becoming a little bit wealthy. I love my refund check and look forward to it each year. It is how I keep score. What fun is a game without a scoreboard? Every year, I try to get a bigger and bigger refund. Some years I win, some years I lose—but mostly I win. As I've said, just don't blow your refund on something stupid. Use it to pay down debt, build your emergency fund, or buy investments. Income is income—it doesn't matter where it comes from.

Unfortunately most of the other tax-reduction tricks depend on your circumstances. If you have children, consider a 529 college savings plan. Buying a home (because it makes sense) can offer a mortgage interest deduction. Large medical expenses can also be deductible. If you are buying and selling investments outside your retirement account, be mindful of short-term and long-term capital gains. If some of your investments become stinkers, consider selling them to harvest the tax loss. The list is long, and if some of this just flew over your head, that's okay. Play the game long enough and you'll learn the rules. The number of tax shelters, tax havens, tax deductions, and tax exemptions are too numerous to list here. Using them is also complicated and often requires a good accountant or lawyer.

Sometimes a pro can easily earn the fee you pay by identifying deductions you don't even know are available to you. If you need simple to moderately complex tax help, hire an enrolled agent (EA). Enrolled agents are licensed, required to have some training, and can prepare and file your taxes for a reasonable fee. EAs are useful if you don't need ongoing advice throughout the year and your situation isn't too complex.

If you run your own business and have lots of deductions, then a certified public accountant (CPA) is the next rung up the ladder. Prices vary significantly, just like when buying a car. It depends on what features you want.

For the truly wealthy, a tax attorney is the very top of the ladder and expensive. In fact, many tax attorneys don't even prepare your taxes; they handle complex legal angles.

Even if you hire a pro, I suggest you take the time to educate yourself a little bit more about taxes. Remember, you can outsource work, but you can never outsource responsibility. No one else cares about your money as much as you do. Also, if you ever get audited, you, not your tax preparer, are on the hook for any mistakes. For a good intro to taxes, try *Taxes Made Simple: Income Taxes Explained in 100 Pages or Less* by Mike Piper.

After clearing up my tax fiasco, then cleaning up the monastery's finances, I got serious about taxes. I dived in with both feet. Tony's example inspired me to maximize every legal deduction I could find. My favorite way to find deductions is to use TurboTax software and let it guide me, step-by-step, through every relevant tax category. The number of ways to game the system are absurd and should probably get fixed if any politician has the guts to tackle that project. I wish our tax system were more efficient and fair, but if you can't beat the system, use it to your advantage.

As a fun experiment and an inexpensive crash course in taxes, try completing your taxes this year with TurboTax or a similar program. Then go to a tax preparer and have them complete your taxes for you. Next, compare the results. Finally, decide who you think did a better job. Either way, you win. If your work is superior, you can save money on tax preparation forever. If the tax adviser wins, you can clearly see the value of their services and now understand what is happening with your money.

The tax game is designed to help make wealthy people wealthier. To win, you need to start thinking like the wealthy. Wealthy people know that taxes are a game with room to negotiate, not a fixed bill with no wiggle room. Like any game, the first few times you play, it is confusing, frustrating, and full of mistakes. But you can't exempt yourself from the tax game. You are going to be playing the game for as long as you live, so why not play it well?

CHAPTER 16

INSURE AGAINST LOSS

Discussing insurance is like being forced to watch a corporate PowerPoint presentation about the benefits of rice cakes—over a slow Internet connection. Christianity preaches that the grace of God can redeem anyone and anything, but I'm not so sure about insurance—it's a dry topic.

Did any kid ever dream of growing up to be an insurance adjuster?

Nonetheless, insurance is the bedrock of becoming a little bit wealthy. Without it, your financial house is built on sand and can crumble at any moment. I used to think insurance was a giant waste of money. During the darkest days of our financial struggles, I dreaded my car insurance bill. I was paying $87 each month for a service I never used. Worse, my cheap car only cost $2,500. After 2.4 years the cost of my insurance premiums exceeded the value of my car! I thought insurance was a rip-off. Besides, I was a good driver, so why did I need it?

Then I made a horrific mistake. As the credit card debt piled up, I struggled to make minimum debt payments, put food on the table, and cover basic living expenses. I couldn't keep up with the avalanche of bills coming in. So some of them stopped getting paid. It is hard to fight basic math—there was more money going out than coming in. Something had to give.

I would pay the phone bill one month, the gas bill the next, and juggle competing needs as best I could. One month I couldn't pay my car insurance. I didn't have the money. Debt payments ate up all disposable income. It was a poor decision in setting priorities. I felt overwhelming pressure to pay the obnoxiously persistent creditors, but my insurance bill was the one thing I absolutely should have paid. Maintaining good insurance is vastly more important than paying on consumer debt— what if I had gotten into a car accident and hurt someone?

What happened next is curious—nothing. Nothing happened. Unlike my credit card or utility bills, when I stopped paying my car insurance, nothing happened. I received a letter with a policy cancellation notice, but the sky didn't fall in, the police didn't show up at my door, and the phone wasn't ringing from my insurance company demanding payment.

Several months went by. Magically making a bill disappear by not paying it was perversely rewarding. I never used my insurance anyway, I thought, so I did a good thing by keeping the money I desperately needed rather than sending it off to a faceless, greedy, multinational corporation that never gave me a darn thing in return for sending them thousands of dollars. Of course, tragedy often strikes at the worst possible time. Murphy's Law doesn't stop for monks.

During a lunch break, I was hastily running around trying to complete some errands, and I accidentally backed into another car in a parking lot. My bumper carved a long, elegant slash down the side of a red Volkswagen Jetta. Fortunately, it was a manageable tragedy. The only damage to my car was psychological; red paint clung shamefully to the bumper in the shape of the letter A. My very own scarlet letter.

I now faced a huge moral dilemma: I was an idiot who didn't have car insurance, nor did I have the money to fix the car I just ruined. What was I supposed to do? The parking lot was empty of people, and no one saw me hit the Jetta, so driving away was an option that I pondered for longer than I'd care to admit.

With my head hung low and no plan, I started looking for the car's owner. I asked around at each business in the immediate area. The second office I entered had a kind young lady behind the reception desk, and I politely inquired about who might own a red Jetta. A deeply pained expression crossed her face as she told me it was her car.

Surprisingly, her reaction was a curious mix of frustration, resignation, and despair—like fate was endlessly punishing her for some past-life crime. She explained: Her car had already been hit six times in the past two years—always while parked. I was unlucky number seven. The law of averages suggests that there is someone who will win the lottery, someone who will get struck by lightning twice and survive, and someone who will get their car banged up seven or more times in random parking lots. But it was still weird.

She wasn't angry, just resigned and exhausted. Then came the hard part: I had to admit that I didn't have any insurance and I didn't have the cash to pay for the repairs. I was thinking on my feet at this point and feeling sorry for her. So I proposed the only solution I could think of—don't report the accident just yet. I suggested she let me go home, re-enroll in my auto policy, then come back and report the accident. It was both an illegal and crazy idea.

Much to my surprise, she agreed. I went home, purchased an auto policy, then we met up the next day and mutually reported the accident one day late. My insurance company paid the bill in full. I can only tell that story because twenty years later the statute of limitation on insurance fraud is long past, and I finally self-reported my transgression to the insurance company out of chronic guilt. They were very kind when I explained what happened. They thanked me for being a loyal, accident-free customer ever since and suggested that I could pay the bill now—if I wanted to. I promptly sent a check for $1,442.67.

Fortunately, they didn't charge me any interest. At an interest rate of 8.7 percent over twenty years, I should have paid them back $7,651.70.

Things could have turned out much worse. One of my colleagues from another school, Paige, was a bright, charming, and talented teacher. While driving home at dusk on a warm spring evening, exhausted from a long day of work, she ran a red light. Tragically, there was a bicyclist in the intersection. She struck him head-on. The cyclist survived but was seriously crippled and promptly sued her for more than a million dollars.

The only good news is that Paige had excellent insurance, including a stand-alone personal liability policy. The insurance company settled the lawsuit, and Paige's life continued, although with great sadness and guilt.

That is why you should always have adequate insurance. Dreadful things happen to good people. And sometimes good people do dreadful things. We all make mistakes, and sometimes they cost more to fix than we can afford. God can always forgive; the court system is less generous.

If I had hit a bicyclist instead of a parked car without insurance, my life would have been turned upside down forever. It is a nightmare scenario I tremble to contemplate.

Buy Insurance for What You Can't Afford to Cover Yourself

To think that you are getting ripped off by your insurance company because you never have a claim is silly. The point of insurance is to outsource risk.

You pay a relatively small recurring fee to an insurance company, and in exchange it takes on the legal liability for some risk you have, like getting into a car accident. The likelihood that you will get into a serious accident is small, but if you do, it's a bill you can't pay.

Most years you make insurance payments and never have a claim, but if you do, the lifetime of payments you make helps cover the cost of that big payment. All the people in the plan who don't have accidents that year also help pay the cost of your big expense.

Outsourcing risk is one of the most important jobs in a free-market economy. So long as the insurance company pulls in more money than they pay out in claims, they make a profit. They deserve to.

The odds are that you'll pay far more in premiums, or payments, to your insurance provider than you will ever get back in claims or payments. If you do end up being paid back more money than you put in, something has gone tragically wrong with your life. That isn't a good thing, but fortunately you have insurance. That's why you purchased it.

All things being equal, it is better not to have any claims and let the insurance company win—and sleep well at night.

However, insurance is expensive, and you never want to pay for goods or a service you don't need. Just because outsourcing risk is important doesn't mean you need to outsource *every* risk. The key to finding good insurance is to always remember what insurance is for: outsourcing a risk you can't afford to take.

If you're diagnosed with cancer, you probably can't afford the treatment on your own, so you need health insurance. Should you run a red light and hit a cyclist, you'll never be able to pay for that. You'd better have good liability insurance.

If the teenager at the checkout counter tries to sell you a $5 insurance policy on your new $35 keyboard, that is a waste of money. Should the keyboard break shortly after purchase, the store's return policy will cover it. If it breaks three or four years down the road, could you afford the risk of replacing it on your own? If the answer is yes, you don't need insurance. You can "self-insure" and replace it. If the answer is no, you've got bigger problems to worry about. Also, if your keyboard does break in a few years, will you even remember about that insurance policy or know how to redeem it? Probably not. You've just thrown $5 into the trash.

I love the convenience of online shopping, but retailers often try to sell an insurance upgrade for items I purchase. Those policies are generally a waste of your money. If one item does break, and you wish you had the insurance, the cost of replacing it is likely less than the price of buying an insurance policy on every purchase.

Self-insure for the small stuff. That is why you have an emergency fund. It is your self-insurance protection for minor accidents and emergencies. Purchase insurance only for those risks or losses you can't afford to pay for on your own.

There weren't a lot of bright spots in the monastery finances in the early years, but one huge blessing is that we had decent health insurance. There were some notably big medical bills, but we dodged a few bullets that could have killed us.

One hospital bill was $217,885. There was no way we could have ever paid that off. It was a bill we couldn't afford, and luckily the insurance company paid most of it. Our out-of-pocket expense was only $42. Yes! That's correct. This is a story with a happy ending.

A second medical procedure cost $21,117. After the insurance paid up, our out-of-pocket cost was zero, nothing, zip, nada! When it works, insurance is more beautiful than wisteria in moonlight.

At this point, you should be asking, which forms of insurance do I need?

The Six Horsemen That Prevent Financial Apocalypse

When purchasing any insurance, finding a good insurance agent or broker can save you time, money, and hassle. They shop around for the best deals and can provide a bundled quote for all your needs while guiding you through a maze of complex decisions. They can also help with complex cost-to-benefit decisions. Many people shop for the lowest rates, but that can leave huge gaps in coverage. Value is always more important than price, and an insurance agent can help frame up those decisions.

If you have a financial adviser, they can likely recommend a good insurance agent/broker or help you find one. If you don't have an adviser, try asking coworkers, friends, or family to see who they've had a positive experience with. Referrals are your best option.

In the meantime, here are some tips I've compiled to help you search for the best insurance and decide what insurance you do need. I call them the Six Horsemen That Prevent Financial Apocalypse.

1. Health Insurance

You must have health insurance at every age. Medical bills are the leading cause of bankruptcy in America. Your physical *and* financial health are chronically at risk without health coverage. It is often disgustingly expensive, and premiums are continually rising. Most people get health insurance through their employer, which is weird if you think about it too hard. You don't get auto or home insurance from your boss, so why health insurance? In any case, if you do get health insurance through work, a group plan from your employer is generally your best option, especially if they pay a portion of the costs.

If you must purchase coverage on your own, or have choices through your employer's plan, the best route is to pick the highest coverage plan you can find that also has a high deductible. For this to work, you need to have a solid emergency fund, self-insure for the small stuff, and let insurance cover the big stuff. If you can afford the risk of a $2,000 deductible for a possible MRI, go with the high-deductible plan. If that is a risk that will devastate your finances, pick a lower-deductible plan. If you don't have an emergency fund yet, pick the highest deductible you can afford. Just be careful that you don't leave yourself exposed with large gaps or holes in coverage. That is a quick way to bankruptcy. If you can't pay smaller expenses out of pocket and need a low deductible, you'll pay much more in premiums.

If you know that you're likely to use a lot of health-care services because you have high risk factors for disease or illness, pre-existing conditions that require significant monitoring and care, or small children with frequent emergency visits, then get the lowest deductible with the highest coverage you can find.

The average American is intuitively aware that health-care costs are spiraling out of control. For some families their monthly health insurance premium is comparable to their rent or mortgage payment. This is an issue whose complexity exceeds the space we have to discuss it here, but I'll say this: health insurance is very different from any other good or service you might purchase.

A hard truth: on its own, a free market, capitalistic economy does many things extremely well—providing affordable health insurance isn't one of them. If it did, we'd have done it already. That is a reality we need to face.

2. Auto Insurance

State laws require almost all drivers to have auto insurance (except New Hampshire and Virginia). However, estimates put the number of uninsured motorists around 13 percent nationwide, which is a problem. If one of those people hits you, they can't pay for the damages, which is why you need to make sure your policy has an uninsured motorist provision. It will fix your car and cover injuries if you are hit by someone who can't pay up or flees the scene of the accident.

The hard question is between comprehensive coverage and just liability coverage. Comprehensive coverage pays for all the damages you cause in an accident (within limits) to other cars, people, and property, along with any damage to your car and even to yourself. It will also cover theft. This is the fullest form of coverage, but also the most expensive.

If you have a car loan, payment, or lease, you need to have comprehensive insurance. This is expensive and one more reason to buy a used car with cash. If you crash your car with a $20,000 outstanding auto loan, you still need to pay that money back, even if your car is totaled. Without comprehensive insurance, your life just got uglier than a drunk warthog at a redneck cookout.

The better option, once you have a strong emergency fund and no debt, is to buy a reliable used car in cash. Then purchase liability and uninsured motorist coverage only. If you hit someone or something, damages you cause are covered, but damages to your car are not.

If you total your car, buy another one. Replacing your used car once or twice over a lifetime will likely cost much less than comprehensive insurance. You are self-insuring your used car while outsourcing the risk of catastrophic damages when you hit a Ferrari and send it crashing into a school bus filled with blind, orphaned kindergarten war refugees.

Paying an extra $100 a month for comprehensive auto insurance will cost $1,200 a year. Over sixty years that's $72,000. However, $100 a month invested using the time value of money over sixty years at 8.7 percent interest is . . . $2,059,076.17. You could replace a lot of cars with that, including a few Ferraris.

3. Homeowner's or Renter's Insurance

It is hard to buy a home without having homeowner's insurance. Any mortgage provider will require it. If you buy a home in cash or have paid off your mortgage, don't drop the homeowner's policy unless you have the money to self-insure and can replace the home and everything in it without creating much stress.

The less used and often-neglected stepchild is renter's insurance.

This will replace your stuff in the event of theft or damage in a rental. Generally, renter's insurance is very affordable and worth the cost. The hard part is deciding between coverage levels and deductible. Again, if you can afford to pay it, take the higher deductible. You'll generally come out ahead even if you have a bad year occasionally.

4. Liability Insurance

Personal liability insurance is something that you'll probably never need to use, but if you do need it, you really, really need it. This is one policy you shouldn't skip. It is also relatively cheap because it is rarely used. You can find good deals by bundling it with your home or auto policy.

Liability insurance is blanket coverage (within reason) for any damages you do to another person or property. You typically get some liability coverage with both home and auto policies, but this takes it a step further. Let's say you are riding your bike, skateboard, unicycle, or unicorn and hit someone, causing significant injury. How will you pay for that? Or you trip and fall into an old lady and break her hip. That is what liability insurance covers, and more. It is for damages you do through your fault or negligence. It also covers any lawsuits you face because of an accident.

The legal terms of fault and negligence lull some very responsible people into skipping liability insurance. Negligently hurting some-one doesn't mean you are a bad or evil person. It means that you had a rough day and, with no malice on your part, someone got hurt. If you hurt someone maliciously and with intent, no insurance policy will cover it. That is called a felony.

You should have, typically, at least $1 million—yes, $1,000,000— in liability coverage. If you have wealth (in other words, if someone might think they can sue you for a lot of money), buy a bigger policy. Cover your rear on the big stuff, self-insure the small stuff.

5. Disability Insurance

Disability insurance is critical if you are supporting a family. If you get injured and can't work for several months or longer, how are you going to pay your bills? If you have an excellent answer to that question, you may not need disability insurance. But if not, get it. Many employers will provide some coverage, but if yours doesn't, go shopping.

Finding the right disability coverage is remarkably complex. Needs and prices vary wildly depending on your income level and profession, so an independent insurance agent is someone you should chat with. Also check with any trade or alumni association you belong to. They may offer a group discount.

6. Life Insurance

Congratulations, you are going to die! For those of us with faith, that should be good news. However, when you have loved ones who are financially dependent on you, your death shouldn't create a money crisis. That would be a rude way to leave the world.

If you have a high net worth, meaning that your loved ones will inherit a big pile of money when you go hang in the hereafter, you probably don't need life insurance. You've already self-insured your death.

Will your death make someone you love financially miserable? If so, get life insurance. The goal of life insurance is to replace the income you provided while living. It isn't to cover funeral expenses or give your family a parting gift.

The biggest mistake I see with life insurance is that most policy amounts are too low. Clients will get offers in the mail for a $20,000 policy that costs just a few dollars a month and get excited. They've found a life insurance policy they can afford. Hoorah! However, that isn't enough coverage to replace your income for even a year! These are legal scams. A life insurance policy should cover five to ten years' worth of your income. For most workers that's at least $250,000 in coverage. If you have kids going to college, you'll need much more.

There are two key types of life insurance: whole life and term life.

I'll avoid the technical jargon and skip to the punchline: go with term life insurance. Whole life is a waste of money and prohibitively expensive for most families at the coverage levels needed. However, insurance salespeople make the most money from selling whole life policies and will push them down your throat at every available opportunity. Just say no.

Term life covers you only as long as you pay your insurance premiums and for the length of the term. It works like homeowner's and auto insurance. If you stop paying the bill, the coverage stops. Which is good. This way you only pay for what you need.

The big goal is to make you a little bit wealthy. Once wealthy, you have money to leave behind and can drop the life insurance. You'll also get wealthy faster by not paying huge whole life insurance premiums. That money is better off invested wisely using the time value of money.

Any life insurance policy worth a darn must be customized to you. It will require a lot of information about your lifestyle and your health. Be ready for a medical exam with blood drawn by a nurse to test for diseases along with an exhaustive medical history questionnaire. These are good things. The insurance company is trying to figure out when you are statistically likely to die and price your insurance accordingly. Any policy that doesn't require a medical exam is likely to assume the worst-case scenario—that's expensive. The coverage limits will also be much lower.

Remember, the point of insurance is to outsource a risk you can't afford to take. Outsourcing risk costs a lot of money. If you can self-insure a risk, you'll likely win in the long run. Just make sure to cover your rear. Wealth is hard to build and easy to lose.

CHAPTER 17

MAKE PLANS FOR YOUR ESTATE

Everyone dies, but not everyone plans on dying. That's a big mistake.

A dear friend, Robert, passed away many years ago. He was a German baker who came of age during World War II and in post-Nazi Germany under the horrific conditions imposed by Russian occupation. His father kicked him out of the house when he was twelve because he didn't want another mouth to feed, and so Robert apprenticed himself to a bakery, sleeping on the storeroom flour sacks at night. Although starving, he baked bread and pastries all day long and would be beaten senseless if caught stealing a roll. He would sometimes eat "roof rabbits," or cats—when he could catch one.

At the first opportunity Robert moved to England where his talent shined, even though the anti-German sentiment at the time was understandably high. He even baked for the queen of England. He was that good.

In time he emigrated across the Atlantic to pursue the American dream. He started off working for other bakers, saved his money, and then opened a shop in Breckenridge, Colorado. His business flourished. We met one day during a trip to visit friends at St. Benedict's Monastery in Snowmass, Colorado. We monks all shared a soft spot for buttery baked goods, so when we passed by the window of a German bakery on our way through the small, high-mountain ski town, we absolutely had to stop. Here we discovered the bliss of a perfect napoleon. Robert made the best napoleon pastries we'd ever encountered, and after this we made long detours to visit him at every opportunity.

Blessed are the pastry chefs, for they make the world happy.

When in Colorado, we always went to Robert's. Over decades of decadent pastries we became close friends. A grim, imposing German persona was his trademark, but he was quick with a laugh and a bear hug if you showed him a hint of kindness. He loved people, but his life was choked with loneliness and sadness. Several marriages failed, and he was estranged from his daughters. A drunk driver killed his only son.

Robert struggled in business because he was semi-illiterate. He could speak four languages, but his formal education was minimal because of the war. Although a genius at making pastries, his money-management skills were appalling. Millions slipped through his fingers. When his kidneys started to fail from diabetes, he retired and sold his business. He began dialysis treatment, and that kept him going for several more years, but his end was coming.

On a lazy summer evening we sat with him in his kitchen, admiring his rose garden. He gazed at the magnificent hybrid tea roses blooming in radiant reds, yellows, and pinks, with an intensity that only the dying can have. Robert made a few false starts at conversation until he gave up on diplomacy and gruffly blurted out, "When I die, make sure my sister back in Germany gets everything." It was a stunning admission of his imminent death but welcome. It was a relief to speak openly about such a taboo subject.

Then he showed us his estate plan to make sure we knew where it was. It was a napkin stuck to his refrigerator with a few illegible lines in blue pen. Even though I was teaching personal finance at the time, I was out of my depth. I strongly suggested Robert contact a lawyer, but he was stubborn, with strong contempt for the legal system. Either I could try to help, or he was going to die without a will. Then his money would likely go to his daughters, with whom he had a chaotic relationship, rather than to his sister who needed the money.

In that moment I became an estate planner. That doesn't mean I was a good estate planner, but I got the job done. We spent the evening working on the key legal documents and had them signed the next day.

An estate is not a mansion in the Hamptons—it is all your stuff. It's the wealth you've built up through your lifetime. An estate plan is your directive of what happens to your stuff and money when you die.

He made us the executors of his will and gave us power of attorney for health care. We guided his medical decisions as he entered hospice care and were with him on his last day. He died at peace while we all prayed at his bedside.

As executors of his will, we guided his estate through the court system, liquidated all his assets, including selling his home, and then made sure his sister received her money. The process took about two years with an incredible amount of work in the first six months. Even with a clear will and estate plan, it was a huge burden. Without a will, it would have been an incomprehensible nightmare. A judge would have made all the decisions about what to do with his money and possessions.

What Your Estate Needs Before You Die

If you don't get your house in order ahead of time, you'll create needless suffering for the people you love. Don't let your fear of death or procrastination stop you. That is selfish and unkind.

In full disclosure, I'm still a little afraid of death, but I'm working on it. It is one more emotional trigger I need to overcome, but relying on my belief in God's love helps me find peace when tackling these tough topics.

You need four key legal documents to prepare for death and to take care of those you love.

Let's go over them.

1. A Will

A will is the most obvious document people think of when doing estate planning, and it is the cornerstone. A will tells the world how you want your possessions distributed when you die.

Excellent software programs will help guide you through the process of creating a will, along with all the other important estate documents. Quicken WillMaker Plus is my recommendation, but there are lots of good options. If you have a complex estate or need a living trust, have a lawyer help with the entire process. Laws vary by state, so having some assistance is crucial, but the basics don't change much.

The best wills are simple, short, and clear. They don't need to be complex or take a lot of time. Only worry about the big stuff and don't sweat the small stuff. You do not need to itemize everything you own or even list specific items in your will. Only do that for important things like a family heirloom or a Picasso painting. Besides, your possessions and accounts are constantly changing. You want a will that will last through the years without needing constant revision. It can be as simple as "I give all my wealth and material possessions to my partner, Jane Doe." Or "I give all my wealth and material possessions to my children in equal shares." In most states, if you don't have a will, your spouse will legally inherit everything.

After deciding who gets your money and stuff, you need to do a few more things:

- Select an executor. This is the person who carries out the directions in your will, which is easier said than done. If married, your spouse is the obvious choice. Otherwise, you need to think hard. The person benefiting the most from your will is another obvious choice, but if they are impaired or a dependent, then you need to keep looking. Ask permission before assigning someone as your executor. It can be a huge burden. The list of duties of an executor is extensive, but in short, they clean up all the legal and financial details for your life, from paying any bills to selling or giving away all your stuff. You'll also need a backup executor in case he or she dies before you or is unable to do the job.
- If you have dependent children, name a guardian in the event your children become orphans. Whoever this person is, you are giving them a tremendous responsibility to shoulder, and you must discuss it with them in detail. With kids involved, get a lawyer to review your will.
- Make sure your will is formatted correctly, according to your state law, signed, and notarized correctly. You'll need at least two witnesses to sign the will, and they cannot be beneficiaries. Pick neutral strangers. Signing your will at your bank or lawyer's office is a good idea since they always have a notary on staff and can rustle up two employees as witnesses. They know the drill.
- Update your will after a big life change, such as a divorce, marriage, death, or birth. One client waited two years after his divorce before updating his will. Had he died, his ex-wife, whom he now detested, would have inherited everything.
- Leave a notarized copy with your executor and/or lawyer. Show a loved one where you keep your copy. Having a will that no one can find is the same as not creating one at all. Don't put it in a safe deposit box. A safe deposit box is automatically sealed

and becomes part of your estate upon death. No one will be able to access it until *after* your estate goes through probate—the legal process where a court validates the will upon your death and then oversees the distribution of assets. Providing a will after probate is useless.

You can include your burial and funeral instructions in your will, but it is often easier to include a "letter of instruction" separate from your will. It will save your family the hassle of digging through a dense legal document in a time of grief.

Funerals can be expensive, so hopefully you've left some wealth behind to cover the costs. How you want your body to be dealt with upon your death is a personal and sometimes religious decision. Traditional burial is usually expensive, and if we all insist on embalming our bodies, we'll turn the planet into a toxic cemetery. I want a cheap and cheerful funeral. Cremate or compost me and then throw a party. I'll have moved on, and I hope everyone else will too.

For most people, writing a will is more than adequate protection and can be a DIY project. For those with significant assets to protect, or who expect to die within ten years, creating a living trust *in addition* to a will allows your estate to skip probate and provides extra legal protections. But living trusts are complex, expensive to set up, hard to change, and require regular maintenance. You'll probably need a lawyer. It is a wise step to consider after you've become a little bit wealthy.

2. Power of Attorney for Health Care

Power of attorney is a strange legal phrase. It means you are granting someone the power to act on your behalf, to represent you as a lawyer would. But the person you give power of attorney to is typically not a lawyer but a relative, friend, or spouse. A spouse is automatically granted power of attorney in the event you are ill, injured, or incapacitated. However, married couples should still have a power of attorney document in the event they are injured together. What happens if you are in the same car when it crashes?

Power of attorney (POA) for health care grants someone the authority to make all your health-care decisions in the event you can't. You may be injured, ill, or mentally incapacitated, and then your POA has the tremendous responsibility to make medical decisions for you. Don't leave home without creating this key document.

Like a will, power of attorney forms are useless if you hide them. All estate documents must be distributed to the people you've granted authority to. And make sure they are all notarized.

3. Power of Attorney for Finances

Your POA for health care covers only health-care decisions. If you become incapacitated for an extended length of time, someone will need to pay all your bills and make financial decisions.

The friend or family member who is your POA for finances will have the legal right to access all your bank accounts and investments, so be very careful to whom you grant this authority. It is perfectly acceptable to grant power of attorney for finances to the same person you've given health-care authority to, but I suggest otherwise. If you have adult children, siblings, or parents, it can be reassuring to distribute these powers to different people. It creates checks and balances to keep everyone aboveboard and honest. It also helps soothe egos so you don't appear to be playing favorites even if you are.

With that said, all these responsibilities are tremendous. Give them to the person or people you trust the most. Family politics can take a back seat.

4. Living Will or Advance Directive

The most emotionally challenging decision is often what to include in a living will. This has nothing to do with a traditional will. A living will expresses your wishes for medical treatment, or the withdrawal of medical treatment, in the event that you are terminally ill and will die without life support.

Some folks want to have every possible intervention to sustain their life, regardless of circumstances or cost. This is their wish, and it should be respected. Others would rather pull the plug if death is inevitable and they can survive only on life support.

Pulling the plug on someone you love is an impossible decision. Most people can't do it, even if it should be done. Some doctors are unhelpful in this regard—they don't want to risk a lawsuit, and end-of-life care is incredibly lucrative. Without an advance directive stating your wishes in this situation, the costs can bankrupt your family or decimate the wealth you spent a lifetime accumulating.

To pull the plug or not to pull the plug, that is the question. Either way, don't leave it unanswered. It is cruel beyond measure to force this choice on someone else. It is yours and yours alone to make. Be brave, decide. Your loved ones can't read your mind when you are in a coma. Give those you love the gift of good estate planning so that your death won't devastate their financial future.

You will sleep a little easier at night knowing that when you die, the people you love can spend as much time as possible comforting one another, remembering you fondly, and moving on to live their own lives without being dragged into a logistical nightmare caused by your procrastination. When a person dies, there will always be practical things to take care of—the point of estate planning is to make it as painless as possible.

Without question, death is the most mysterious thing that will happen to us in this life. Hope lies in believing that death isn't the end of the story. It sure as heck isn't the end of your financial life. That lives on, so don't mess it up. Even when your soul moves to the great beyond and your body returns to the earth, the ghosts of your financial life will linger. Your financial afterlife can be heaven or a fiery hell for those you love. What will your legacy be?

PART 5

HELP OTHERS BECOME A LITTLE BIT WEALTHY TOO

CHAPTER 18

BUILD A BUSINESS

Companies are designed to make money—they are money-generating machines. That is their purpose for existence. For all the inherent flaws in corporations and risks of investing, they are the best place to grow your wealth. And owning your own business is often the hallmark of a capitalist. All the great fortunes of the world were created by visionary founders of companies, such as Steve Jobs, Bill Gates, Mark Zuckerberg, Jeff Bezos, and Warren Buffett.

The best companies also solve a problem. That is why we willingly give them our money. They are not evil, and they are not the enemy some make them out to be.

Entrepreneurship, when wedded to *agape-argyria*, turns companies into more than just money-making machines. It turns them into suffering-prevention machines. Invent a new blockbuster drug, a productivity app, or a better mattress, and you've found a way to make money and solve a problem for people. That problem could even be where to find a good cup of coffee; hence we now have a Starbucks on every corner. As a caffeine addict and writer, I'm grateful to have a convenient place to get coffee, free Wi-Fi, a quiet space to work, and a clean bathroom. In fact, the clean bathroom is what I love most about Starbucks—to heck with the coffee. (Just don't sacrifice your financial future by spending all your money on consumer goods, especially lattes.)

Entrepreneurship is the most powerful money-generating investment in the history of human civilization. But it also carries the highest risk. It isn't for the faint of heart. If an entrepreneur is successful, a big *if*, then they can generate a lot of money.

If You Want to Become an Entrepreneur

It isn't easy to be an entrepreneur. Fifty percent of new businesses fail in the first five years, and only a third make it to ten years or more.[1] That shouldn't discourage you too much; rather it should set realistic expectations. Most successful business owners try and fail several times to get it right. The learning curve is steep, and the factors required for success are numerous—and that's another book. We can't delve into that too much here.

However, here is the hard truth: most people shouldn't start their own companies as a full-time gig. They don't have the time, resources, or talent for it. Just like most people don't have the talent to be a professional athlete. Not becoming a pro football player, though, doesn't mean I can't be an amateur athlete, enjoy sports, and be in great physical shape. A company you start may never get listed on the NASDAQ, but it can still be a great side gig or hobby.

Being an entrepreneur is a calling, just like being a monk. If you feel the call, nothing will stop you. If you aren't sure, hold off awhile and think about it. Better to do it right with mindful intention than to jump in too fast and take a beating.

Here is a cheat sheet on how to start a successful business:

1. Find a pain point. Is there a problem that causes suffering that you can help solve?
2. Build or find a solution to the pain point.
3. Make sure it is a profitable solution.
4. Nail your solution and scale it out as much as possible.

For example, I discovered that most teacher retirement plans are junk. This causes pain for teachers, professors, and most academic institutions. When a teacher can't retire on time, everyone suffers—the teacher, the school, and the students. I figured out how to build a better mousetrap (i.e., a better retirement plan) while making a profit. After a lot of trial and error, I nailed my solution. Now I scale it out to as many institutions as possible.

It wasn't easy. It took me a decade to implement. The extreme failures were heartbreaking. I failed to win a contract to manage the retirement plan of the school where I worked for eighteen years, even after successfully building and running their plan pro bono for several years. (Office politics got in the way.) That was a kick in the seat of my pants that almost sent me flying off a high bridge into heavy traffic. Be ready for lots of failures. They are always the first steps to success.

New businesses generate individual wealth but also spur innovation, help the economy grow, and create jobs. Companies are the specialized teams we form to help make the world a little bit better for ourselves and others.

The downside of companies is that they have a strong incentive to perpetuate the problems they are being paid to solve or exchange one problem for another. For example, we have a problem called transportation. We need to move our bodies and stuff around, so we invented one of the most remarkable machines in human history to help with our transportation problem: the combustion engine. Most of modern civilization is based on the work of combustion engines, in one form or another, especially the electricity generated from power plants. The need for energy in a modern society should be obvious. Until recently, when we discovered that greenhouse gases cause climate change, the combustion engine was generally a positive force for good.

But most combustion engines run on fossil fuels, especially internal combustion engines like in cars. Those fossil fuel emissions are destroying our global ecology and threatening all our economic and social development. Pollution is what economists call an "externality." Running cars, machines, and power plants is a very good thing. However, they produce an unhelpful side effect, or externality, such as pollution. It is the job of governments to help regulate and prevent externalities.

It is also the job of businesses to solve problems. Innovative businesses can solve the problem of externalities caused by other industries. For example, pollution from fossil fuels can be reduced by developing alternative energy sources. This can solve our transportation and energy needs while protecting God's creation. Unfortunately, established industries, like coal, gas, and oil, will fight against new solutions—those solutions can put them out of business. They fight back by controlling government regulations, blocking disruptive technologies, and disdaining innovative business practices and empirical truths that threaten their very profitable business model.

The great irony is that the process of fighting innovation is anti-capitalistic. A fair and free market will embrace and push for innovation, allow groundbreaking technologies to prosper, solve critical problems, and generate even more wealth while reducing the suffering of the world. A well-regulated free market is a beautiful thing. It pushes society forward. It brings tears to my eyes when I think of how far we've come since the brutal times of Jesus—the Lord works in mysterious ways.

When Businesses Sin

Despite the benefits that a well-regulated free market provides, not every business solves a problem well, and they can sin. Businesses sin when they deliberately, or through negligence, cause grievous harm to others and the planet.

No person and no corporation should be judged solely by their worst behavior on their worst day. Accidents and mistakes happen, and businesses that sin need to make reparations and ask forgiveness for mistakes. The legal system and courts help ensure they repent adequately.

A more serious situation arises when the problems a business creates exceed the value of the problems they solve. For example, cigarettes help relieve stress and provide pleasure to smokers. There is nothing inherently wrong in that, but the problems they create, such as addiction, cancer, and death, far exceed the benefits they provide. I have firsthand experience with the sins of these companies: they helped kill my grandfather, and they ruined the health of my father. I've never met an executive from Philip Morris, but if I did, it would take all of my monastic training to override my Marine Corps training . . . and not rip out his throat with my bare hands.

The US Supreme Court has ruled that corporations are legally people and have the right to certain protections granted to citizens, like free speech. It is high time that we started treating them spiritually like people too. You can't have one without the other. Rights are always attached to responsibilities. If corporations are people, then they can sin and perpetuate evil. We put people in jail or execute them if their crimes are heinous enough, and there are a few companies that need to die. Remember, corporations and companies didn't exist in their current form during the time of Moses, Buddha, or Jesus. This is new spiritual territory that religious texts couldn't cover.

Corporations are legally people because they represent the collective action of an organized group of people. Those people have the right to work together for a common cause and can't be denied their constitutional rights, even as a collective. Fine with me. But then every employee and investor in a company that does something wrong shares a proportional piece of their collective sin. Which means some folks have a lot of repenting to do.

Remember, there are no shortcuts or loopholes in the spiritual journey. We are responsible for all our actions. When we employees and business owners engage in a collective sin, we each own our piece of that. It is one reason why pure index funds, discussed in chapter 12, are highly problematic—they don't screen out any of the bad apples.

It is the job of governments to referee the playing field for people and companies. We need government to help make sure that no one, either willfully or through negligence, grievously harms others—especially their right to be prosperous. We also need government to ensure that companies only solve problems, not create new ones through their business models, production, or labor practices. Please vote your values. Don't sit out on these issues.

If we strive to build and invest in sustainable companies that solve problems, we can grow our personal and collective wealth and make the world a wonderful place. Then everybody wins. What's not to like about that?

CHAPTER 19

THINK BIG

My hope and prayer are that you will reassess your approach to money, become a little bit wealthy, and use that wealth to help others do the same. Helping people solve their money problems doesn't fix everything, and the world will still never be perfect or happy because happiness is not the absence of suffering. But if we can help eliminate the suffering of poverty and money stress, wouldn't that free up time and energy for more important things like loving and caring for one another?

Here's a radical idea: Instead of focusing on anti-poverty programs, what about teaching wealth-creation programs? Think what could happen if we all pull in one direction toward what we want: wealth. Besides, building wealth, especially for others, is way more fun than trying to stop poverty. It's my attempt to reframe a persistent problem.

You may not agree with all the ideas I'm about to present, but it's important to consider them in the context of how they affect wealth. With that, here are some attitudes and policies we can adopt at home and in our communities that can put us on that path.

Investment, Not Consumerism, Grows Wealth

If you love money, you'll want to keep as much of it as you can to use in service to others.

Consumerism erodes wealth and can make you very unhappy, especially if it leads to consumer debt. Our cycle of purchasing things that depreciate and then throwing them away needs to stop. It is bad for our wallets, but it has the horrible side effect of destroying the planet. Purchase stuff that has lasting value and aligns with your values; then you can become wealthy and protect God's creation. This principle is so important that I've devoted much of chapter 6 to it.

Building Wealth Is a Marathon, Not a Sprint

In truth, it's more like an ultra-triathlon: making money, saving money, and investing money. You have to win at all three, and that requires fortitude to take real action. Attitudes like those displayed by the Dreamer and the Gambler (see chapter 4) produce a shortcut mind-set that makes you hope for an easy and quick solution that skips the work required to build wealth. It also ignores the other two parts of the race, saving and investing. There are no shortcuts.

There is a cliché in spirituality that the path is the goal. Being on the path is what matters and will produce impressive results. The same is true for money and wealth. If you won the lottery tomorrow, you may not be happy in the long term. Why? Because 90 percent of lottery winners are broke within ten years of hitting it big. Why do they go broke? The money came too easily, and they never learned proper money management techniques. If you become wealthy the slow and steady way, you're unlikely to make that mistake.

During the darkest days of our financial struggles in the monastery, I would occasionally sneak off to the grocery store to buy a few dollars' worth of lottery tickets. I never spent much, so I figured it couldn't hurt. Financially, it wasn't a big deal. But emotionally it was crippling. It gave me false hope, and I wasted countless hours dreaming about how great life would be if we could win a small fortune. It robbed me of time and energy I could have spent taking real action.

If you are in so much financial pain that your only hope comes from gambling, stop and rest in your pain. Then lean into the pain. Embrace it as your best friend because that has the power to get you off your duff and take meaningful action. Don't try to shortcut or dismiss your suffering. You are in pain for a reason: something in your life is broken. Instead of denying your pain and looking for a magic solution, try to fix the problem.

The Secret of Success Is Delayed Gratification

You've probably heard about the famous Stanford marshmallow experiment, but if not, here is a quick recap. In the 1960s and 1970s, a Stanford professor conducted a series of experiments with young children. He would place a child alone in a room with a marshmallow on a plate. The child was given a simple option: eat the marshmallow now or wait a few minutes and then get two marshmallows. The experimenter would leave the room while recording the child's reactions. The videos of these kids are hysterical as they try to avoid eating the marshmallow, and modern versions are available online. I highly recommend viewing them. It is a simple example of "delayed gratification."

The important part of the study occurred when they followed these kids into adulthood. What did they find? The kids who could delay gratification and wait to get the second marshmallow tended to have better life outcomes as measured by test scores, educational achievement, and body mass index.

If you want to be wealthy, you'll need to make some sacrifices. If you struggle to delay gratification, those sacrifices will be difficult to make.

Perhaps the greatest gift I received from my time in the Marine Corps was increased self-discipline. For example, when practicing an ambush attack, we had to lie in wait for the opposing force. While camouflaged in our carefully chosen spot, I had the sudden and uncontrollable urge to sneeze. It wasn't a sniffle or run-of-the-mill nose itch. This was a monster sneeze, perhaps several monster sneezes, that threatened to shake my whole body. The sound would have revealed our position. While it was only a combat simulation, the firestorm that awaited me from both the drill instructors and my platoon were too horrific to contemplate. I had to hold it in. But I couldn't hold it—that was a paradox with no easy solution.

The struggle between my body and my mind lasted for almost an hour. But we had a mission to carry out, and my reputation was at stake. No one wants a person in their platoon who can't be trusted in a critical situation. I had expected that the hardest part about Marine training would be the athletic challenges, but those were relatively easy compared to mastering discipline and self-control under extreme pressure. But that is the self-control necessary to carry out difficult tasks. I'm still not sure how I stifled that sneeze. Let's just say, ambushes and allergies don't mix.

To build wealth, or achieve any greatness, you'll need to endure some short-term sacrifices. Delayed gratification sometimes requires skipping expensive vacations, avoiding fancy restaurants, and bagging your lunch. No one likes living on a budget, or even doing a budget, but short-term discomfort can help you achieve long-term financial freedom.

Addiction Is an Enemy of Wealth

No one ever plans on becoming an addict. But if you consistently use drugs or alcohol, that is what will happen biologically. It's inevitable. If you suffer from an addiction issue, as millions of Americans do, then seeking treatment and committing to a healthier lifestyle should be your first imperative on your path toward wealth.

Addiction interrupts the reward processing centers of your brain and makes delayed gratification difficult. This can make all life goals difficult. Instead of getting a reward from your brain for a job well done and a challenging task accomplished, drugs and alcohol provide a reward "hit" right now, for no reason. In the long term this can stop you from achieving financial security. Your priorities will get mixed up.

The folks at Harvard Medical School sum this up well:

> In nature, rewards usually come only with time and effort. Addictive drugs and behaviors provide a shortcut, flooding the brain with dopamine and other neurotransmitters. Our brains do not have an easy way to withstand the onslaught.
>
> Addictive drugs, for example, can release two to 10 times the amount of dopamine that natural rewards do, and they do it more quickly and more reliably. In a person who becomes addicted, brain receptors become overwhelmed. The brain responds by producing less dopamine or eliminating dopamine receptors—an adaptation similar to turning the volume down on a loudspeaker when noise becomes too loud.[1]

The end result of this process is predictable and tragic—normal life achievements become empty and meaningless compared to the pleasure of getting high.

Addiction is complex, but it is often a symptom of loneliness, isolation, depression, and disconnection. In our fracturing world, it is no surprise that addiction is rising, with almost one in ten Americans suffering from drug or alcohol addiction.[2] And some of the hardest hit areas from the opioid crisis are rural communities we've neglected economically.

I don't advocate for complete abstinence from all drugs or alcohol because I don't want to be a hypocrite. But it's not a bad idea. Please be mindful about substance use. Make sure your actions align with your values. If you value being wealthy, drugs and alcohol are not your best friends.

Education Creates Intellectual Capital and Builds Wealth

Intellectual capital is the sum of all your talents and skills inside your brain. It includes the ability to read, write, complete a crossword puzzle, cook a meal, make friends, kiss like Casanova, solve a business problem, and so on. If your house burned down, and you lost all your material possessions, lost your job, and lost your money, what would you have left? For some of us, a lot! If you know how to hustle and perform a valuable skill or service, you can bounce back. If you don't have any marketable skills, then you are in a total mess. Intellectual capital includes intangibles, like kindness, patience, the ability to dance, practice law, or perform surgery. It's why people go to school.

Education isn't about getting a degree or a piece of paper—it is about creating intellectual capital. Here is a secret: Most of the world's wealth isn't in banks or the stock market. It is inside our brains! Our intellectual capital is the most valuable thing we have and is responsible for most of the world's riches. The more intellectual capital you have, the wealthier you are likely to be.

Intellectual capital is the brainpower behind economics, and it is perhaps the greatest driver of the disparity between the rich and poor. Look at it this way, modern economics rewards specialization, and specialization requires education. In addition to specialization, a rapidly changing economy requires the ability to adapt quickly to new information, which involves critical thinking and a love of learning new things. So classical liberal arts majors who earn a rigorous, multi-disciplinary degree can rejoice. Being a great generalist, in an age of specialists, is a unique specialty.

A broken educational system destroys personal wealth, which is really bad. Failure to provide children with intellectual capital that a free market wants to pay for will leave them outside of the wealth-generating machine of capitalism, creating permanently poor people.

We also are moving to a world where the need for physical capital, the capacity to earn a living from physical labor, is disappearing. If your primary asset is the ability to move boxes in a warehouse, then a robot will be able to do that cheaper and faster. If your primary source of income is from mining coal, then a younger worker can replace you when you age and accomplish the job better and cheaper. If you make a living working in a factory assembling stuff, then a company in China can do that cheaper too. Our historical economy was based on physical capital, like farming or building cars. Our modern economy is based on knowledge.

Any job based on your physical ability is a precarious one. As a simple example, a friend of mine was a yoga instructor. Then she ruptured several disks in her lower spine. In an instant, her yoga career was over. Physical capital is fleeting; intellectual capital is durable. It can even get better with age. Stephen Hawking unlocked the scientific mysteries of black holes while needing tubes to breathe and eat.

This doesn't mean you shouldn't pursue your passion, but for heaven's sake, please have a fallback option based on intellectual capital!

Everyone Needs Health Care

If you aren't healthy, you can't work at your optimal efficiency. Medical bills without insurance can quickly bankrupt almost anyone, which destroys personal wealth. How we pay for and distribute health care is tricky, but we all need it—it's a requirement. So support lawmakers and politicians who are seeking ways to make health care as cost effective, affordable, and efficient as possible.

Refocusing Our Incarceration Values Can Protect Wealth

There aren't many people arguing that crime is good, but maybe we can focus our crime reduction efforts more tactically. Perhaps we can have a better definition of what a crime is. The laws that protect people, communities, public goods, and wealth make sense, but imprisoning people who self-harm by using drugs doesn't.

America incarcerates more people and a larger proportion of its population than any other country in the world. Are we that much worse than other nations, or do we have a broken criminal justice system? Imprisoning people destroys a lot of taxpayer wealth, and prison ruins the lives of the people we incarcerate, along with their current and future income potential. Would you hire a former convict? That has repercussions far beyond a prison sentence, including lost productivity and tax revenue from the work an ex-convict can't get. What if we focused our incarceration efforts only on people who truly need to be there?

Anyone who messes with another person's physical safety and well-being, wealth, potential wealth, and overall prosperity needs to pay for their actions. What happens to people who are permanently crippled from acts of violence or abuse? What kind of mental horrors and loss of productivity result from sexual assaults alone? Any violence, except in self-defense, violates our right to pursue happiness and prosperity. It is painful and costly to fix broken bodies. Violence also erodes the social bonds that hold us all together. I include financial violence in this category.

But anyone who wants to destroy his own body, wealth, and prosperity should be left to his own devices. If this was our model of justice, we'd incarcerate fewer poor people and more greedy, selfish, power-hungry scoundrels.

Equality of Opportunity Is Better for the Economy than Discrimination

If you discriminate against a class of people, any people, then you limit their ability to join the global economy and build wealth. Discrimination creates severe economic disadvantages, lowering standards of living, reducing purchasing power, and limiting how much people can spend. If they spend less, that hurts the entire economy. Gender equality is a simple example. If you discriminate against half of the population and limit the ability of women to go to school and earn a fair living, you are reducing your national gross domestic product (GDP) by half. That is crazy horrible for wealth creation—for everyone. There is a direct correlation between women's rights and national GDP. Oppression of any kind hurts us all.

We can either tear one another down, making ourselves collectively poorer, or strive for economic justice and a fair playing field, making everyone increasingly wealthy. As a nation, and global community, we need to make wealth creation as easy as possible, not create institutional barriers to success. As I said in part 1, wealth is not a zero-sum game! Help one person become wealthy, and they have more money to spend, save, and invest, which creates more jobs, which makes more people wealthy, ad infinitum. Making wealthy people wealthier does help the economy a little, but not nearly as much as moving more people into the middle and upper classes.

For some communities the likelihood of individuals becoming wealthy due to systemic social injustice is negligible. It is possible for some people who are born into extreme poverty to bootstrap themselves up. But when you create an iterative game, one that is played over and over again, where one player consistently loses, eventually they quit playing. What's the point? I strongly suspect that the same phenomena plays out over communities as well. When your world keeps kicking you in the teeth for arbitrary reasons, one natural response is to give up and then resentfully want to tear the game down to the ground. That won't end well for anyone.

Racism, sexism, and prejudice of any kind hold us all back and are both anti-Christ and un-American. Jesus commands us to love our neighbors, and so does macroeconomics!

Or look at it this way: How would you feel if most people you met hated you just because of who you are—for how you were born? It's something you have no control over, something you can never change. No self-help book will alter basic biology, even if you desperately want it to change. So why hate someone for something they have no control over? It isn't their fault. It makes no sense, and every decent religious leader, in every religion, of every faith, agrees on this point.

(One small caveat: The goal of equality means equality of opportunity for all. Not equal outcomes. Equality of outcomes can be achieved only by force and denies us the free will to make our own choices, even bad choices. We all deserve to be treated equally under the law and be provided equal opportunity to succeed, *and* we are each a unique, autonomous individual with a range of talents and interests who will have varied degrees of success in life.)

For me, God is everywhere, in everyone. So let's stop hating God in the form of our brothers and sisters. And stop hating yourself, too—you are infinitely loved. Don't let anyone tell you otherwise.

Good Political Systems Increase Wealth

As mentioned several times already, the key role of government is to set the rules that we all live by and build strong communities. Governments also provide public goods that no one can afford to pay for on their own. An example is 911 services. If I need the police or the fire department, I can't afford to pay for the entire 911 network on my own. Instead, my local government requires me to pay a small portion of my income as a tax, and those emergency services are made available on demand to everyone. By requiring everyone to buy into the system, the system is there when we need it.

The reason we don't let private industry take over our emergency services and then charge each person who uses them is it creates too many secondary problems. For example, if we privatize the fire department, what happens if a poor person has a house fire? If they can't afford to have the fire department put it out, nothing. The house burns down, but then the fire can spread, and the entire city can burn down too. Or if you live in California, entire communities can get wiped out. Not smart. Some problems are both individual and collective. Which is why we pay taxes, and why taxes are a good thing, although we all still hate them.

Public goods that governments provide also have another characteristic. They typically suffer from a "free rider" problem. Think of the military. If I pay for a strong military, assuming I had the money to do that alone, then the military protects our entire country from our enemies. Fine. But if I protect the nation with my army, you get that service for free. You are then a free rider. You get that protection, but don't need to pay for it. I've already done it. Same thing is true with clean air, trash-free streets, and parks. Once the good or service is in place, it is hard to prevent other people from reaping the benefits. This is a problem because the free market does a terrible job of providing any good or service that has a free-rider issue.

Capitalism alone will not provide public goods because the cost-to-benefit ratio is wildly skewed. While I like the benefit of clean air, the cost is too high for me to purchase clean air for my entire city. Even if I could afford to pay for clean air, I probably wouldn't. I'd just move. It's cheaper. We need excellent forms of government to provide public goods and services. For governments to provide public goods and services we need taxes. Those taxes need to be fair and uniformly applied, or people won't pay them. For the government to collect taxes fairly, and spend the money appropriately, we need effective forms of governance and political stability.

Corruption and political instability mess with all that. If taxes don't get applied fairly, or the political system is used to enrich government officials, the system breaks down. When governments stop working, or become highly inefficient, wealth is quickly destroyed. Perhaps the biggest wealth destroyer on the planet is a lack of government accountability, lack of transparency, and corruption. They distort the distribution of wealth and concentrate it into too few hands. If you don't believe me, ask the North Koreans. Oh, that's right, you can't! Their government imprisons them.

You will notice, if you look carefully, that I always state that a well-regulated, free-market economy is the best path to global wealth. You can't remove the regulated part of the equation. Somalia is a very free market. But there are no rules, and you can do pretty much anything you want, including shooting people you don't like. I know that I'm first in line on several people's hit lists, so no thanks. Our regulations and good government make the game fair and keep it free.

Those who only want to remove or roll back regulations from our government tend to see government as the enemy. While they have ample reason to hold this view, it is shortsighted. It is like getting mad at the referee who makes a bad call during a football game. It feels good to rant and rage, and you may hate the referee and want him removed. But that is very different from saying you don't want any rules or referees at all.

I don't understand why so many Americans love their country, love the Constitution, but hate government. That is a logical fallacy. Again, it is like loving football but hating all the rules and the refs. This is a complex topic, but try to make sure the politicians you support are committed to putting Americans first (not themselves) and to keeping the game well regulated and fair. The refs must be impartial. If you choose football players with strong team allegiances as the refs, the game stops being fair and then falls apart.

It Would Benefit All to Consider War Only as a Final Resort

War destroys lives, industries, and communities, which destroys intellectual capital and wealth. Just look at Europe after each world war. Look at Syria now.

This truth should be self-evident, but it is worth discussing briefly. We often frame wars as a breakdown in political systems and lament the loss of life they produce. Sending soldiers to war to defend your country is sometimes a harsh but necessary reality. However, we forget the economic impact that war produces on the global economy. If we kill people, we also destroy their earning potential, all their purchasing power, and often their property. I wish we could end warfare on purely moral grounds, but that hasn't worked very well so far in human history. Since capitalism reveres money and wealth, could we avoid more wars by understanding that wars will (overall) make the world poorer and destroy vast amounts of wealth? Some industries do profit from war, but what serves the greatest good for the greatest number of people?

I was perfectly happy to fight for my country as a Marine, and some of my friends and family were as well. But was it worth it? The Vietnam, Iraq, and Afghanistan wars cost the US taxpayers around $3.5 trillion. That doesn't include the damage we inflicted on the countries we invaded. Not to mention the loss of life and unspeakable human suffering inflicted on all sides. War may be necessary to protect our national interests, but as with any investment, let's do an *accurate* cost-to-benefit analysis first.

Better Economic Infrastructures Can End Global Poverty

You can't be productive or healthy if you are starving, dehydrated, or malnourished. These circumstances impede a person's ability to generate and secure wealth. They also force people to think of only short-term necessities, like cutting down rain forests or hunting elephants as a necessity to feed their children. We need to give people around the world better pathways to wealth than exploiting natural resources.

Desperate people make desperate decisions, and much of the world lives in not-so-quiet desperation. The way to end global poverty is by building better economic infrastructures. Prosperous people also buy more goods and services, which generates more global wealth, which makes us all wealthier. It is a virtuous cycle, which is why we should encourage and cheer plans that help countries and communities thrive economically all around the world.

Many people don't realize that caring for the environment is a *luxury good*. Yes, you read that right. The environment is a luxury good. Why? Because a luxury good is defined as a good or service you spend more money on as your income increases. How much of your income do you spend on a professional masseuse to give you back massages? If you are poor, the answer is likely zero. If you are wealthy, you might spend a lot of money at spas for back rubs and Botox. Luxury goods and services are things we spend more dollars on as our income increases.

How much do you contribute to environmental causes? If you are poor, probably nothing. You don't have the luxury because you are busy trying to feed your family. The irony and opportunity is that if we help the global economy grow sustainably, then a side effect is an increased concern for the environment.

Why is the air pollution in much of India so bad? In part because the per capita income is around $1,670 per year. Wealthy people don't want to breathe that mess and will protest or pay to make it go away. Wealthy people will also pay for clean water, green grass, and trash-free streets. It's why downtown Detroit looks different from Carmel-by-the-Sea.

Regulations also impact growth. There is no denying that. It is just a question of trade-offs. You can't have pollution-free cities without regulations. And many poor communities fight regulations because they don't want to risk losing jobs from the increased costs of running businesses. We need to help the world become wealthier so everyone has the financial stability to afford good regulations, thereby saving themselves and the planet.

We also need to stop environmental degradation from pollution and protect global biodiversity. How do we accomplish that? The most effective way is to increase the well-being of people around the world so they have an incentive to protect the environment rather than destroy it. The dark side of capitalism is that almost everything can be a commodity, even water, air, soil, and trees. If someone can make more money cutting down a tree than saving the tree, capitalism will cut down the tree. If it is cheaper to dump our pollution into a river or burn it away into the smog-o-sphere, then dump and burn it we will.

Capitalism is all about "incentives." Incentives are the things that motivate us, like money, fame, comfort, not going to jail, and love. If the incentives for Option A are greater than the incentives for Option B, then all other things being equal, people will choose Option A. If we give people incentives to pollute and destroy the planet, they will pollute and destroy the planet. If we provide incentives to protect the environment and natural resources, then God's creation will be maintained responsibly in perpetuity. This is what governments are supposed to do. They are rule makers that provide incentives for helpful behavior.

The best way to protect God's creation is to make it more profitable for communities to protect the environment than destroy it. For example, if villages in Kenya can make more money from elephant-related tourism than from poaching elephants, elephants will flourish. If they can make more by shooting them and harvesting tusks, expect bullets to fly.

But the point of this section is about endemic poverty. Sadly, starvation is often a weapon of war. It is easier and cheaper to starve people than to shoot them. When you try to shoot them, they typically shoot back. Starvation, or sieges, are a time-tested way to destroy people. Sieges also take the form of trade embargos, blockades, and economic sanctions. While there are exceptions, when you see a large group of people starving around the world, not just individuals struggling in extreme poverty, it is because political engineering created that situation.

Clean water is another complex matter and will likely become a dominant issue in the future. Cities like Cape Town in South Africa are already facing critical water shortages that make daily life extremely challenging. Water is necessary for life, and water makes societies function. Without water, creating wealth is an afterthought because survival takes precedence.

In Ahmednagar, India, droughts are common. In 2013, while on a spiritual retreat, I met a translator there who woke up early every morning to get water for his family. He rode his bike an hour to a water collection point, filled up large containers strapped to the sides of his bike, then spent two hours pedaling home. This was their daily water supply. The loss of human productivity is astounding. How much national productivity is lost when citizens need to struggle for hours a day to procure water?

What we know about human biology is that if you put polluted water into people, their bodies don't work right. And if you put polluted water into children, they don't grow up healthy and will have serious issues and possible brain damage. That destroys productivity and global wealth because the capacity for intellectual capital is reduced or destroyed. If we destroy intellectual capital, by any means, including lack of food and water, everyone gets poorer. That includes you. Those poor people can't buy the goods or services your business sells, nor those of the companies in which you invest.

Too often we see poverty as an individual problem, at best worthy of our charity. But it is a collective problem too. If poor people across the globe have an increased standard of living, they have more disposable income for things like the environment, but they also have money for other goods and services, like books on finance. The more people there are around the globe who can afford to purchase my books, the more money I make. It is a "multiplier effect" and a virtuous cycle. The more money I make, the more likely I am to go out to dinner or buy new clothes. That makes other people a little bit wealthier, who spend more, and so on, ad infinitum.

Wealth cannot exist in isolation. Like it or not, we are all interconnected, and the more altruistic our economic infrastructure is, the wealthier we all become. Moving more people up the economic ladder creates more overall wealth, giving them more money to spend, making it easier for the rest of us to become even wealthier. That is a win-win situation.

Agape-argyria is good for the soul, but also good for the bottom line. Try to support politicians and policies committed to improving our economic infrastructure and building a more inclusive economy. It can help all of us grow wealthy together.

CHAPTER 20

GIVE
CHARITABLY

The divine love of money requires charity. But, more importantly, the spiritual journey is about moving from selfishness to selflessness and reducing our egoism. *Agape-argyria* is one of many ways of achieving that goal.

Most economists argue that money is morally neutral. It is simply a tool, and there is much truth in that worldview. However, the pragmatic reality is more nuanced—money in action is like a spiritual sponge, absorbing the values and intentions of the user. When we put money into action, it always reflects our values. Spending, receiving, and giving money is never morally neutral. That is why it helps me to give thanks and say a quick prayer each time I use money. It keeps me mindful of the spiritual and moral power of money.

What do you value? Do you value becoming a little bit wealthy? Then your work, savings, and investing habits should reflect that. Do you value serving, loving, and caring for others? Then your spending and charitable giving should reflect that.

Here is the hardest truth for people of any faith to accept: charitable giving and building personal wealth are antagonistic to each other. For example, if you are a median US household and donate 10 percent of your annual income every year, you'll donate 10 percent of $57,000. That's $5,700 per year. Over sixty years, using the time value of money at an 8.7 percent rate of return, that's a lifetime of giving worth $10,161,485. That's a lot of money that could otherwise be in your investment portfolio! You still need to give of your wealth, but it will always be a sacrifice, so make sure it goes to a worthy cause.

Agape-argyria requires us to be charitable, but let's be honest about it. It hurts! And it should, or it isn't an act of selflessness. Some of the more disreputable and unscrupulous preachers pervert the spiritual message of religion to hide this simple mathematical reality. Too often we hear some religious leaders claim that by giving away our wealth (to them), we'll become wealthier. If we give more, we'll get more. That's not true, and it also perverts the entire spiritual journey from selfishness to selflessness. You can't give stuff away as an act of charity and selflessness and expect to selfishly gain more. That is your ego looking for a spiritual loophole.

I call this the Give More to God Fallacy. It is the notion that if you only give more, God will love you more and provide you with a miracle. In my opinion, God already loves you—you can't change that. So stop waiting for a miracle and start taking action. We give as an expression of our love, not to be loved.

The Give More to God Fallacy is the Weaponizer money monster at work in the spiritual domain. It is an attempt to use money to manipulate the Divine. That is *philargyria* and is some tricky stuff. Preachers who promise wealth in exchange for donations, which they claim are to God, are liars, frauds, charlatans, con artists, tricksters, snake-oil salesmen, and anti-Christs. But they are also preying on the greed or desperation of their followers. It's a two-way street.

News flash: Warren Buffett did not get wealthy by donating his money to televangelists.

As I said in part 1, growing wealthy requires math, not miracles.

And being ethically wealthy means using your money and power to relieve suffering, especially the suffering of the poor. However, ministers who take from the poor, creating suffering for their personal gain, are abusive. If your pastor is living in a mansion while you struggle to make ends meet, then, to quote Shakespeare, "Something is rotten in the state of Denmark." They aren't serving you; they are serving themselves and twisting God's message to do it.

There is no correlation between austerity and spirituality, but there is a correlation between spirituality and kindness. Taking money from poor people, promising them their donation will grant them God's favor, and then living an opulent lifestyle is not kind. It is not spiritual. It's wrong.

The Real Purpose of Charity

Charity is more than just giving money. It also means loving all our brothers and sisters wholeheartedly. Charity is not a miserly parsing out of affection to members of your social clique.

I didn't grow up with any religion at all, so I had to find my way to God solo. I had a close friend in high school, Luke, and I spent much of my free time at his home. Any opportunity to get out of my house was a blessing. On weekends and summer breaks, Luke and I would spend the afternoons riding his dirt bikes through the fields behind his house, and at night we'd binge watch bad '80s movies. Luke was in a rebellious phase and wasn't very religious at that point in his life, so the subject of God rarely came up.

As I spent more and more time at his home, his family quietly adopted me, like a stray puppy who showed up at their door. When I'd sleep over on a Saturday, the family would get up for church every Sunday morning and invite me to join them. At first, I declined. I wasn't interested. Their overwhelming kindness and generosity of spirit, however, made me curious to know more about their faith. They took in strangers who were homeless or people who were struggling and needed help. They even put up with me hanging around all the time.

Sitting at their breakfast table, as they generously cooked for me and shared their scrumptious homemade jams, I learned about the Bible and Jesus. They talked about God's love, which they expressed through mindful service to others. I decided that if God was the source and strength of their love, I wanted more of that! I also wanted more of their homemade strawberry jam each Sunday morning, so I started going to church with them in Wheaton, Illinois, a town that supposedly has the second most churches per capita in America.

Their church community provided the fellowship, love, and support I desperately needed. It was wonderful. In time I was baptized and made Wheaton my spiritual home. The best part was that Luke's older brother, David, was a student at Wheaton College. David took me under his wing and invited me to join him for lectures, concerts, and community events, introducing me to the wider Christian community. I'd found a mentor, community, and God.

I converted because I felt loved. I found a family that supported and encouraged me. Yes, the theology was very orthodox, but the community was a life raft that saved me from drowning in loneliness. The evangelical Christian community pulled me in and held on tight. They rescued me from my worst impulses and gave me a home when I needed one. They welcomed a lonely stranger into their midst and treated me like family. If I'm ever Dispossessed, I know where I'm going to move: Wheaton, Illinois. If you are a sincere seeker, you can find a home there. I will always love them for that. And I will never forget the many gifts they gave me.

Luke's family preached love and practiced love, and their example has always stayed with me. They proved that political and religious viewpoints are irrelevant if you strive to love and serve everyone you meet, without judgment. Without charity, religion can become twisted and hateful. Philosopher and author Rabbi Abraham Joshua Heschel beautifully captures this sentiment in his poem "What of the Night":

> This is a time to cry out.
> One is ashamed to be human. One is embarrassed to
> be called religious in the face of religion's failure to
> keep alive the image of God in the face of man . . .
> We have imprisoned God in our temples and slogans,
> and now the word of God is dying on our lips.
> There is darkness in the East, and smugness in the West.
> What of the night?
> What of the night?[1]

If you want to know what "the night" is, there is a book by that title written by Elie Wiesel, describing his experience in a Nazi concentration camp.

The great challenge is to love those we hate, to be kind to those we would rather destroy, and to forgive. That's arduous work. If you want to sacrifice something as a spiritual practice, how about giving up your prejudices and hatred? Which human beings do you hate the most? Are you brave enough to give up that hatred out of charity?

Perhaps the greatest spiritual challenge of our time is learning to love those with differing political views. If we fail to find a moral bridge that allows both sides of the political spectrum to communicate and cooperate, the social bonds that hold us together may completely break.

I eventually left my church in Wheaton because I began experiencing more judgment than love there. I was spiritually adrift for many years. It seemed hip to be Buddhist, so I pretended I was really into Zen meditation, even though I never had the patience to sit in zazen more than a few minutes at a time. I always ended up falling asleep. Then I bounced between atheism and agnosticism until I met "the Benedictine brothers" during college. One of the brothers was my mathematics professor and senior thesis adviser.

My senior thesis explored the path that the French author and mathematician Blaise Pascal took to find God. While I often disagree with Pascal, studying him so closely led to some great conversations with the brothers over long dinners when they invited me into their home. The food was just as good as the conversation.

The brothers were great cooks. They may have been austere in other aspects of their lives but not with food. The first time they invited me for a meal, they cooked a special recipe they called "spiedini." It is an Italian classic, but theirs was spectacularly unique and unlike any version I've seen in a restaurant or cookbook. (You can find the recipe on my website.)

Is it hypocrisy to become a monk for the food? Okay, the food at the monastery was great, but I really joined the community and converted to Catholicism for one reason: I felt unconditionally loved. Food was just one expression of their love. I didn't care as much for the rites and rituals, but I was deeply loved. That was worth sacrificing the world for. Even though they made poor money decisions, and some other bad choices as well, they always tried to love more and more. If we can share that kind of enthusiastic love with the world, God can walk the earth again in the hearts of his lovers everywhere.

In fact, many will be surprised to learn that I entered the monastery as an agnostic-atheist. I didn't have any faith, but I was wrestling with an age-old problem: If God doesn't exist, why am I here? What is the meaning of life? My life, *like all our lives*, is filled with suffering. If that suffering has no meaning, I'd rather not keep doing this life thing. I really have had enough.

J. S. Bach, in my translation of his Cantata BWV 82, best captures this sentiment:

> I eagerly look forward to my death.
> Oh, how I wish it had already come!
> Only then will I escape this ceaseless suffering
> Which imprisons me wherever I roam.

This is why we are supposed to love our neighbors—*because everyone we meet is having a really hard time.* The monastic brothers intuitively understood this and offered a compelling solution. I felt called to give it a try. The alternative wasn't very appealing.

How to Give Well

Since this book is primarily about money management, the question we need to answer is how to give your time and money to charity. There is no simple answer to that question. Much depends on your faith tradition, family circumstances, and overall wealth. I don't like strict formulas because they are too rigid and can force some poor people into financially gut-wrenching decisions while letting many wealthy people off the hook too easily. However, 10 percent is a good place to start the conversation, just don't get legalistic about it. Leave that to the Pharisees.

Charitable giving should be like taxes: the more you have, the more you should be donating. That is what helps justify your wealth—it allows you to do more good in the world. A billionaire who donates half their wealth may sacrifice less than a poor person who donates a hundred dollars.

> As Jesus looked up, he saw the rich putting their gifts into the temple treasury. He also saw a poor widow put in two very small

copper coins. "Truly I tell you," he said, "this poor widow has put in more than all the others. All these people gave their gifts out of their wealth; but she out of her poverty put in all she had to live on." (Luke 21:1–4)

The point of this passage isn't that the poor should give generously from their poverty, but that the rich need to step up their game.

But remember: charity is selfless—not selfish. Otherwise, it's not charity. Don't use charity as an extension of your ego to dominate others or seek rewards for yourself. That misses the mark.

Also remember the first rule of a water rescue: don't jump into the water (see chapter 11). Avoid putting yourself in a dangerous position where you can become a victim as well. Be mindful that your charity doesn't risk your wealth, health, or family security. You can't stand up for others until you've learned to stand up for yourself.

If you are deep in debt, especially on credit cards, you get a pass on donating money to charity until you get your house in order. If you have a negative net worth, you have no wealth to share. However, the trade-off is you should be giving more *time* to charity. The knowledge that you can't help others financially until you clean up your mess first should provide extra motivation to get your debt under control. Just don't use debt as an excuse to ignore charity and splurge selfishly without fixing your money problems. That would be an ego trap too.

I think the best way to donate to charities is by giving your time first and your money second. Start by volunteering at your local church, school, homeless shelter, soup kitchen, environmental group, or animal rescue. Get to know a charity well, learn about their needs, and then the how-much question will answer itself. With mindfulness and empathy you'll see suffering and want to help as best you can.

When you have skin in the game by giving your time and talent, your charity becomes more mindful and powerful. Take a passionate interest in one cause and throw the weight of your charitable efforts behind it. Then giving becomes easy, natural, and graceful. When you are ready to give to a specific charity, do a little fact-finding first.

1. Make sure they are a legitimate tax exempt 501(c)(3) public charity.
2. Research their finances to ensure they are financially stable and use all donations effectively, not just on marketing and high salaries. Look at the "efficient ratio" to see what percentage of their income goes to their stated mission and how much goes to expenses.
3. Be sure they are transparent and accountable in all they do.

There are several websites that can help with this process. The largest and most popular right now is Charity Navigator: www.charitynavigator.org.

Agape-argyria requires charity: share the money that you love, with the people and causes that you love, in the spirit of love. Then you'll live a good, honorable life and can look back at the end and enjoy it a second time.

CHAPTER 21

PUT YOUR VALUES IN ACTION

The real trick to building lasting wealth, wealth you can live on forever and pass on to your loved ones, is to think of wealth as a personal endowment. Just like at a college or a foundation, an endowment is a large pile of money carefully invested. Those investments generate income, and a portion of the income is reinvested in the endowment. The rest of the income generated is money to live off. If the endowment is large enough, the income generated replaces your income from work. Then you have a beautiful retirement—in other words, you are financially liberated to spend your time in whatever activities bring the most value to your life, without having to worry about where your next paycheck will come from. And living your values is what brings the most meaning and happiness.

Why reinvest some of the income? To help maintain your purchasing power over time. Inflation and market changes will erode the value of an endowment. For example, a bottle of Coke when I was a kid cost $0.25 from a vending machine. Now it costs $1.50 or more. That is inflation. A quarter buys less stuff now and will keep buying less stuff over time.

If you want to maintain the purchasing power that your investments generate, your investments need to produce more and more money. To accomplish this, reinvest a small portion of the income generated by your endowment to keep the "principal," or core assets, growing to match the pace of inflation. Once you take care of inflation, everything else you make is money to live off. But to do that successfully takes a lot of money. The sooner you want to retire, the more wealth you need to make it happen.

How Much Wealth Do I Need?

If you want to live comfortably on an annual income of $60,000 a year, then your endowment needs to generate $60,000 of income, plus extra to reinvest. The typical rule of thumb for maintaining an endowment is to never withdraw more than 4 percent of the total value per year. Since inflation averages around 2 percent to 4 percent per year, your endowment needs to generate around 6 to 8 percent in returns. You need a little bit of wealth. If you invest in a balanced ESG index-based fund, your endowment should (hopefully) generate around 8.7 percent interest, on average. That gives you 4 percent to withdraw, 4.7 percent to reinvest, and a cushion for when the market goes crazy.

So how much money are we talking about? A lot. If you want your endowment to comfortably generate $60,000, simply divide $60,000 by 0.04, or 4 percent. That's $1,500,000. Ouch! But it's doable. Not easy, but doable. If it were easy, everyone would be doing it already. However, if you earn an average of $57,000 a year, save 15 percent pre-tax for 33 years at 8.7 percent interest, you'd have $1,511,720. It can be done!

If you earn more and save more, the time frame gets shorter and shorter. If you earn $100,000 per year, you'd need to save 15 percent pre-tax for 27 years to reach $1,535,572. Play with the numbers online and see what scenario makes sense for you. There is a free calculator on my website: douglynam.com.

Simply divide the amount of money you want to live off annually by 0.04. That gives the total amount needed for your endowment. Then use the compound interest calculator to figure out the savings rate and time frame you need to reach that goal.

Desired Annual Income / 0.04 = Total Amount of Endowment

I've simplified a very complex process, which is why having a good financial adviser is helpful. Some investing nuances require continual adjustment, like the fact that there are no average years in the stock market or average years for inflation. For example, the average mom has 2.4 children in her lifetime.[1] But, there is *no* mother with 2.4 children—averages are tricky and potentially misleading. There are really good years and some really bad years in the market, but the averages are in your favor.

Remember the nighttime navigation techniques in the Marine Corps? When moving forward in the dark, set a long-term goal, but then aim for small, manageable goals you can see right in front of you, and continually course correct. As your financial circumstances change and market conditions change, you must be ready to improvise, adapt, and overcome.

For me, being a little bit wealthy means having enough money to live off of indefinitely without needing to work. Most people call this retirement, and it can happen at any age. Many people never generate enough wealth to retire comfortably, so they delay retirement as long as possible to run down the clock. The shorter your expected lifespan in retirement, the less money you need.

Retire to Something

I want everyone to retire with dignity and retire as early as possible to focus on projects they find meaningful. If you can generate enough wealth, there is no reason to wait until you are older to retire. You can then work only at what you love to do and be of greater service to the world.

Here is a personal secret: I never want to retire in the traditional sense. I may want to slow down, work on fewer projects, and focus my energy, but I never want to stop working completely. That would be dreary. I find meaning, pride, and delight in my work. It brings me joy to serve others, so why would I ever want to stop doing what I value?

I once took a solo vacation to Zanzibar in Africa, where I toured on a motorcycle around the island, then holed up in a remote tropical beach resort with a stack of books. Each day I camped out on a wide expanse of pure white beach, with crystalline azure waves, and sipped tall fruity drinks with little umbrellas. It was paradise—for about three days. Then I was bored as heck.

Leisure is great but only as a counterpoint to mindful activity. We all need to rest and rejuvenate, but an endless vacation isn't paradise; it's vacuous. We also need meaning, connection, and purpose, no matter how old we are. Sitting around, doing nothing meaningful, and waiting to die sounds awful to me. I've seen too many friends, family, and clients disintegrate in retirement when deprived of connection and activity.

I tell clients to never retire *from* something—always retire *to* something. It's great to leave a job you are burned out on for a new adventure. That adventure may involve paid work, or not. It may include more time with family and friends, but in the *agape-argyria* model it should also involve charity and service to others. That is where we find the greatest meaning and purpose, by sharing our love and God's love with the world. Just quitting on life, with nothing to move toward, is one type of hell.

Your Wealth as the Root of LOVE

Money is the clearest expression of our values in action. Money is not the root of all evil, our ego-driven selfishness is. A spiritually rich life is always about living according to your values. Monks take that to an extreme, trying to make every day and every action a reflection of love, compassion, and kindness.

One of the original intentions behind monastic poverty was that by renouncing all material goods and worldly ambitions, the monk would be free to act selflessly and without ulterior motives. They could be free agents of love, mercy, and kindness, serving God all day in all things. For a monk, the deepest spiritual values shape every moment of every day.

Another way forward can accomplish the same: Instead of having everyone live in poverty, which isn't going to work out well, what if we all had a little bit of wealth? Wouldn't that allow us to achieve the same objective? My prayer is that everyone can live like a true monk, a free agent of love and kindness, beholden to no one. With no strings attached.

You don't need any money to make that happen, but having a personal endowment makes it much easier. Otherwise, you'll live a precarious existence. Wealth, wisely invested, allows you to live your values more fully, not be stuck in a workaday grind that leaves many of us angry, frustrated, and exhausted.

A life where your deepest spiritual values shape each day and each act is what I call a **LOVE** life. **LOVE** is an acronym for **L**ive **O**nly **V**alue-based **E**xperiences. You should know by now that buying stuff will not make you happy. However, meaningful value-based experiences do make us happy. They also make the world a better place. Money is the catalyst that makes value-based experiences happen. The more wealth you have, the more valuable experiences you can pack into your life. Wealth can help make life **LOVE**-ly.

My hope is that you have a life filled with meaningful value-based experiences that bring you greater contentment, joy, and peace while serving others to the best of your ability—without having to stress about money or running the daily rat race.

Is a **LOVE** life always pleasant and happy? Nope. Not at all.

For example, someone who needs cancer treatment is going to value that treatment highly, even though it is devastating. They need to focus on their health and quality time with family, not on paying medical bills, earning an income, or even cleaning the house. Money can remove the unvaluable experiences from your life, allowing you to focus on what you truly value.

My first job after college involved tedious legal work that I detested. I was also on the wrong side of a big legal battle. While I valued the paycheck, I never valued the work. I had more fun flipping burgers at Wendy's in high school. We often do things we dislike out of necessity, but it's wonderful to avoid those situations, if possible. It certainly isn't how I want to live my entire life. Too much of that and you LOSE at life, where you Live Only Sad Experiences.

The list of value-based experiences is endless. You may value working in a homeless shelter, helping foster children, running aid missions around the world, helping people build stronger retirement plans, or training service dogs for veterans struggling with PTSD. It should also include, in moderation, spending time on a tropical beach sipping fruity cocktails with your friends and family. Those experiences add value to your life and to the world too. They strengthen social and family bonds, bringing joy into the world.

Personally, I find value in building my business, praying, writing, doing yoga, cooking great food, spending time with friends and family, and looking for ways to make the world a little bit better. Wealth is a catalyst that makes that possible.

One of my favorite **LOVE** stories is the time a group of students at my old school, on their own initiative, made a cake and threw a party for a seven-year-old girl whose family moved into a homeless shelter on her birthday. That was LOVE-ly. I value every moment of that day. I still get teary eyed every time I think about that little girl's surprise, and the joy it gave to every guest in the shelter that night. It made a tragically dreary day into a celebration. The students also made dinner for the whole shelter. It was spontaneous and brought a small miracle into the world. And if you don't think that was a real miracle, just ask the little girl's mother.

That LOVE story required a little money, but it also took time and energy. And it is hard to find the time or money when all your energy is devoted to making ends meet. With a little bit of wealth, your entire day can be filled with LOVE stories, not just with hours clocked at a job you don't like. We all are required to do unpleasant things, but money, used wisely, can drastically reduce our suffering and provide us with the time and resources to help others more effectively. For me, an abundant, blessed life is one where I move closer and closer to living only the experiences I value and that reflect my deepest held beliefs. That means climbing Jacob's Ladder, moving from selfishness to selflessness, and mastering the sublime art of serving others.

There are people everywhere living a LOVE life, bringing abundant joy and compassion into the world. One client worked in a high-powered law firm in Manhattan for many years until her children were grown. She then retired in her fifties to become a Presbyterian minister in a religious school. One friend retired as the CEO of a media corporation and now runs disaster relief missions around the world. Another friend left a lucrative Wall Street job and now builds and designs radically inexpensive and portable homeless shelters.

In an ironic twist, one of the founding partners at LongView Asset Management retired shortly before I arrived—to become a nun! It was a karmic swap. I believe that we are the hands of God. In the monastic tradition, God loves us, blesses us with his grace, and needs us to share that love with the world. We are responsible for delivering God's love—and God surrounds us. With time, resources, and compassion in our hearts, we are each a powerful tool for change in the world.

God knows, our world needs it.

> "May the LORD bless you
> and keep you;
> may the LORD cause His face to shine upon you
> and be gracious to you;
> may the LORD lift up His countenance toward you
> and give you peace."
> —NUMBERS 6:24–26 BSB

ACKNOWLEDGMENTS

Writing a book requires the work of many hands. In chronological order, I owe a profound debt to the Your Money staff at the *New York Times*, in particular, Tara Siegal Bernard, who introduced me to Ron Lieber. Ron's article, "The Monk Who Left the Monastery to Fix Broken Retirement Plans," featuring me, went viral. That connected me to my outstanding agents at Folio Literary Management, Jamie Chambliss and Steve Troha. Their hard work introduced me to an equally superb publishing house, Thomas Nelson and the W Publishing Group, where I met acquisitions editor Debbie Wickwire and publisher Daisy Hutton. That put me in the hands of Erin Healy of WordWright Editorial Services. Erin's contribution to this book can't be overstated. Helping me create a coherent narrative, then blending in some of the most controversial topics in the history of human civilization (money, religion, and politics) without annoying too many readers, is no small accomplishment. Her tongue lashings whipped this book into shape. Then, of course, is the ever-critical editorial and marketing support from Paula Major and Kristi Smith.

Not least of all is my personal support and editing staff: Molly Talbert, Leah Cantor, and Ginna Clark. Thank you all! I am forever grateful for your hard work and encouragement. A special shout-out goes to John Wasik for his wisdom and council.

And finally, to the principals of LongView Asset Management, David Cantor and Harlan Flint: thank you.

Sometimes honesty is cruel, and one must be cruel to be kind. I'm deeply grateful to everyone involved who shared their honest opinions in the spirit of excellence.

NOTES

Chapter 2: Money Isn't Bad—Poverty Is

1. Lisa Esposito, "The Countless Ways Poverty Affects People's Health," *U.S. News and World Report*, April 20, 2016, https://health.usnews .com/health-news/patient-advice/articles/2016-04-20/the-countless -ways-poverty-affects-peoples-health.
2. Rob Wile, "These Three Charts Show Why Middle Class Workers Are Struggling to Get Ahead Today," *Money*, April 17, 2017, http://time.com /money/4742648/middle-class-workers-struggle-financial-diaries/.
3. Jessica Dickler, "Six-Figure Income and They Can't Make Ends Meet," CNBC, July 14, 2017, https://www.cnbc.com/2017/07/14/the-middle -class-is-struggling-even-on-six-figures.html.
4. Preston Ni, "How Money Issues Predict Divorce (& How to Prevent Them)," *Psychology Today*, April 14, 2013, https://www.psychology today.com/us/blog/communication-success/201304/how-money-issues -predict-divorce-how-prevent-them.
5. National Council on Drug Abuse, "Drug Talk," http://ncda.org.jm /index.php/publications/drug-talk/66-poverty-a-drug-abuse; Avelardo Valdez, Charles D. Kaplan, Russell L. Curtis Jr., "Aggressive Crime, Alcohol and Drug Use, and Concentrated Poverty in 24 U.S. Urban Areas," *American Journal of Drug and Alcohol Abuse*, July 7, 2009, https://www.ncbi.nlm.nih.gov/pmc/articles/PMC3015237/; David Francis, "Poverty and Mistreatment of Children Go Hand in Hand," National Bureau of Economic Research, accessed September 14, 2018,

http://www.nber.org/digest/jan00/w7343.html; Heather D. Boonstra, "Abortion in the Lives of Women Struggling Financially: Why Insurance Coverage Matters," Guttmacher Institute, July 14, 2016, https://www.guttmacher.org/gpr/2016/07/abortion-lives-women -struggling-financially-why-insurance-coverage-matters; GPE Secretariat, "5 Ways Education Can Help End Extreme Poverty," Global Partnership for Education, October 17, 2016, https://www .globalpartnership.org/blog/5-ways-education-can-help-end-extreme -poverty; Dan Simon, "Poverty Fact Sheet: Poor and in Poor Health," Institute for Research on Poverty and the Morgridge Center for Public Service, accessed September 14, 2018, https://www.irp.wisc.edu /publications/factsheets/pdfs/PoorInPoorHealth.pdf.

6. Claire Conway, "Poor Health: When Poverty Becomes Disease," University of California San Francisco, January 6, 2016, https://www .ucsf.edu/news/2016/01/401251/poor-health.

7. Desmond Brown, "10 Reasons Why Cutting Poverty Is Good for Our Nation," Center for American Progress Action Fund, December 6, 2011, https://www.americanprogressaction.org/issues/poverty/news /2011/12/06/10771/10-reasons-why-cutting-poverty-is-good-for-our -nation/.

8. BBC, "Welby 'Embarrassed' by Wonga Link," July 26, 2013, http:// www.bbc.co.uk/religion/0/23448808.

9. Michael Hoffman, *Usury in Christendom: The Mortal Sin that Was and Now Is Not* (Independent History and Research, 2012).

10. The Dutch East India Company was the first modern corporation, founded in 1602.

11. John Parker, "Burgeoning Bourgeoisie," *The Economist*, February 12, 2009, https://www.economist.com/special-report/2009/02/12 /burgeoning-bourgeoisie.

12. I'd like to acknowledge that the current US economic structure does have flaws that need fixing, and those flaws do cause poverty. But those are systemic issues that aren't necessarily caused or perpetuated by my earning, saving, and investing behavior.

13. Charles Wheelan, *Naked Economics* (New York: W. W. Norton & Company, 2010).

14. Michael Curtin, "Using Food as a Weapon of War," *International Policy Digest*, November 27, 2017, https://intpolicydigest.org/2017 /11/27/using-food-as-a-weapon-of-war/.

15. Michael Massing, "Does Democracy Avert Famine?" *New York Times*, March 1, 2003, https://www.nytimes.com/2003/03/01/arts/does -democracy-avert-famine.html.

16. Jessica Haynes, "What Would Happen to the Economy If We All Stopped Spending Money?" ABC News, March 6, 2017, http://www .abc.net.au/news/2017-03-07/what-happens-to-the-economy-when -we-stop-spending-money/8297724.

17. Jessica Dickler, "Six-Figure Income and They Can't Make Ends Meet" (see chap. 2, n. 3).

Chapter 3: Loving Money with the Right Kind of Love

1. Scholars of the ancient Greek may dislike how I've created the word *agape-argyria*. Linguistically it should probably be *agapargyria* or perhaps *argyragape*, but it's hard enough to pronounce as it is. Also, for an English-speaking audience, I think it's helpful to keep the word *agape* distinct.

2. Some Christians believe Judas took the money not out of greed but as a necessary action to fulfill prophecy. However, that isn't in the original text. Unfortunately, the negative portrayal of Judas has been used to justify anti-Semitism, which is certainly not my intent.

3. "Towards the End of Poverty, *The Economist*, June 1, 2013, https://www.economist.com/leaders/2013/06/01/towards -the-end-of-poverty.

Chapter 5: Assess Your Team

1. Kelley Holland, "Fighting with Your Spouse? It's Probably About This," CNBC, February 4, 2015, https://www.cnbc.com/2015/02/04 /money-is-the-leading-cause-of-stress-in-relationships.html; Stephen Little, "Money Worries Biggest Reason for Marriages Ending, Survey Finds," *Independent*, January 8, 2018, https://www.independent.co.uk /news/business/news/money-marriage-end-divorce-day-relationships -personal-finances-slater-gordon-a8147921.html.

Chapter 7: Consider Whether to File for Bankruptcy

1. David U. Himmelstein, Deborah Thorne, Elizabeth Warren, Steffie Woolhandler, "Medical Bankruptcy in the United States, 2007: Results of a National Study," *The American Journal of Medicine*, 2009, http://www.pnhp.org/new_bankruptcy_study/Bankruptcy-2009.pdf.

2. *Huffington Post*, "Top Ten Reasons People Go Bankrupt," May 24, 2015, https://www.huffingtonpost.com/simple-thrifty-living/top-10 -reasons-people-go-_b_6887642.html.

3. United States Courts, "Just the Facts: Consumer Bankruptcy Filings 2006–2017," March 7, 2018, http://www.uscourts.gov/news/2018/03 /07/just-facts-consumer-bankruptcy-filings-2006-2017.

4. See R.K. Hammer, "Payment Cards Analyst," April 22, 2018, http:// rkhammer.com/ for the latest numbers.

5. According to the United States Federal Reserve, 44.2 million students owe $1.52 trillion in college loans. The Brookings Institute estimates that almost 40 percent of student loans may be in default by 2023. (See Gail Gardner, "Student Loan Crisis: Are Small Businesses Impacted?" Small Business Trends, June 20, 2018, https://smallbiztrends.com/2018/06/student-loan -crisis.html.) It is a huge crisis. The lack of basic consumer protection on student loans is creating a debtor's prison for millions of Americans.

6. United States Department of Justice, "Census Bureau, IRS Data, and Administrative Expenses Multipliers," April 2017, https://www.justice .gov/ust/means-testing/20170401.

7. Note: President Trump filed for business bankruptcy six times, not personal bankruptcy.

8. Career Builder, "More Than 1 in 4 Employers Do Not Conduct Background Checks of All New Employees, According to CareerBuilder Survey," November 17, 2016, https://www.careerbuilder.com/share/aboutus /pressreleasesdetail.aspx?sd=11/17/2016&siteid=cbpr&sc_cmp1=cb_pr975 _&id=pr975&ed=12/31/2016.

Chapter 9: Live Below Your Means

1. H. Claire Brown, "The Top Five Meat and Dairy Companies Emit More Carbon than the Gasoline Giants," New Food Economy, July 18, 2018, https://newfoodeconomy.org/meat-dairy-greenhouse-gas-emissions/.

Chapter 10: Run from Credit

1. Assuming an 8.7 percent rate of return in a balanced portfolio and a 19 percent interest rate on a credit card.

Chapter 11: Pay Yourself First

1. Retirement savings calculator, http://douglynam.com/.

Chapter 12: Grasp the Basics of Investing

1. Monique Morrissey, "The State of American Retirement," Economic Policy Institute, March 3, 2016, https://www.epi.org/publication /retirement-in-america/#charts.
2. Fidelity, "A Couple Retiring in 2018 Would Need an Estimated $280,000 to Cover Health Care Costs in Retirement, Fidelity Analysis Shows," April 19, 2018, https://www.fidelity.com/about-fidelity/employer-services /a-couple-retiring-in-2018-would-need-estimated-280000.
3. Vanguard, "Vanguard Portfolio Allocation Models," accessed September 14, 2018, https://personal.vanguard.com/us/insights /saving-investing/model-portfolio-allocations?lang=en.
4. Aye M. Soe and Ryan Poirier, contributors, SPIVA U.S. Scorecard, "Summary," S&P Dow Jones Indices, downloadable PDF available: SPIVA U.S. Year-End 2017 at https://us.spindices.com/search/?Content Type=SPIVA&_ga=2.196484460.1734890763.1521559714-1488324395 .1521382159.

Chapter 13: Invest Sustainably

1. Gordon L. Clark, Andreas Feiner, and Michael Viehs, "Report Highlights," in *From the Stockholder to the Stakeholder: How Sustainability Can Drive Financial Outperformance*, (SSRN, March 5, 2015), 9. PDF available at http://dx.doi.org/10.2139/ssrn.2508281 or https://ssrn.com/abstract=2508281.
2. The MSCI data contained herein is the property of MSCI Inc. (MSCI). MSCI, its affiliates, and its information providers make no warranties with respect to any such data. The MSCI data contained here is used under license and may not be further used, distributed, or disseminated without the express written consent of MSCI.

3. Investment Leaders Group, "The Value of Responsible Investment," University of Cambridge, 2014, https://www.cisl.cam.ac.uk/resource s/publication-pdfs/ilg-the-value-of-responsible-investment.pdf.

4. United States Department of Defense, "National Security Implications of Climate-Related Risks and a Changing Climate," July 23, 2015, http:// archive.defense.gov/pubs/150724-congressional-report-on -national-implications-of-climate-change.pdf?source=govdelivery.

5. United States Central Intelligence Agency, "CIA Opens Center on Climate Change and National Security," September 25, 2009, https:// www.cia.gov/news-information/press-releases-statements/center-on -climate-change-and-national-security.html.

6. Max Roser, "Life Expectancy," Our World in Data, accessed September 14, 2018, https://ourworldindata.org/life-expectancy.

7. Emily Wirzba, "35 National Religious Leaders Applaud Republican Climate Resolution," Friends Committee on National Legislation, March 15, 2017, https://www.fcnl.org/updates/35-national-religious -leaders-applaud-republican-climate-resolution-687, https://www.fcnl .org/documents/289.

8. Don Draper is a fictional character from the TV show *Mad Men*. His role was inspired by the life of Draper Daniels, an advertising executive who worked on the Marlboro Man campaign.

Chapter 14: Get Good Help

1. The Law Dictionary, 2nd ed., "Three Potential Consequences of Breach of Fiduciary Duty," accessed September 14, 2018, https://thelawdictionary .org/article/three-potential-consequences-breach-fiduciary-duty/.

2. Richard G. Netemeyer, Dee Warmath, Daniel Fernandes, John G. Lynch Jr., "How Am I Doing? Perceived Financial Well-Being, Its Potential Antecedents, and Its Relation to Overall Well-Being," *Journal of Consumer Research*, November 7, 2017, https://academic.oup .com/jcr/article-abstract/45/1/68/4600084?redirectedFrom=fulltext.

3. "Interpretive Bulletin Relating to the Exercise of Shareholder Rights and Written Statements of Investment Policy," Department of Labor, Employee Benefits Security Administration, December 29, 2016,

https://federalregister.gov/d/2016-31515, https://www.dol.gov/sites
/default/files/ebsa/2016-31515.pdf.

4. "Field Assistance Bulletin No. 2018-01," Department of Labor,
Employee Benefits Security Administration, April 23, 2018, https://
www.dol.gov/agencies/ebsa/employers-and-advisers/guidance
/field-assistance-bulletins/2018-01.

5. Ibid.

6. ASPPA Net Staff, "U.S. Retirement Assets Reach $26 Trillion,"
ASPPA, June 28, 2017, https://www.asppa.org/news-resources
/browse-topics/us-retirement-assets-reach-26-trillion.

Chapter 18: Build a Business

1. Glenn Kessler, "Do Nine Out of 10 New Businesses Fail, as Rand Paul
Claims?" *Washington Post*, January 27, 2014, https://www
.washingtonpost.com/news/fact-checker/wp/2014/01/27/do-9-out-of
-10-new-businesses-fail-as-rand-paul-claims/?noredirect=on&utm
_term=.b5a62a9498e6.

Chapter 19: Think Big

1. Harvard Health Publishing, "How Addiction Hijacks the Brain,"
July 2011, https://www.health.harvard.edu/newsletter_article/how
-addiction-hijacks-the-brain.

2. Ibid.

Chapter 20: Give Charitably

1. Abraham Joshua Heschel, "What of the Night?", republished with
permission of Crossroad Publishing Company, from *I Asked for
Wonder: A Spiritual Anthology*, 1983; permission conveyed through
Copyright Clearance Center, Inc.

Chapter 21: Put Your Values in Action

1. Gretchen Livingston, "Family Size Among Mothers," Pew Research
Center, May 7, 2015, http://www.pewsocialtrends.org/2015/05/07
/family-size-among-mothers/.

ABOUT THE AUTHOR

Doug Lynam is Director of Educator Retirement Services at LongView Asset Management in Santa Fe, New Mexico. He is a graduate of St. John's College in Santa Fe, the "Great Books" school, where he earned a degree equivalent to a double major, one in the History of Mathematics and Science and one in Philosophy, as well as a double minor, one in Classical Studies and the other in Comparative Literature. He is also a graduate of the Marine Corps Officer Candidate School.

Douglas has devoted his life to service. He was a Benedictine monk for twenty years, while working as a math and science teacher for eighteen years, and math department chair at Santa Fe Prep for over a decade. His work with teacher retirement plans and individual investors combines his desire to make the world a better place with his fascination for economics.

Before becoming a teacher, Doug worked as a legal analyst for Los Alamos National Laboratory. He was the vice president of the St. John's College Search and Rescue Team and is a certified cycle instructor and an avid yoga practitioner. He continues to work as a pro bono financial adviser to low-income families, which he has done since 2005, and he has won awards for his volunteer efforts for the homeless.